Where every meal becomes a quiet celebration.
I0816228

Glorious Table

Glorious Table

Beautiful Food for a Delicious Life

GLORIA JANG

Publisher Mike Sanders
Art & Design Director William Thomas
Editorial Director Ann Barton
Senior Editor Brook Farling
Senior Designer Jessica Lee
Developmental Editor Christy Wagner
Copy Editor Melissa Haskin
Photographer Sungmin Kim
Food and Prop Stylist Gloria Jang
Proofreaders Bianca Bosman, Mira S. Park
Indexer Michael H. Goldstein

First American Edition, 2025
Published in the United States by DK Publishing
1745 Broadway, 20th Floor, New York, NY 10019

The authorized representative in the EEA is Dorling Kindersley Verlag GmbH. Arnulfstr. 124, 80636 Munich, Germany

25 26 27 28 29   10 9 8 7 6 5 4 3 2 1
001–345671–NOV2025

A catalog record for this book
is available from the Library of Congress.
ISBN 978-0-5939-6333-3

Printed and bound in China

www.dk.com

This book was made with Forest Stewardship Council™ certified paper – one small step in DK's commitment to a sustainable future.
Learn more at
www.dk.com/uk/information/sustainability

I dedicate this book to my family.

Thank you to my father, who instilled in me the best habit of integrity, and to my mother, who taught me to cook from an early age and made me realize the value of food. You showed me that food made with love and care is the most precious thing.

I would also like to dedicate this book to my husband, Sungmin, who has always believed in me and nurtured my culinary dreams, and to our daughters, Haena and Haelin.

To Anne and Jake, our extended family who have always cheered us on and cared for us with unwavering love. Thank you, and we love you.

Without all of you, none of this would have been possible.

Contents

Introduction.. 8

Vegetables

Caprese Salad Rolls............................ 13
Preserved Lemon 14
Balsamic Marinated Tomatoes 17
Baked Beet Salad with Warm Cottage Cheese............................... 18
Creamy King Oyster Mushroom Steaks 21
French Tian 22
Baked Eggplant Rollatini 25
Black Red Onion Pies 26
Whole-Wheat Shiitake Mushroom Pasta with Cheese Crisps............... 29
Eggplant Parmesan 30
Mushroom Wings with Garlic Honey Hot Sauce........................... 33
Beet Tortilla Mushroom Tacos with Mango Salsa 34

Seafood

Grilled Shrimp with Louie Sauce..... 39
Creamy Mussels 40
Phyllo-Wrapped Seafood Papillote.. 43
Black Squid Ink Pasta 44
Fish and Chips 47
Beetroot-Cured Salmon 48
Deep-Fried Lobster with Lemon Cream Sauce.................................. 51

Beef, Pork & Lamb

Prime Rib Roast................................. 54
Steak with Pine Nut Sauce................ 57
Beef Tenderloins with Diane Sauce 58
Corned Beef and Cabbage 61
Beef Bourguignon 62
Bone Marrow Meatballs.................... 64
Sweet Soy-Marinated Boneless Beef Short Ribs 66
Spicy Pork Ribs with Melting Cheese 69
Crispy Porchetta 70
Hamburger Steaks with Aligot......... 73
Herb-Marinated Pork Shoulder Roast 74
Rack of Lamb Crown Roast 76
Rack of Lamb Cutlets 79
Lamb Chop Birria Tacos.................... 80

Poultry

Balsamic Glaze–Marinated Roasted Chicken Legs with Olives and Potatoes 85
Chicken Breast Rolls.......................... 86
Creamy Chicken with Green Pasta 89
Lollipop Drumsticks with Sweet Chili Oil Sauce and Jalapeño Coleslaw.. 90
Chicken Soup with Spicy Green Onion Soy Sauce............................ 93
Turkey Breast with Orange Sauce.... 94
Roasted Turkey with Stuffing and Candied Lemon Peel Cranberry Sauce 96

Breads

No Butter, No Egg Sandwich Bread 100
Hotel Bread 103
Pide Bread with Kaymak.................104
Braided Cinnamon Loaf..................107
Pumpernickel Bread........................108
Herbed Flatbread with Beet Hummus......................................110
Sweet Garlic Butter Leaves Bread 112
Cheesy Caramelized Onion Bread 115
Monkey Bread...................................116
Raspberry Babka 119
Chocolate Bread with Pearl Sugar 120
Candied Orange Peel Chocolate Babkas..123

Buns

Crunchy Cinnamon Balloon Buns 127
Butter Eye Buns................................128
Pretzels with Smoked Paprika Cheese Sauce.................................131
Brioche with Lemon Whipped Cream...132
Meringue Cinnamon Rolls 135
Butter Crumble Buns with Strawberry Cream 136
Cardamom Butter Buns 139
Anchovy Grilled Naan.....................140
Olive Fougasse 143
Apple and Cream Cheese Filled Buns 144

Sandwiches

Tamago Sandwiches with Wasabi Mayonnaise 149
Porchetta Sandwiches 150
Rack of Lamb Sandwiches 153
Black Ciabatta Egg Sandwich 154
Reuben Sandwiches with Spicy Garlicky Sauerkraut.....................157

Butter Shrimp and Black Bun Sandwiches....158
Open-Faced Baked Eggplant Sandwiches....161
Picnic Sandwiches....162

Scones & Biscuits

Country White Gravy and Biscuits....167
Sunflower Biscuits....168
Cinnamon Kouign-Amann Biscuits....171
Strawberry and Chocolate Scones....172
Cheese and Leek Scones....175
Black Cheese Scones....176

Cakes

Black Forest Cake (Forêt-Noire Gâteau)....180
Whipped Ganache Cake....182
Strawberry Jelly Cake....185
Mini Pistachio Baklava Cakes with Lemon Diplomat Cream....186
Carrot Loaf Cake....188
Chocolate Loaf Cake....191

Desserts

Peach Cookies....194
Koesisters (Spiced Doughnuts)....197
Pineapple Cupcakes with Sweet Coconut Cream....198
Red Pear Chocolate Turnovers....201
Apple Tarte Tatin....202
Beignets....205
Orange Custard Cream Éclairs....206
Cinnamon Twist Doughnuts....209
Cookie Choux with Cinnamon Chocolate Ganache Drip....210
Panna Cotta with Fruity Gin Jellies....213
Lime Pavlovas....214
Rochers Coco....217
White Chocolate–Coated Candied Lemon Peels....218
Chocolate Baklava with Hazelnuts....220
Lemony Nougat....223
Gin-Filled Pavé Chocolates....224

Frozen Desserts

Pomegranate Sorbet....229
Orange Thyme Sorbet with Blood Orange Compote....230
Lemon Basil Sorbet....233
Lime Cheesecake Gelato....234
Brown Butter Ice Cream with Pumpkin Spice Puree....237

Liquors

Apple Liquor....241
Pomegranate Liquor (Original and Cream Versions)....242
Limecello (Original and Cream Versions)....245
Pineapplecello (Original and Piña Colada Cocktail Versions)....246
Strawberry Whiskey....248

Index....250
Acknowledgments....255
About the Author....256

How to Use This Book

There are more than 100 recipes in this book, organized so that one recipe can be expanded into another. I don't want the recipes to be just an instruction manual, but rather a way for you to try new combinations of foods and discover their unique flavors.

There's no one right way to use this book. You can follow the recipes exactly as they are written, or you can add or change ingredients to make them your own. For example, if you're a vegetarian, try substituting vegetables or tofu in dishes that call for meat. You can also play around with sauces to try new combinations. The important thing to remember is that this book is meant to be a guide to help you create your own flavorful experiences.

Each recipe is organized with a sense of seasonality and harmony in mind. Choose a dish that fits your mood for the day or that you want to share with family and friends. Cooking isn't about special skills; it's about putting your heart into what you're creating.

I hope this book will be a longtime favorite in your kitchen and bring you many precious moments with those you love.

Introduction

I welcome you all with open arms.

What I thought was only a vague dream more than a decade ago has become a reality, and here I am, writing to you in this book. I am grateful and overwhelmed to be able to share with you the love of cooking that I have nurtured for so many years.

I believe that food is not just for survival, but also a special language that enriches life and captures emotions. I have many fond memories of warm meals from my childhood, and I learned to cook when I was young, naturally, by my mother's side. My mother made all the basic ingredients for traditional Korean food at home. She created doenjang, gochujang, and soy sauce – the most common sauces in Korean cuisine – herself, and she grew vegetables in the garden to prepare meals for our family. Watching her, I learned that cooking is both a process and a labor of love. As a child, when I was bored, I took out my mother's cookbooks and "helped" her by pretending to chop vegetables with my tiny hands, and the best part of my day was cooking and then eating with her.

Over the years, I've come to appreciate so many other cuisines, not just traditional Korean food. On my first trip to Europe, for example, I remember the sandwich of avocado on bread that the lady next to me on the train shared with me, the hot European coffee I drank in the morning after spending the night on that train, the simple but delicious breakfast of fresh cheese and bread the owner of a small hostel in Switzerland prepared for me, and a pasta with olive oil (which was just store-bought olive oil but tasted so good) with just the right amount of salt and pepper. These experiences were more than just new tastes. They taught me the importance of fresh ingredients, and it made me feel the emotion of that food with my whole body.

After I got married and had my own kitchen, cooking became the center of my life. My mother encouraged me to get a certificate as a Korean cuisine chef; as a lover of bread, I bought a small used oven, learned to bake at a local school, and got both certificates. My own kitchen was more than just a space to cook, it was a world of its own, a place where I could unleash my creativity without interference. I loved the hours I spent watching and studying cooking shows, experimenting in the kitchen, and immersing myself in cooking.

Then I moved to Canada and started working as a chef in a Japanese restaurant to pursue my culinary dreams. I'll never forget the excitement of walking into the kitchen for the first time – the wide stainless-steel countertops, the roaring fire pits, the shiny chef's knives and cutting boards . . . it all felt like a scene from a movie.

I worked in that restaurant for years, learning how to fillet fish, cut sashimi with precision, and collaborate with my co-chefs to complete dishes quickly during peak times. I spent my days in kitchens: working in the restaurant kitchen during the week, and baking and studying recipes from videos and books in my own kitchen on the weekends.

One day I realized that I wanted to do more than just cook; I wanted to document and share my cooking, and so Glorious Table was born. It started out as a small @glorioustable channel on Instagram, but as more and more people loved my cooking, my dream grew. My love for cooking began to be expressed through my videos, and it was inspiring to see how one shot, one recipe, or one plate of food could bring comfort and joy to so many people.

For me, cooking is more than just a job; it's a way of expressing love, a tool for communicating emotions. I believe that a meal made with love can bring true comfort to someone, healing to a broken heart, and happiness to our lives.

This book is the culmination of everything I've learned and loved about cooking over the past 15 years. Through it, I want to connect with you on a deeper level. I want to share with you my love of cooking, my love of food, and the joy a meal can bring. I hope that every time you open this book, you will begin to feel that same love and joy and be inspired to try your hand at cooking, too.

I hope that cooking will make your days more special and your life more delicious.

Are you ready to cook together? I invite you to join me at the Glorious Table.

– Gloria Jang

CHAPTER 1

Vegetables

Caprese Salad Rolls

PREP TIME: 5 minutes • **COOK TIME:** none • **MAKES:** 2 rolls

Even slight modifications to a recipe can create new textures and tastes. This recipe creates a unique flavor experience and a fresh take on the traditional caprese salad by transforming the classic combination of fresh tomatoes and mozzarella into a roll!

1 large or 2 medium heirloom tomatoes (any color)
½ tsp (2.5g) kosher salt, divided
⅛ tsp (0.1g) freshly ground black pepper
8 oz (225g) ball fresh mozzarella
24 fresh basil leaves
Grated Parmesan cheese
Balsamic glaze
Truffle-infused olive oil

SPECIAL EQUIPMENT
Mandoline

1. Use a mandoline to slice the tomatoes ⅛ inch (2mm) thick.
2. Place an 8 × 12-inch (20 × 30.5cm) sheet of parchment paper on a large cutting board. Arrange half the tomato slices in rows on the parchment paper, with each slice overlapping the next by about ½ inch (1.25cm).
3. Sprinkle ¼ teaspoon salt and a pinch of pepper over the tomatoes. Tear half of the mozzarella into small pieces, and layer them on top of the tomatoes. Add half of the fresh basil leaves to the top of the mozzarella.
4. Starting on one of the long sides of the parchment paper, grasp the edge of the paper and begin rolling the ingredients gently and tightly until you've formed a roll. Let sit for 5 minutes.
5. Remove the parchment paper, and cut the roll into 8 equal-sized pieces. Place the pieces on a plate, cut sides down, and repeat with the remaining tomatoes, mozzarella, and basil.
6. Sprinkle with Parmesan, ¼ teaspoon salt, and a pinch of pepper, followed by a drizzle of the balsamic glaze and truffle oil. Serve.

Preserved Lemon

PREP TIME: 15 minutes plus 16 days to age • **COOK TIME:** none • **MAKES:** 1 (1-quart/1-liter) jar

Sour is the number-one contributor to stimulating our sense of taste and increasing the pleasure of eating. This recipe captures the refreshing scent and sour taste of a lemon by preserving fresh lemons and an orange with salt and submerging them in lemon juice and oil. The resulting sauce, which combines the sweetness of the orange and the tartness of the lemon, goes very well on salads, fish, meats, and even in sandwiches.

8 large lemons
1 orange
2 tsp (12g) baking soda
2 cups (473ml) cups boiling water
4 tbsp (60g) kosher salt
3 tbsp (45ml) extra-virgin olive oil

Notes

I recommend using organic lemons. If you use regular lemons, be sure to wash them thoroughly before using.

You also can add some of your favorite fresh herbs with the salted lemons for a rich, herbaceous flavor. Any herbs will work; use about 10 sprigs to make an herb bouquet, and add to the jar with the lemons.

1. Fill a medium bowl with ice water and set aside. Place the lemons and orange in a medium bowl. Sprinkle the baking soda over the top, and pour in boiling water. Using tongs, roll the citrus in the hot water until all sides have been submerged, then immediately transfer to the ice water and roll again. Pat dry with paper towels.
2. Cut 4 or 5 lemons into quarters, starting at one end and cutting down through the lemon, leaving about ⅜ inch (1cm) intact at the bottom.
3. Open the lemon quarters like a flower, and sprinkle the flesh all over with salt. Place the salted lemons in a 1-quart (1-liter) jar.
4. Cut the orange in half. Cut one half in half again. Sprinkle both quarters with salt, and arrange the quarters in the jar with the lemons.
5. Peel the remaining orange half (orange part only) and the remaining 4 or 5 lemons (yellow part only). Set the peels aside.
6. Juice the peeled lemons and orange half.
7. Pour the lemon and orange juices over the salted lemons and orange in the jar. The citrus should be fully submerged. Add the peels and the remaining salt, and close the lid.
8. Allow the jar to set at room temperature for 48 hours. Turn the jar upside down a few times to disperse and dissolve the salt.
9. Remove the lid and add the olive oil to the jar. Close the lid again, and set aside at room temperature for 2 weeks.
10. Enjoy in your favorite recipe. Store any leftovers in the refrigerator for up to 6 months. When you store it, be sure the lemons are submerged under at least a ½ inch (1.25cm) of olive oil.

Balsamic Marinated Tomatoes

PREP TIME: 15 minutes plus 6 hours to marinate • **COOK TIME:** none • **MAKES:** 18 oz (500g) marinated cherry tomatoes

The combination of tomatoes, basil, olive oil, and balsamic vinegar is a classic pairing. This simple, healthy, flavorful dish can be served as is, as a side dish, as a salad dressing, or even as a sandwich topping. It's so fresh and delicious.

TOMATOES

18 oz (500g) cherry tomatoes
1 tbsp (15ml) white vinegar

BALSAMIC SAUCE

1 small shallot, finely chopped
¼ cup (59ml) balsamic vinegar
¼ cup (59ml) extra-virgin olive oil
2 tbsp (42g) honey
10 fresh basil leaves, chopped
Juice of ½ lemon
1 tsp (1g) dried oregano or thyme
¼ tsp (1.25g) kosher salt
½ tsp (0.5g) freshly ground black pepper

1. Place the cherry tomatoes in a medium bowl, cover with water, and add the vinegar. Let sit for 3 minutes.
2. Strain the tomatoes. Using a sharp knife cut a shallow X in the top of each tomato. Return the cut tomatoes to the bowl.
3. Pour boiling water over the tomatoes until they are submerged, and gently stir with a spoon.
4. Meanwhile, fill a medium bowl with ice water.
5. After a few minutes, the skin will begin to loosen from the tomatoes. Once all skin is loosened, transfer the tomatoes to the prepared ice water and cool for 10 minutes.
6. Use your fingers to peel each tomato. Place the peeled tomatoes in a clean bowl with a lid. Set aside.
7. In a small bowl, whisk together the shallot, balsamic vinegar, oil, honey, basil, lemon juice, oregano or thyme, salt, and pepper. Pour the mixture over the tomatoes, and gently mix to combine. Cover and marinate in the refrigerator for at least 6 hours.
8. Serve. Store any leftovers in an airtight container in the refrigerator for up to 7 days.

Baked Beet Salad

with Warm Cottage Cheese

PREP TIME: 10 minutes • **COOK TIME:** 30 minutes • **SERVINGS:** 2 or 3

This roasted beet and warm cottage cheese salad highlights the unique charm of warm salads. Beets are a nutrient-packed superfood, rich in nitrates that help improve blood circulation and may even prevent or dissolve blood clots. Full of antioxidants that reduce inflammation and boost immunity, this dish is as healthy as it is delicious. Simple yet elegant, it's perfect for a light lunch or as a side dish for special occasions. Roast the beets ahead of time for an easy, fuss-free meal. One bite, and you'll feel the warmth and comfort filling your heart and soul.

3 medium beets
1 tsp (2g) fresh thyme
¼ tsp (1.25g) kosher salt
½ tsp (0.5g) freshly ground black pepper, plus more for seasoning
2 tbsp (30ml) extra-virgin olive oil
2 cups (450g) cottage cheese
1 tsp (2g) lemon zest

Note

You can roast a batch of six beets, store them in the refrigerator, and enjoy them for a healthy snack every day! Oven-roasted beets have a sweet flavor and pair well with cheese and olive oil for a great side dish. Remove them from the refrigerator, let them stand for 10 to 15 minutes, and experiment with adding them to your favorite foods!

1. Preheat the oven to 400°F (200°C). Line a baking sheet with a 15-inch (38cm) piece of parchment paper or foil, fold in half, and open.
2. Peel the beets and cut each into about 12 small pieces. Place the beets on one side of the paper or foil.
3. Sprinkle evenly with the thyme, salt, pepper, and 1 tablespoon (15ml) of the olive oil. Fold over the paper or foil and fold inward again two or three times (about ¼ inch/6mm) to close and seal the edges.
4. Bake the beets for 20 minutes. Let cool for about 10 minutes.
5. Meanwhile, place the cottage cheese in a small, ovenproof dish, and bake for 10 minutes. (The cheese curds and whey will separate, and the sour cheese flavor will disappear.)
6. Transfer the cottage cheese to a fine-mesh sieve and drain. Add the solids to a serving dish. Top with the beets, drizzle with the remaining 1 tablespoon (15ml) of olive oil, sprinkle with the pepper and lemon zest, and serve.

Creamy King Oyster Mushroom Steaks

PREP TIME: 10 minutes • **COOK TIME:** 15 minutes • **SERVINGS:** 2 or 3

Mushrooms often serve as the protein in meatless dishes, and lucky for us, there are so many different kinds of mushrooms to choose from. In this recipe, large, nutty, earthy king oyster mushrooms are the star alongside fresh herbs and a creamy white wine sauce. Because of their size and texture, cooked king oyster mushrooms are similar to scallops or even chicken breast, when shredded with a fork. I think you'll love them in this dish. (Look for them in an Asian market if you can't find them in your grocery store.)

4 king oyster mushrooms
1 tsp (5g) kosher salt
¼ tsp (0.25g) freshly ground black pepper
½ tsp (0.5g) garlic powder
1 tbsp (6g) lemon zest
2 or 3 sprigs fresh sage
2 or 3 sprigs fresh thyme
2 or 3 sprigs fresh rosemary
¼ cup (58g) unsalted butter
1 shallot, chopped
2 garlic cloves, minced
⅓ cup (79ml) white wine
⅓ cup (79ml) heavy cream
1 tsp (5ml) fresh lemon juice
1 tbsp (3.5g) fresh sage, thyme, or rosemary, or a combination, chopped
Fresh flat-leaf parsley, chopped, for garnish
Warm mashed potatoes, to serve

SPECIAL EQUIPMENT

Kitchen string

1. Gently wipe the mushrooms with a wet paper towel to remove any grit, and cut off the bottoms. Cut the stems and caps into 1-inch (2.5cm) thick slices, and then score each piece about ⅛-inch (2mm) deep on one side in a small grid pattern.
2. Place scored side up on a baking sheet, and season on all sides with ¾ teaspoon (3.75g) of the salt, ⅛ teaspoon (0.125g) of the pepper, the garlic powder, and the lemon zest. Let sit until the water starts to release, 5 to 10 minutes.
3. Meanwhile, tie together the sprigs of sage, thyme, and rosemary with kitchen string to make a mini herb brush.
4. Heat a medium skillet over medium-high heat, and add the mushrooms and butter. When the butter is melted, use the mini herb brush to brush the melted butter onto the mushrooms.
5. Cook the mushrooms on one side until golden, about 5 minutes. Turn over the mushrooms, use the brush to baste the mushrooms again with melted butter, and cook until golden, 3 to 5 minutes. Remove the mushrooms from the pan, and keep warm.
6. Add the shallot, garlic, white wine, and heavy cream to the pan, and stir well. Bring to a boil over medium heat.
7. Add the remaining ¼ teaspoon (1.25g) of salt, the remaining ⅛ teaspoon (0.125g) of pepper, the lemon juice, the entire mini herb brush, and the chopped herbs. Cook, stirring often, until sauce is thick, about 5 minutes.
8. Serve the mushroom steaks over warm mashed potatoes, pour the creamy lemon-herb sauce over the top, garnish with fresh parsley, and serve.

French Tian

PREP TIME: 40 minutes • **COOK TIME:** 55 minutes • **SERVINGS:** 4

Although often mistaken for ratatouille, as popularized by the animated film of the same name, this dish is actually called a "tian," according to my French followers. Whatever it's called, it's a healthy and mouthwatering meal. The vibrant layers of tomatoes, zucchini, and eggplant, combined with a rich tomato sauce and herb-infused olive oil, make it a delightful and nutritious choice. This is my take on the classic French tian, beautifully arranged in a flower pattern and delicious when served with goat cheese and a baguette.

HERBED OLIVE OIL

¼ cup (59ml) extra-virgin olive oil
2 tbsp (10g) chopped fresh basil
2 tbsp (10g) chopped fresh parsley
2 tsp (4g) fresh thyme leaves
½ tsp (2.5g) kosher salt
½ tsp (0.5g) freshly ground black pepper

ROLLED VEGETABLE FLOWERS

1 yellow squash
1 zucchini
3 Roma tomatoes
1 medium eggplant
1 tbsp (15ml) white vinegar
1 tsp (5g) kosher salt

TOMATO SAUCE

2 tbsp (30ml) extra-virgin olive oil
3 cloves garlic, minced
½ medium white onion, finely chopped
2 (15oz/425g) cans crushed tomatoes
10 fresh basil leaves, plus more for garnish
½ tsp (2.5g) kosher salt
½ tsp (0.5g) freshly ground black pepper

1. To make the herbed olive oil, whisk together the olive oil, basil, parsley, thyme, salt, and pepper in a small bowl. Set aside.
2. Place the yellow squash, zucchini, tomatoes, and eggplant in a large bowl, and cover with water. Add the vinegar, and let sit for a few minutes. Rinse and transfer to a tea towel.
3. Cut two-thirds of the yellow squash into 1½-inch (3.75cm) lengths (columns), and slice the rest into thin circles. Do the same with the zucchini. (You will have a total of 8 zucchini columns.)
4. Place the sliced zucchini on a large platter, and sprinkle with a pinch of salt.
5. Holding a zucchini column in one hand, begin slicing it as thinly as possible, from the skin inward toward the center in one long continuous spiral cut; stop when you reach the seeds, and cut away the seed part, but do not discard. You should have at least a 6-inch (15cm) long sheet of very thinly sliced zucchini. Sprinkle the inside of the skin with a pinch of salt, and set on a plate. Repeat with the remaining columns.
6. Slice the tomatoes and eggplant as thinly as possible into rounds, sprinkle with a pinch of salt, and arrange on the plate with the zucchini slices.
7. Chop the remaining zucchini (including the seeds) into small pieces.
8. To make the tomato sauce, heat a medium ovenproof skillet over medium heat, and add the oil. Add the garlic, chopped zucchini, and onion, and sauté until the onions are soft, about 5 minutes.
9. Add the crushed tomatoes, basil leaves, salt, and pepper. Reduce the heat to medium-low, and simmer for 10 to 15 minutes. Remove from the heat.
10. Preheat the oven to 350°F (180°C).
11. Lay the zucchini strips lengthwise on a cutting board with the skin down. Place the sliced tomato, eggplant, and zucchini on one end of the zucchini strip in a random pattern so they overlap about halfway. You will need 12 to 14 vegetable slices per strip of zucchini. Roll the zucchini strip from the bottom up and over the vegetable slices so when viewed from the side, it looks like a flower. Make a 1½-inch (3.75cm) cut in the center of the zucchini, and place the cut side down to hold the flower upright. Lean the flowers against each other to keep them from unraveling. Repeat with the remaining zucchini strips and vegetables, so you have 16 flowers total. If you have any leftover vegetables, chop them finely and stir them into the tomato sauce.
12. Nestle the flowers in the tomato sauce, and drizzle the herb oil over the top. Cover with foil and bake for 40 minutes.
13. Remove from the oven. Scoop out the flowers with some tomato sauce, garnish with basil leaves, and serve.

Baked Eggplant Rollatini

PREP TIME: 30 minutes • **COOK TIME:** 1 hour 20 minutes • **SERVINGS:** 5

Even my eggplant-averse husband can't resist the deliciousness of this rollatini. The grilled eggplant, filled with a creamy ricotta and Parmesan mixture, is perfectly complemented by a rich tomato sauce and melted mozzarella. It's a dish that transforms simple ingredients into a family favorite.

EGGPLANT

- 3 medium eggplants, washed, trimmed, and cut into ¼-inch (6mm) thick slices
- 1 tsp (5g) kosher salt
- 1 tsp (5ml) extra-virgin olive oil
- 1 (15oz/425g) can tomato sauce
- 3 tbsp (60g) tomato paste
- 1 tbsp (5g) chopped fresh basil
- 2 cups (250g) shredded mozzarella

FILLING

- 1 cup (246g) ricotta cheese
- ½ cup (56g) grated Parmesan cheese
- 2 tbsp (10g) chopped fresh basil
- 1 garlic clove, minced
- ¼ tsp (1.25g) kosher salt
- ¼ tsp (0.25g) freshly ground black pepper

1. Season the eggplant all over with salt, and let sit for 10 minutes to sweat. (This removes excess moisture from the eggplant and prevents a watery rollatini.)
2. Pat the eggplant all over with paper towels and wipe off any remaining salt.
3. Lightly oil a heavy skillet or grill pan with a brush, and set over medium-high heat. When the pan is hot, working in batches, add the eggplant. Cook until golden brown or until grill marks appear, about 3 or 4 minutes. Flip and cook for 3 to 4 minutes more. Transfer to a wire rack (this softens the eggplant so you can easily roll it with the filling) and repeat until all of the eggplant is cooked.
4. Preheat the oven to 400°F (200°C).
5. To make the filling, add the ricotta, Parmesan, basil, garlic, salt, and pepper to a small bowl, and mix well with a wooden spoon.
6. Place the eggplant slices on a work surface. Add 1 or 2 tablespoons of the filling to the center of each eggplant slice, and roll the eggplant over the filling. Repeat with the remaining slices and filling.
7. In a small bowl, combine the tomato sauce and tomato paste. Whisk to combine. Spread a ¼-inch (6mm) layer of tomato sauce in the bottom of a 9 × 13-inch (23 × 33cm) casserole or baking dish. Arrange the eggplant rolls side by side in the tomato sauce.
8. Top each eggplant roll with ½ tablespoon of tomato sauce, sprinkle with chopped basil, and sprinkle with mozzarella.
9. Cover with foil and bake for 30 minutes. Uncover and bake for 10 to 15 minutes more.
10. Remove from the oven and serve hot.

Black Red Onion Pies

PREP TIME: 30 minutes plus 1 hour 10 minutes to rest • **COOK TIME:** 55 minutes • **MAKES:** 6 pies

This visually striking dish combines a crispy black squid ink pastry with a flavorful red onion and cheese filling. Red onions are rich in antioxidants and have anti-inflammatory properties, which can help boost your immune system, while blue cheese and smoked Gouda are excellent sources of calcium and protein. Hidden in the filling is a soft-poached egg, adding a creamy texture that enhances the richness of each bite. These pies are perfect for a special brunch or unique dinner.

PIE DOUGH

½ cup (120g) sour cream
⅓ cup (79ml) cold water
500g all-purpose flour, plus more for dusting
1¼ tsp (5g) baking powder
½ tsp (3g) baking soda
2 tsp (10g) kosher salt
2 cups (454g) cold unsalted butter
1 tbsp (24g) squid ink
1 tbsp (14g) unsalted butter, at room temperature

RED ONION AND CHEESE FILLING

3 large red onions, thinly sliced
½ tsp (2.5g) kosher salt
¼ tsp (0.25g) freshly ground black pepper
2 tsp (3g) dried oregano
1 tsp (1.5g) dried thyme
½ cup (115g) unsalted butter
1 cup (120g) grated smoked Gouda cheese
½ cup (60g) crumbled blue cheese
½ cup (60g) cheese curds
6 large eggs
1 tbsp (15ml) white vinegar

SPECIAL EQUIPMENT

Dough scraper
Six 4-inch (10cm) springform pans

Note

Squid ink can add natural color and flavor to dishes. It's not readily available in regular supermarkets, but you can find it in Italian markets or online.

1. Whisk together the sour cream and cold water in a small bowl until no lumps remain. Place in the refrigerator until ready to use.
2. Mix together the flour, baking powder, baking soda, and salt in a large bowl.
3. Sprinkle about 1 cup (120g) of the flour mixture onto a floured work surface. Add the cold butter, and use a dough scraper to cut the butter into ¼-inch to ½-inch (0.5cm to 1.25cm) pieces, sprinkling the butter with the flour mixture as you cut the butter. Return the butter and flour mixture to the bowl, mix well, and place in the freezer for about 10 minutes.
4. Use your right hand to cut the butter into small pieces and your left hand to dig the buttery flour from underneath and pour it on top, mixing until all the dough is crumbly and fluffy with butter pieces.
5. Add the squid ink. Crumble the mixture using the same technique used to crumble the butter, mixing until it is evenly distributed and the mixture resembles black sand. Add the cold sour cream mixture in 4 or 5 equal-size portions, mixing with a wooden spoon until the dough is lumpy.
6. Turn out the dough onto a work surface, divide it in half, and pound and press the dough pieces into two 1-inch-thick (2.5cm) disks (do not knead the dough). Cover the dough pieces with plastic wrap, and place them in the refrigerator for 1 hour.
7. Meanwhile, to make the filling, add the onions, salt, pepper, oregano, and thyme to a medium bowl. Toss until the onions are evenly coated, then squeeze the onions a few times with your hands. (This process will infuse them with the herbs and tenderize them a bit.) In a medium skillet over medium heat, add the butter and cook the onions until softened, about 15 minutes.
8. Spread the onions in a large bowl and allow to cool slightly. Add the Gouda, blue cheese, and cheese curds, and mix well. Allow to cool to room temperature and then place in the refrigerator until ready to use.
9. Remove the dough disks from the refrigerator. Turn out one piece of the pie dough onto a floured work surface, and roll out with a rolling pin to ⅛-inch (3mm) thickness. Cut the dough into three 6-inch (15cm) rounds. (These are for the bottom piecrusts.) Roll the trimmed dough into single piece and roll out three more 6-inch (15cm) rounds. Place a piece of parchment paper between each round, and transfer to the refrigerator.
10. Roll the remaining disk out to ⅛-inch (3mm) thickness, and cut three 5-inch (12.5cm) rounds. (These are for the tops of the pies.) Roll the trimmed dough into single piece and roll out three more 5-inch (12.5cm) rounds. Place a piece of parchment paper between each round, and transfer to the refrigerator.
11. To poach the eggs, place a slotted spoon over a small bowl and crack an egg into the spoon. (This will separate the watery white and create a cleaner surface after cooking.) Transfer the egg to another small bowl. Place a small saucepan over medium heat, add enough water to cover the eggs, and bring to a boil. Add the vinegar, stir the water with a spoon about five times in one direction, and then add the egg in the center. Cook the egg for 2 minutes and then transfer to a plate. Repeat with the remaining eggs.

12. Preheat the oven to 380°F (190°C).
13. Remove the crusts from the refrigerator.
14. Butter the sides and bottoms of the six 4-inch (10cm) springform pans. Place a 6-inch (15cm) piece of dough in a pan and gently press down with your fingers to help the pastry adhere to the pan.
15. Divide the filling into six equal portions. Place half of one portion in the pastry shell. Carefully add a poached egg on top, and cover with the second half of the filling.
16. Cover the filling with a 5-inch (12.5cm) piece of pastry. Brush the top of the bottom pastry with water, and press the two doughs together. (If the doughs do not overlap well, use your fingers to press and stretch the edge of the top pastry.) Fold the edges of the doughs from the outside in to seal them together. Finish by pressing with your fingers to create a decorative squiggly edge. Repeat with the remaining dough and filling. Place in the refrigerator until ready to bake.
17. Remove the pies from the refrigerator, and place on a baking sheet. Using the tip of a small knife, make a hole in the center of each for venting, and score the top of each pie four to six times.
18. Bake for 30 to 40 minutes. Serve warm.

Whole-Wheat Shiitake Mushroom Pasta

with Cheese Crisps

PREP TIME: 10 minutes • **COOK TIME:** 20 minutes • **SERVINGS:** 2

This pasta is a comforting blend of nutty, whole-wheat spaghetti and the rich, earthy flavors of shiitake mushrooms. Each forkful further delights with crispy cheese crisps, which add a crunchy contrast to the silky pasta and tender mushrooms. The garlic-infused olive oil and meaty shiitake mushrooms come together to deliver a deeply satisfying, umami-rich taste that's perfect for any occasion. This recipe is quick to prepare, too, making it ideal for busy weeknight dinners.

- ⅓ cup (40g) plus 1 or 2 tbsp (15–20g) grated Parmigiano-Reggiano
- 6 to 8 (100g) shiitake mushrooms
- ½ cup (118ml) extra-virgin olive oil, plus more for drizzling
- 3 garlic cloves, minced
- ½ medium white onion, diced small
- ½ tsp (2.5g) kosher salt
- 1 tbsp (15g) chicken or vegetable bouillon powder or paste
- 7 oz (200g) whole-wheat spaghetti
- ¼ tsp (0.25g) crushed hot red pepper
- ¼ tsp (0.25g) freshly ground black pepper

Notes

You can substitute salt for the bouillon powder or paste using a 1:1 ratio.

You can use any mushrooms you like, but I recommend shiitake mushrooms for their rich flavor. If you use dried mushrooms, rehydrate them first. To do so, add them to a medium bowl, cover them with boiling water, and allow them to soak for 20 minutes. Gently squeeze dry before using.

The power of the whole-wheat pasta in this recipe is that it adds a nutty flavor. I do not recommend using plain pasta for this recipe.

1. Pour 6⅓ cups (1.5 liters) of water into a large pot, set over high heat, and bring to a boil.
2. Meanwhile, to make the cheese crisps, set a large skillet over low heat. Using a measuring spoon, place 1 teaspoon (5g) of the Parmigiano-Reggiano in a pile in the skillet and press down lightly. After 2 or 3 minutes, the cheese will melt and form a crust. Using a thin spatula, remove the crisp from the skillet, and place on a piece of parchment paper to cool. Repeat with remaining Parmigiano-Reggiano, working in batches of 10 crisps at a time, until you have a total of 20 crisps.
3. Gently wipe the mushrooms clean with a wet paper towel, and cut them into ¼-inch (0.5cm) slices.
4. Add the olive oil, garlic, and onion to the skillet, and sauté until the onion is translucent, about 3 minutes. Add the mushrooms and salt, and cook until the mushrooms are lightly golden, about 5 minutes. Remove the pan from the heat, and let stand.
5. When the water in the large pot is boiling, add the bouillon and spaghetti, and cook for 8 minutes. Drain the pasta, reserving about 1 cup (237ml) of the pasta water.
6. Return the skillet with the mushrooms to medium heat. Add the cooked pasta, and half of the water and stir. Add the remaining half of the water, stir well, and remove the pan from the heat. Add the remaining 1 or 2 tbsp (15 to 20g) of Parmigiano-Reggiano, crushed red pepper, and black pepper, and stir to combine. Transfer the pasta to a serving dish, top with the cheese crisps, drizzle generously with olive oil, and serve.

Eggplant Parmesan

PREP TIME: 15 minutes • **COOK TIME:** 30 minutes • **SERVINGS:** 2 or 3

Eggplant Parmesan, a delightful combination of fresh eggplant and melted Parmesan, is a traditional dish that hails from Naples, Italy. The soft texture of the eggplant pairs beautifully with the rich flavor of the cheese, and it's crispy on the outside and tender and juicy on the inside. Enjoy the perfect marriage of eggplant and Parmesan, and bring some joy to your table!

2 small eggplants (about 14-oz/400g total weight)
¾ tsp (3.75g) kosher salt
1 cup (60g) breadcrumbs
6 sprigs of fresh parsley, finely chopped
4 sprigs of fresh thyme, finely chopped
2 sprigs of fresh oregano, finely chopped
1 sprig of fresh sage
2 medium eggs
2 tsp (9g) everything bagel seasoning
¼ cup (30g) all-purpose flour
½ lb (227g) chestnut mushrooms, cleaned, ends trimmed
3 tbsp (42g) cold unsalted butter
½ tsp (0.5g) freshly ground black pepper
2 cups (473ml) extra-virgin olive oil
7 oz (250g) fresh mozzarella, torn
¼ cup (28g) freshly grated Parmesan cheese
½ lemon, cut into wedges

TOMATO SAUCE

1 (28 oz/794g) can whole tomatoes
1 tbsp (15ml) extra-virgin olive oil
3 garlic cloves, thinly sliced
2 shallots, sliced
½ tsp (2g) sugar
2 or 3 springs each of fresh thyme, oregano, parsley, and sage, tied in a bundle with kitchen string

SPECIAL EQUIPMENT

Kitchen string
Food processor
Deep-fry thermometer

Notes

Sprinkle a little sugar on the lemon wedges, heat them a bit with a blowtorch, and squeeze them just before you eat to provide an extra boost of flavor from the caramelized lemon juice.

To melt the cheese, you can also use a kitchen torch.

1. Wash the eggplants under running water, and pat dry with a towel. Place on a cutting board. Starting at the stem end, make 4 cuts through each eggplant, ½ inch (1.25cm) apart, being careful not to cut the pieces away from the stem. Fan out the slices, and season each side with ¼ teaspoon (1.25g) of salt. Allow the eggplant to rest for 10 minutes.
2. Meanwhile, stir together the breadcrumbs, parsley, thyme, oregano, and sage in a baking dish. Spread the mixture into an even layer.
3. Beat the eggs in another similar-sized dish. Set aside.
4. Pat the eggplant dry with a paper towel. Sprinkle all over with the everything bagel seasoning. Use a fine-mesh sieve to dust the eggplant pieces with the flour and then gently shake off any excess. Dredge the eggplant in the egg and then in the breadcrumb mixture until evenly coated. Transfer the eggplant to a baking sheet, cover with a tea towel, and set aside.
5. Place the mushrooms in a food processor or chopper, and process until finely chopped.
6. Melt 1 tablespoon (14g) of butter in a small skillet over medium heat. Add the mushrooms, the remaining ¼ teaspoon (1.25g) of salt, and ¼ tsp (0.25g) of pepper, and toss to combine. Sauté until the mushrooms have released their moisture, about 5 minutes. Remove from the heat, and set aside.
7. To make the tomato sauce, set a strainer over a medium bowl, and pour in the tomatoes. Chop the tomatoes into small pieces, and return them to the tomato juice.
8. Heat the olive oil in a medium skillet over medium heat. Add the garlic and shallots, and sauté until translucent, about 5 minutes.
9. Add the chopped tomatoes and juice, the sugar, and the herb bundle. Increase the heat to medium-high, and simmer, stirring occasionally, for about 10 minutes. Remove from the heat, and keep warm.
10. Preheat the broiler with a rack in the center position.
11. Pour the 2 cups (473ml) of olive oil into a medium skillet, set over medium-high heat, and bring to 340°F (170°C). Add the eggplant, and cook until brown on both sides, 3 to 5 minutes. (The eggplant should be at least half submerged in the oil.)
12. Transfer the eggplant to a wire rack. Grate the remaining 2 tablespoons (28g) of cold butter, sprinkle the butter over the eggplant, and allow to melt completely, 2 or 3 minutes.
13. Place the eggplant in an ovenproof dish, and spread the fresh mozzarella evenly over the top. Broil for 3 to 5 minutes until the cheese is melted (see Note).
14. Spread the prepared mushrooms in an even layer over the eggplant, cover with the warm tomato sauce, and sprinkle with grated Parmesan cheese and the remaining ¼ teaspoon (0.25g) of black pepper. Squeeze with lemon just before serving.

Mushroom Wings

with Garlic Honey Hot Sauce

PREP TIME: 25 minutes plus 6 hours to freeze • **COOK TIME:** 25 minutes • **SERVINGS:** 3 or 4

Who says wings have to be chicken? King oyster mushrooms are low in calories but rich in vitamin D, antioxidants, and immunity-boosting beta-glucans. Coated in a crispy golden crust, tossed in a finger-licking garlic honey hot sauce, and paired with a creamy Dijon blue cheese dip, these wings hit all the right notes—savory, spicy, sweet, and tangy. Perfect for sharing (or not!), they're a crowd-pleaser for game nights, parties, or weeknight meals. Once you try these, you'll never look at mushrooms the same way again!

MUSHROOM WINGS

6 king oyster mushrooms

2 qt (2 liters) canola oil, for frying

DIJON BLUE CHEESE DIPPING SAUCE

⅔ cup (90g) crumbled blue cheese

½ cup (123g) sour cream

¼ cup (58g) mayonnaise

¼ cup (59ml) buttermilk

2 tbsp (30g) whole-grain Dijon mustard

2 tbsp (42g) honey

1 tbsp (6g) lemon zest

1 tbsp (15ml) lemon juice

GARLIC HOT HONEY SAUCE

2 tbsp (30ml) extra-virgin olive oil

5 garlic cloves, finely diced

¼ cup (58g) unsalted butter

½ cup (118ml) hot sauce

½ cup (170g) honey

1 tsp (2g) cayenne

BATTER

2 cups (240g) all-purpose flour

½ cup (80g) cornmeal

½ cup (60g) cornstarch

2 tbsp (15g) onion powder

1 tbsp (15g) kosher salt

2 tsp (2g) freshly ground black pepper

1½ tsp (7g) baking powder

1 tsp (3g) garlic powder

½ tsp (1g) smoked paprika

½ tsp (1g) cayenne

1 cup (237ml) buttermilk

SPECIAL EQUIPMENT

Deep-fry thermometer

1. Wipe the mushrooms with a paper towel to remove any grit and slice into ovals about 3 or 4 inches (7.5 or 10cm) long and 1½ inches (3.75cm) thick. You should get about four slices, or wingettes (the middle part of a chicken wing), per mushroom. Arrange on a tray, set in the freezer, and freeze for about 6 hours.
2. Whisk together all the ingredients for the Dijon blue cheese dipping sauce in a medium bowl. Cover with plastic wrap, and set in the refrigerator.
3. To make the garlic hot honey sauce, place a small saucepan over medium heat, add the olive oil and garlic, and sauté for 3 minutes. Stir in the butter, hot sauce, honey, and cayenne, and simmer, stirring constantly, for 5 minutes. Keep the sauce warm or reheat over low heat just before tossing with the mushroom wings.
4. Pour the canola oil into a wide, deep skillet or large wok over medium-high heat, and heat to 350°F (177°C).
5. Whisk together the batter ingredients, except the buttermilk, in a large storage container. Transfer ⅔ cup (80g) of the batter mixture to a medium bowl, add the buttermilk, and whisk to make a wet batter.
6. Remove the mushrooms from the freezer. Toss in the dry mixture to coat evenly, dip in the wet batter, and return them to the dry mixture. Add the lid to the dry mixture and shake vigorously until well coated. Remove the lid and gently shake off the excess flour and set the coated mushrooms aside on the tray for about 5 minutes.
7. Set a wire cooling rack inside a baking sheet. Working in batches to maintain the heat of the oil, fry about eight mushrooms at a time for 3 to 4 minutes and then transfer to the wire rack to cool. Repeat with the remaining mushrooms.
8. Increase the heat to high, and heat the oil to 360°F (185°C). Add all the mushrooms and deep-fry again until golden brown, about 2 minutes. Use a strainer to transfer the mushrooms to the wire rack again, and pat with a paper towel to absorb some of the oil.
9. Pour the warm hot sauce into a large bowl, add the fried mushrooms, and roll them in the sauce to coat. Transfer the coated wings to a serving platter, and serve with the blue cheese dipping sauce.

Beet Tortilla Mushroom Tacos

with Mango Salsa

PREP TIME: 50 minutes • **COOK TIME:** 1 hour • **MAKES:** 14 tacos

The vibrant red of beets adds a beautiful pop of color to your table, while shredded king oyster mushrooms perfectly mimic the texture of meat, making each bite hearty and satisfying. Sweet and tangy mango salsa brings a refreshing balance to the dish, and the creamy sour cream sauce ties everything together. Beets support heart health and energy, and mushrooms are packed with nutrients, making these tacos flavorful and wholesome.

MANGO SALSA

½ large mango, peeled and diced
2 small Roma tomatoes, diced
¼ medium red onion, diced
2 small bell peppers, ribs and seeds removed, diced
1 jarred hot and sweet jalapeño, diced
1 garlic clove, finely diced
2 tbsp (12g) fresh cilantro, chopped, plus more for serving
1 tbsp (15ml) fresh lime juice
½ tsp (2.5g) kosher salt
1 tsp (1g) freshly ground black pepper

SOUR CREAM SAUCE

1 cup (225g) sour cream
¼ cup (59ml) jarred hot and sweet jalapeño juice
3 tbsp (45ml) fresh lemon juice
2 tsp (8.5g) sugar
¼ tsp (0.5g) garlic powder
½ tsp (0.5g) onion powder
¼ tsp (1.25g) kosher salt
½ tsp (0.5g) freshly ground black pepper

HOMEMADE TACO SEASONING

1 tbsp (7.5g) chili powder
1 tbsp (5g) crushed hot red pepper flakes
1 tbsp (7g) smoked paprika
2 tsp (6g) onion powder
2 tsp (10g) kosher salt
1 tsp (1g) freshly ground black pepper
1 tsp (3g) garlic powder
1 tsp (2g) dried oregano
½ tsp (1g) ground cumin

MUSHROOM BALLS

1½ cups (235g) baby bella mushrooms
1 garlic clove
1 shallot
2 tbsp (30ml) extra-virgin olive oil
1 (15.5 oz/440g) can chickpeas, drained and rinsed with hot water
½ lb (227g) tofu, patted dry with paper towels
⅔ cup (80g) breadcrumbs
¼ tsp (1.25g) kosher salt
2 tbsp (20g) homemade taco seasoning (see above)

SHREDDED MUSHROOMS

1 lb (454g) king oyster mushrooms
¼ tsp (1.25g) kosher salt
1 tbsp (10g) homemade taco seasoning (see above)
¼ cup (59ml) extra-virgin olive oil

BEET TORTILLAS

1 medium beet, peeled and cut into 1-inch (2.5cm) pieces
½ tsp (2.5g) kosher salt
240g corn flour (I like MASECA corn flour)
2 limes, cut into wedges, for serving

SPECIAL EQUIPMENT

Chopper
Disposable kitchen gloves
Tortilla press
Taco stands

1. To make the mango salsa, place the mango, tomatoes, onion, bell peppers, jalapeño, garlic, and cilantro in a medium bowl. Add the lime juice, salt, and pepper, and mix with a spoon until combined. Cover with plastic wrap, and set in the refrigerator.
2. To make the sour cream sauce, whisk together all the ingredients in a small bowl, cover with plastic wrap, and set in the refrigerator.
3. To make the homemade taco seasoning, add all the ingredients to a small jar, cover, and shake to combine.
4. To make the mushroom balls, cut off the base of the baby bella mushrooms, dust them with a towel or brush, and put them in a food chopper. Add the garlic and shallot, and chop finely.
5. Heat a medium skillet over medium heat. Add the oil. Once shimmering, add all the chopped mushrooms and cook, stirring constantly, until the mushrooms release their moisture, about 5 minutes. Remove from the heat, and allow to cool slightly.
6. Place the chickpeas in a large mortar and pestle, and mash to a fine paste. (You also can use a food processor for this.) Transfer the chickpea paste to a large bowl, and add the cooked bella mushrooms, the tofu, breadcrumbs, salt, and homemade taco seasoning. Put on a pair of disposable kitchen gloves. Hand-mash the tofu and mix all the ingredients until well combined.
7. Line a baking sheet with parchment paper. Form 1 tablespoon (18g) of the mixture into a ball, and place on the prepared baking sheet. Repeat with the remaining mixture. Cover the mushroom balls with plastic wrap to keep them from drying out.
8. Next, make the shredded mushrooms. Cut the bottom off the king oyster mushrooms, brush off any dust, and place the mushrooms on a cutting board. Shred the mushrooms using

a fork, starting at the bottom of the mushroom. You'll end up with a texture that is similar to shredded chicken.

9. Transfer the mushrooms to a small baking dish, add the salt, homemade taco seasoning, and olive oil, and toss with gloved hands to combine. Cover with plastic wrap, and set aside.

10. To make the beet tortillas, place the beet in a small saucepan. Add the salt, and cover with water . Bring to a boil over high heat. Cook until tender, about 15 minutes.

11. Allow the beet to slightly cool, then transfer it to a blender along with 1½ cups (355ml) of the cooking water. Blend on high until smooth, about 2 to 3 minutes.

12. Use a wooden spoon to stir together the corn flour and ground beet in a large bowl until the dough comes together. Knead with your hands. Cover the dough with plastic wrap, and let rest for 10 minutes.

13. Open the plastic wrap halfway. Pull out some dough, weigh it out to 40 grams, flatten it slightly with your hands, and return it to the bowl. Do the same with the rest of the dough, keeping the plastic wrap in place to help retain the dough's moisture. You should have about 14 pieces of dough (soon to be tortillas).

14. Preheat a large skillet over medium-high heat. Line a tortilla press with a 7 × 7-inch (17.75 × 17.75cm) piece of parchment paper. Roll one piece of dough into a ball between the palms of your hands, place it on the parchment paper, cover with another piece of parchment paper, and press down. (Cut 6 to 8 pieces of parchment paper, and change them as they get soggy.)

15. Remove the parchment paper, transfer the dough to the preheated skillet, and cook, turning every 30 to 40 seconds, for a total of 2½ to 3 minutes. Immediately transfer the cooked tortilla to a plate lined with a tea towel, and cover with another tea towel to retain moisture. Repeat with the remaining dough.

16. Preheat the broiler to 550°F (290°C) for 5 minutes. Remove the plastic wrap and add the mushroom balls and shredded mushrooms to the oven, and broil for 10 minutes.

17. Place the tortillas on taco stands. Top with the mushroom balls, shredded mushrooms, mango salsa, and sour cream sauce, and serve with extra cilantro and lime wedges.

Note

For quick, even dicing, a vegetable chopper comes in handy when cutting the ingredients for the mango salsa.

CHAPTER 2

Seafood

Grilled Shrimp
with Louie Sauce

PREP TIME: 40 minutes plus 2 hours to marinate • **COOK TIME:** 10 minutes • **SERVINGS:** 3 or 4

I'll never forget the first time I tasted a shrimp cocktail with Louie sauce in a restaurant—the perfectly grilled shrimp and tangy, rich sauce left an unforgettable impression. This recipe recreates that magic with juicy, lemongrass-marinated shrimp and a zesty Louie dipping sauce. Paired with a refreshing lettuce veggie cube bowl, this dish brings a bit of that restaurant magic to your table.

SHRIMP AND MARINADE

1 tbsp (15g) plus ¾ tsp (3.75g) kosher salt

12 unpeeled raw colossal shrimp with tails on

1 tsp (1g) freshly ground black pepper

1 tbsp (15ml) extra-virgin olive oil

3 stalks lemongrass, cut into 4-inch (10cm) pieces

LOUIE DIPPING SAUCE

6 tbsp (30g) fresh flat-leaf parsley leaves

3 tbsp (18g) chopped fresh chives

2 garlic cloves

1 tsp (5g) kosher salt

1 tsp (1g) freshly ground black pepper

1⅓ cups (300g) mayonnaise

⅓ cup (75g) ketchup

1 tbsp (15ml) Worcestershire sauce

2 tbsp (30g) prepared horseradish

3 tbsp (45g) sweet pickle relish

2 tbsp (30g) nonpareil capers

2 tbsp (30ml) fresh lemon juice

LETTUCE VEGGIE CUBE BOWL

½ tbsp (7.5ml) white vinegar

¼ head of lettuce

½ small red onion, diced

1 medium tomato, diced

2 mini cucumbers, diced

1 avocado, peeled, pitted, and diced

1 tbsp (15ml) red wine vinegar

½ tsp (2g) sugar

½ tsp (2.5g) kosher salt

½ tsp (0.5g) freshly grounded black pepper

SPECIAL EQUIPMENT

Mortar and pestle

Pizza oven or grill

1. Combine enough cold water to cover the shrimp and 1 tablespoon (15g) of salt in a large bowl, and stir well to dissolve the salt. Add the shrimp, toss, and gently shake the shrimp with your hands to wash. Drain.
2. Line a cutting board with paper towels. Peel the shrimp, but leave the tails intact. Be careful not to tear the inside of the head. Place the shrimp on the prepared cutting board, and insert a knife into the center of the back of each shrimp from head to tail. Pick up each shrimp and remove the vein by pulling it out with a paper towel. (You can remove the vein with your fingers, but it's slippery, so a paper towel comes in handy.)
3. Sprinkle the shrimp with the remaining ¾ teaspoon (3.75g) salt and the pepper, and drizzle with olive oil.
4. Crush the lemongrass with a mortar and pestle to release the zest. Line a medium bowl with the lemongrass, and arrange 3 or 4 shrimp on top. Continue to add layers of the remaining lemongrass and shrimp until all shrimp and lemongrass are used. Cover the bowl with plastic wrap, and place in the refrigerator for 2 hours.
5. To make the Louie dipping sauce, place all the ingredients in a food processor and pulse to combine and finely chop the herbs. Transfer the sauce to a bowl, cover, and place in the refrigerator.
6. To make the lettuce veggie cube bowl, combine enough cold water to cover the vegetables and the white vinegar in a large bowl. Remove 2 or 3 leaves of lettuce from the head, add to the water, and let soak for a few minutes. Rinse under running water and drain in a colander.
7. Add the onion, tomato, and cucumbers to a medium bowl. Add the avocado, red wine vinegar, sugar, salt, and pepper, and mix with a wooden spoon until well combined. Cover the bowl with plastic wrap, and place in the refrigerator.
8. Preheat a pizza oven or grill to 350°F (180°C).
9. Remove the shrimp from the refrigerator, and discard the lemongrass. Place the shrimp on the grill and cook until opaque, about 5 minutes. Flip and cook for about 5 more minutes.
10. Transfer the shrimp to one side of a large platter, with the Louie sauce in a bowl alongside. Arrange the lettuce in a circle like a bowl, spoon the diced vegetable salad into the lettuce bowl, and serve. Enjoy with a cold beer, if you'd like.

Note

The Louie sauce is also delicious as a nacho dip. Don't forget the chips!

Creamy Mussels

PREP TIME: 20 minutes • **COOK TIME:** 15 minutes • **SERVINGS:** 3

The city where I live is in a mountainous area, so it's hard to find fresh seafood. Luckily, however, I can buy mussels—which I really love—at my local supermarket. Mussels are rich in nutrients such as calcium, phosphorus, and iron. (Bonus: they're helpful in relieving hangovers!) Indulge in the rich flavors of these creamy mussels, in which a luxurious cream sauce coats the mussels and pairs perfectly with a warm baguette. For a unique twist, try substituting coconut cream for the heavy cream. It brings a new depth of flavor to the sauce.

2 lb (1kg) mussels
1 tbsp (15g) plus ½ tsp (2.5g) kosher salt
10 sprigs fresh flat-leaf parsley, stems removed and set aside, leaves roughly chopped
3 or 4 sprigs fresh thyme
3 or 4 sprigs fresh oregano or sage
1 bay leaf
1 tbsp (14g) unsalted butter
2 shallots, thinly sliced
2 garlic cloves, finely chopped
1 cup (237ml) white wine
¼ cup (59ml) heavy cream
1 cup (150g) cherry tomatoes, halved
1 Thai red chile, sliced

SPECIAL EQUIPMENT
Kitchen string

1. Place the mussels in a large bowl with enough water to cover. Discard any mussels that float and those with broken shells. Pull out the beard of each mussel by grasping it between your thumb and index finger and pulling firmly.
2. Add 1 tablespoon (15g) of salt to the water, and clean the mussels by rubbing them for 2 minutes. Drain the water and rinse the mussels again with clean water. Drain them once more using a fine-mesh sieve, and set aside.
3. Tie the parsley stems, thyme, oregano, and bay leaf together with kitchen string.
4. Heat a large skillet over medium-high heat, and add the butter and herb bouquet. Stir for 2 minutes to infuse the herbs into the butter.
5. Add the shallots, garlic, and the remaining ½ teaspoon (2.5g) of salt, and stir-fry until soft, about 3 minutes.
6. Pour in the wine, and bring to a boil. Add the mussels and all but 1 tablespoon (6g) of chopped parsley leaves, cover, and cook until the mussels open, 7 to 10 minutes.
7. Uncover, and remove the herb bouquet. Add the heavy cream, and stir well.
8. Add the cherry tomatoes, the remaining parsley leaves, and the red chile, and stir.
9. Serve with your favorite toasted bread.

LA COQUETTE

Phyllo-Wrapped Seafood Papillote

PREP TIME: 20 minutes plus 5 hours to thaw • **COOK TIME:** 1 hour • **SERVINGS:** 2 or 3

This recipe brings together the bounty of the sea in a dish that's both elegant and comfortingly rustic. Tender seafood, crispy potatoes, and aromatic herbs are wrapped in flaky phyllo pastry for a meal that feels as special as it is satisfying. The preparation may seem a bit involved, but the flavors are more than worth the effort. The natural sweetness of the seafood is elevated by the Old Bay Seasoning, and the buttery phyllo pastry provides the perfect contrast to the juicy seafood inside. With a variety of seafood options to choose from, each bite brings a new burst of texture and flavor.

- 3 tbsp (45ml) extra-virgin olive oil
- 1 tbsp (6g) chopped fresh thyme, plus 2 stems for garnish
- ½ tbsp (3g) chopped fresh rosemary, plus 1 stem for garnish
- 8 frozen phyllo pastry sheets
- 2 large red potatoes, peeled
- 1 tsp (5g) plus 2 tbsp (30g) kosher salt
- ½ lb (227g) octopus legs
- 6 (340g) colossal (8–12 count) black tiger shrimp
- ⅓ lb (150g) clams, scrubbed
- 6 scallops
- 1 cup (185g) pearl onions
- ½ lb (227g) cherry tomatoes
- 1 tsp (1g) freshly ground black pepper
- 1 cup (227g) unsalted butter, melted
- 2 tbsp (30ml) cooking wine or white wine
- 3 tbsp (21.5g) Old Bay Seasoning

SPECIAL EQUIPMENT

- 9-inch (23cm) oval-shaped baking dish
- Kitchen string

1. Combine the olive oil, chopped thyme, and chopped rosemary in a small heatproof bowl, and microwave on high for 1 minute. Allow to cool, cover with plastic wrap, and set aside at room temperature.
2. Let the pastry sheets stand at room temperature for about 1 hour.
3. Place the potatoes in a small saucepan. Cover with water, add ½ teaspoon (2.5g) of salt, and simmer over medium-high heat for 20 minutes.
4. Add about 1 quart (1 liter) of water and 2 tablespoons (30g) of salt to a large bowl, and stir to dissolve the salt. Add the octopus legs, shrimp, clams, and scallops, and stir gently with your hand. Transfer the seafood to a colander to drain. Set aside.
5. Cut the cooked potatoes into ½-inch (1.25cm) slices. Set aside.
6. Arrange the pearl onions and cherry tomatoes in a single layer in a medium baking pan. Arrange the seafood on top, being careful not to overcrowd or overlap. Season the seafood evenly with ¼ teaspoon (1.25g) of salt and ½ teaspoon (0.5g) of the pepper. Flip over the seafood only, and season with the remaining ¼ teaspoon (1.25g) of salt and ½ (0.5g) teaspoon of pepper. Drizzle with the reserved herbed olive oil, and let rest for a few minutes.
7. Preheat the oven to 350°F (180°C).
8. Line a work surface with parchment paper. Place one full sheet of thawed pastry on the parchment paper, brush it with melted butter, cover with another sheet, brush with butter again, and repeat until you have eight layers. (Be sure to brush thoroughly so the edges don't dry out and crack.) Cut the eight layers of 13 × 16-inch (33 × 40cm) pastry in half to make two stacks of 13 × 8-inch (33 × 20cm) sheets.
9. Line a 9-inch (23cm) oval baking dish with one of the pastry pieces. Trim the second pastry piece to be about 1 inch (2.5cm) larger than the shape of the dish, and set aside.
10. Set a large skillet over high heat, and heat for about 5 minutes. Add the seafood and pearl onions, and cook for 3 minutes. Add the wine, and cook for another 2 minutes. Mix the Old Bay Seasoning with the remaining melted butter, drizzle over the ingredients in the skillet, and toss to combine. Remove from the heat, and set aside.
11. Add the potatoes to the baking dish. Next, add the tomatoes and then the seafood and onions, then top with the octopus. Add the second sheet of pastry and gently tuck the dough into the dish to create a lid. (The pastry should hug the ingredients.)
12. Tie both ends of the phyllo pastry pieces together with kitchen string, and seal the filled pastry with the trimmed pieces of dough from step 9.
13. Bake for about 30 minutes or until the pastry is golden brown.
14. Garnish with thyme and rosemary stems, and serve immediately.

Black Squid Ink Pasta

PREP TIME: 20 minutes plus 30 minutes to rest • **COOK TIME:** 10 minutes • **SERVINGS:** 2

This pasta dish showcases the unique harmony of whole squid and squid ink and delivers an unforgettable flavor experience. The chewy texture of the squid perfectly complements the rich, deep, briny flavor of the ink, creating a delightful sensation with every bite. Squid ink is not just flavorful; it's also rich in antioxidants and can have positive effects on health, including supporting immune function and reducing inflammation. Note that you will need a pasta maker for this recipe.

SQUID INK PASTA DOUGH

1 cup (125g) all-purpose flour
¾ cup (135g) semolina
2 large eggs, beaten
1 tbsp (24g) squid ink
1 tbsp (15ml) extra-virgin olive oil
1 tsp (5g) kosher salt

PASTA SAUCE

¼ cup (59ml) extra-virgin olive oil, plus more for drizzling
1 shallot, minced
2 garlic cloves, minced
½ lb (227g) whole squid
½ tsp (2.5g) kosher salt
¼ cup (59ml) white wine
2 tbsp (30g) tomato paste
⅛ tsp (0.1g) crushed hot red pepper
¼ tsp (0.25g) freshly ground black pepper
¼ cup (20g) grated Parmigiano-Reggiano

SPECIAL EQUIPMENT

Pasta maker

Notes

Because you're cooking the pasta and making the sauce at the same time, it's helpful to prepare all the ingredients for the sauce and have them ready by the stove.

When making the sauce, you can add ½ teaspoon (2.5ml) of oyster sauce for extra flavor.

You can make spaghetti noodles from the remaining half of the dough. Dust them generously with flour, place them in a container lined with a paper towel, cover, and refrigerate for up to 3 days.

1. To make the pasta dough, place the flour, semolina, eggs, squid ink, 1 tablespoon (15ml) water, olive oil, and salt in a medium bowl and mix with a spatula. When the dough starts to come together, use your hands to fold and knead the dough for 10 minutes. (The dough will be a little stiff, but it will get softer after resting.) Form the dough into a ball, cover with plastic wrap, and let it rest for 30 minutes.
2. Bring a large pot of 6⅓ cups (1.5 liters) water to a boil over high heat.
3. Turn out the dough onto a lightly floured work surface, and roll out with a rolling pin to ¼-inch (0.5cm) thickness. Divide the dough into two halves with a scraper. Wrap one half of the dough in plastic wrap for later use (see Note). Put the other half of the dough through a pasta maker and roll it out thinly, working from level 0 to level 3 and running the dough through the pasta maker twice for each level. Cut the pasta with a spaghetti cutter, or fold into two or three layers, dust each layer with flour, and cut with a knife to a thickness of ⅛ inch (3mm).
4. Add some salt to the pot of boiling water. Drop in the pasta, and cook for 3 to 5 minutes.
5. Start making the sauce at the same time the pasta is added to the water. Heat a large skillet over medium heat, and add the olive oil, shallots, and garlic. When the pan starts to sizzle, add the squid, salt, white wine, and tomato paste. Cover and cook for 2 to 3 minutes. Turn the squid and cook 2 to 3 minutes more or until the squid changes from translucent white to completely white, and the squid is plump and taut. Transfer the cooked squid to a bowl and cover with plastic wrap.
6. Using tongs, remove the cooked pasta from the pot (do not discard the pasta water), and add it to the skillet the squid was cooked in. Add ¼ cup (59ml) of the pasta water, stir, and then add ¼ cup (59ml) more of the pasta water, stir, and cook for 3 to 5 minutes.
7. Remove from the heat, add the crushed red pepper, black pepper, and Parmigiano-Reggiano, and toss to combine. Transfer the pasta to a serving dish.
8. Cut the squid into thin slices and place on top of the pasta. Pour the rest of the sauce from the saucepan over the squid, and serve with a generous drizzle of extra-virgin olive oil.

Note

Maintaining the temperature of the oil is essential for the crispness of the fish and the potatoes. Aim for a temperature of about 345°F (175°C) at all times. A deep-fry thermometer is a must for this recipe.

Fish and Chips

PREP TIME: 10 minutes plus 1 hour to chill • **COOK TIME:** 40 minutes • **SERVINGS:** 3 or 4

Fish and chips hold a special place in my heart, reminding me of the times my husband and I spent together in Darling Harbour in Sydney, Australia. This classic dish, featuring crispy fried fish and golden chips, or french fries, is complemented by a tangy tartar sauce and creamy mashed peas. The combination of fresh fish, a light beer batter, and perfectly seasoned potato chips makes this a true comfort food.

CHIPS

3 large russet potatoes
1 tbsp (15g) kosher salt, divided

TARTAR SAUCE

4 baby cucumbers, diced
2 (6g) anchovies, minced
2 hard-boiled eggs, peeled and diced
1 shallot, diced
¼ cup (58g) mayonnaise
2 tbsp (18g) nonpareil capers
1 tbsp (6g) chopped fresh parsley
1 tbsp (6g) chopped fresh dill
1 tbsp (6g) lemon zest
1 tbsp (15ml) fresh lemon juice
½ tbsp (7.5ml) maple syrup
1 tsp (2.5g) crushed red pepper

MASHED PEAS

1 cup (185g) frozen summer sweet peas
2 tbsp (28g) unsalted butter
1 shallot, chopped
⅛ tsp (0.6g) kosher salt
¼ cup (59ml) 2% milk or water
2 tbsp (12g) chopped fresh mint leaves

FISH

2 qt (2 liters) canola oil
3 cod or haddock fillets (about 14 oz/400g)
½ tsp (2.5g) kosher salt
¼ tsp (0.25g) freshly ground black pepper
3 tbsp (23.5g) cake flour or all-purpose flour

BATTER

1 cup (120g) cake flour or all-purpose flour
1 tsp (4.8g) baking powder
½ tsp (2.5g) kosher salt
¼ tsp (0.25g) freshly ground black pepper
1 cup (237ml) cold light beer

SPECIAL EQUIPMENT

Potato masher
Deep-fry thermometer

1. Wash the potatoes under running water, slice into ½-inch (1.25cm) sticks, and immediately soak in a large bowl filled with cold water to remove the starch.
2. Bring 2 quarts (2 liters) of water to a boil in a large pot over medium heat. Transfer the soaked potatoes to the boiling water, and add 2 teaspoons (10g) of salt. Return to a boil, and cook until the potatoes are tender but not falling apart, about 15 minutes. Transfer the potatoes to a paper towel–lined baking sheet, and place in the freezer for 1 hour.
3. To make the tartar sauce, combine all ingredients in a small bowl, cover with plastic wrap, and place in the refrigerator.
4. To make the mashed peas, briefly rinse the frozen peas under running water. Line a medium bowl with a paper towel, and place the peas on top.
5. Heat a small skillet over medium heat. Add the butter and chopped shallot, and cook until translucent, about 2 minutes. Add the peas and salt, and cook for about 3 minutes.
6. Remove from the heat, and use a potato masher to mash the peas, adding the milk (or water) to moisten the mixture. Add the mint, stir to combine, and transfer the pea mixture to a bowl to cool.
7. To prepare the fish, pour the oil into a large, deep skillet, and heat over high heat to 350°F (180°C).
8. Preheat the oven to 200°F (93°C).
9. Line a cutting board with a paper towel, place the cod or haddock fillets on top, and pat dry with another paper towel. Season the fish with salt and pepper and then dust both sides with the flour. Set aside.
10. To make the batter, whisk together the flour, baking powder, salt, and black pepper in a medium bowl. Pour in the cold beer, and whisk to combine.
11. Working in two or three batches, coat the fish with the batter and carefully place in the hot oil. When the batter is firm, turn the fish and fry until golden brown on both sides, 5 to 7 minutes. Transfer the cooked fish to a wire rack, and transfer to the oven to keep warm. Repeat with the remaining fish, making sure the oil temperature does not drop below 340°F (170°C).
12. Remove the potatoes from the freezer. Working in two or three batches, fry the potatoes in the remaining oil in the skillet until golden brown, about 5 minutes. Transfer the cooked potatoes to a plate, and immediately sprinkle with the remaining 1 teaspoon (5g) salt.
13. Serve the fish with the chips and peas on the side and the tartar sauce for dipping. Pair with an ice-cold beer, if you'd like.

Beetroot-Cured Salmon

PREP TIME: 30 minutes plus at least 24 hours to cure • **COOK TIME:** none • **SERVINGS:** 20

Beets contain a wealth of nutrients, among them betaine, a nutrient found in beets' red color, which is excellent for helping prevent cancer and relieving inflammation. Salmon also has health benefits, including helping prevent vascular diseases. In this healthy recipe, salmon is wrapped in beets and served with pickled cucumbers and horseradish sauce, taking care of not only your health but also your taste buds!

SALMON

1 (2 lb or 1kg) salmon fillet
9 oz (250g) peeled and chopped beets
1 tsp (2g) whole black peppercorns
1 tsp (2g) dill seeds
1 tsp (2g) coriander seeds
1 cup (240g) kosher salt
1 cup (213g) brown sugar, firmly packed
Zest of 1 lemon
½ cup (118ml) gin

PICKLED CUCUMBERS

¼ cup (59ml) white wine vinegar
¼ cup (50g) granulated sugar
½ tsp (2.5g) kosher salt
4 mini cucumbers, cut into long, thin slices

HORSERADISH SAUCE

½ cup (123g) sour cream
2 tbsp (30g) prepared horseradish
2 tbsp (30g) cream cheese
½ tsp (2.5g) kosher salt
½ tsp (0.5g) freshly ground black pepper

SPECIAL EQUIPMENT

Food processor
Spice grinder or coffee grinder

1. Pat the salmon dry with a paper towel. Set aside in the refrigerator.
2. Add the beets to a food processor and process until finely chopped. Transfer to a bowl, and set aside.
3. Using a spice or coffee grinder, grind the black peppercorns, dill seeds, and coriander seeds. Transfer to a medium bowl.
4. Add the salt, brown sugar, and lemon zest to the ground spices, and mix well. Add the beets and gin, and mix again with a spoon.
5. In a large airtight container that will hold the salmon, add an even layer (about ½ inch [1.25cm] deep) of the salt mixture.
6. Arrange the salmon on top of the salt and cover with remaining salt, fully covering on all sides.
7. Place a piece of parchment paper over the container, and press down to squeeze out any air bubbles. Cover the dish with plastic wrap or a lid, and cure in the refrigerator for at least 24 hours and up to 36 hours.
8. To make the pickled cucumbers, combine the vinegar, sugar, and salt in a small bowl. Add the cucumbers to a container with a lid, and pour the vinegar mixture over the top. Cover and refrigerate until ready to use.
9. To make the horseradish sauce, combine the sour cream, prepared horseradish, cream cheese, salt, and pepper in a small bowl. Cover and refrigerate until ready to use.
10. To serve, remove the salmon from the refrigerator, rinse well, and pat dry with paper towels.
11. Place the salmon on a cutting board, and slice as thinly as possible. The outside of the salmon should be beet red, and the inside will be deep orange.
12. Serve the salmon with the pickled cucumbers and horseradish sauce on your favorite crackers or baguettes. Add some fresh dill and capers to make it even more delicious!

Deep-Fried Lobster

with Lemon Cream Sauce

PREP TIME: 40 minutes • **COOK TIME:** 12 minutes • **SERVINGS:** 3 or 4

There's something truly special about deep-fried lobster. The first time I tasted this dish, I was amazed at how perfectly the textures and flavors came together. The crispy, golden lobster shell gives way to tender and juicy meat. Then, the bright and creamy lemon sauce brings it all to life—it's the perfect balance. This dish feels luxurious and comforting at the same time. It's the kind of meal that impresses guests yet is surprisingly easy to make. Once you try it, you'll never think of lobster the same way again.

1 cup (190g) potato starch
1 head of iceberg lettuce
1 tbsp (15ml) white vinegar
1 (1½ lb or 680g) lobster
2 tbsp (30ml) white wine or cooking wine
½ tsp (2.5g) kosher salt
1 tsp (1g) freshly ground black pepper
2 qt (2 liters) canola oil, for frying
¼ cup (59ml) vegetable oil

LEMON CREAM SAUCE

Zest of 1 lemon
3 tbsp (45ml) fresh lemon juice
¾ cup (173g) mayonnaise
2½ tbsp (50g) sweetened condensed milk
2 tbsp (30ml) maple syrup
¼ tsp (1.25g) kosher salt
½ tsp (0.5g) freshly ground black pepper

SPECIAL EQUIPMENT

Deep-fry thermometer
Disposable kitchen gloves

1. Place the potato starch in a large bowl, add enough water to cover, and let the starch soak for 30 minutes.
2. Meanwhile, remove the core from the lettuce by pressing firmly to break it apart from the leaves. Discard. Place the lettuce cored side up in a medium bowl, add the vinegar to the core cavity, and cover with cold water. Let the lettuce soak for about 3 minutes, then lift the lettuce to drain, and discard the water. Repeat with fresh water, and drain again. Using your hands, break the head of lettuce in half, place the lettuce broken-side down on a paper towel–lined plate, cover with plastic wrap, and refrigerate.
3. Cut the lobster in half, shell side first, using heavy-duty scissors. Place the lobster on a cutting board, and use a knife to cut it in half all the way through. Cut the lobster into 2-inch (5cm) pieces (the shell will still be attached), and place in a medium bowl. Drizzle with the wine, season with salt and pepper, and toss to coat. Set aside.
4. To make the lemon sauce, whisk together all the ingredients in a small bowl. Cover with plastic wrap, and place in the refrigerator until ready to serve.
5. Pour the canola oil into a large pot or wok over medium-high heat, and heat the oil to 340°F (170°C).
6. Drain and discard the water from the potato starch. Put on a pair of disposable kitchen gloves. Add the vegetable oil, and use your gloved hands to mix until a thick, dripping batter forms.
7. Set a wire cooling rack inside a baking sheet. Place the lobster in the batter and toss to coat. Working in two or three batches, remove the lobster from the batter, allow any excess to drip off, and place the lobster pieces in the hot oil one at a time. Maintain a temperature of at least 330°F (165°C). You may need to increase the heat to high and then reduce it back down to medium-high once it reaches 330°F (165°C) to 340°F (170°C). Fry the lobster until the shell is crisp, about 3 minutes. Transfer to the prepared baking sheet, and repeat with the remaining lobster.
8. Increase the heat to high, and heat the oil to 355°F (180°C). Add all the lobster at once, and deep-fry again until extra crispy, about 1 or 2 minutes. Transfer to a clean wire rack to rest for 2 or 3 minutes.
9. Tear the head of lettuce by hand and add to a serving bowl. Place the fried lobster on top, drizzle with the lemon cream sauce, and serve.

CHAPTER 3

Beef, Pork & Lamb

Prime Rib Roast

PREP TIME: 2 hours 40 minutes • **COOK TIME:** 2 hours 45 minutes • **SERVINGS:** 4 or 5

There's nothing quite like a beautifully cooked prime rib roast—it's my absolute favorite cut of beef. With its rich marbling and melt-in-your-mouth tenderness, this dish is a true showstopper for any occasion. The slow, gentle roasting method ensures a perfectly juicy interior with a crisp, flavorful exterior crust. To make it a complete meal, I pair it with vibrant green beans tossed in a bright, buttery lemon sauce and golden cheesy potato balls that are crispy on the outside and irresistibly gooey inside. To bring it all together, a luscious maple jus sauce adds just the right touch of deep, savory sweetness. Every bite is pure indulgence!

ROAST

1 (4½ lb or 2kg) prime rib roast
¼ cup (60g) whole-grain mustard
2 tbsp (30ml) extra-virgin olive oil
1 tbsp (15g) kosher salt
2 tsp (4g) finely ground black pepper
2 tsp (4g) onion powder
2 tsp (8g) sugar
1 tsp (2g) garlic powder

CHEESE POTATO BALLS

4 medium red potatoes, peeled and chopped into large pieces
1 tsp (5g) kosher salt
½ cup (125g) shredded cheddar
½ cup (125g) shredded mozzarella
¼ cup (28g) grated Parmigiano-Reggiano
½ tsp (2g) sugar
2 tbsp (30ml) extra-virgin olive oil

MAPLE JUS SAUCE

¼ cup (59ml) red wine
1 cup (237ml) no-salt-added beef broth
3 tbsp (45ml) maple syrup
2 tbsp (30ml) Worcestershire sauce
1 tsp (1g) freshly ground black pepper

SAUTÉED GREEN BEANS WITH LEMON BUTTER SAUCE

2 tbsp (28g) unsalted butter
1 tsp (5ml) extra-virgin olive oil
½ shallot, finely chopped
⅛ tsp (1g) kosher salt
½ lb (227g) fresh green beans, ends trimmed
1 tbsp (15ml) lemon juice
1 tbsp (15ml) maple syrup

1. To make the roast, allow the prime rib to rest at room temperature for 2 hours.
2. Preheat the oven to 450°F (230°C).
3. Pat the meat dry with paper towels. Trim the fascia away from the bone and trim off any large pieces of fat. Tie the meat three or four times with kitchen string. Place the meat in a roasting pan.
4. Combine the mustard, olive oil, salt, pepper, onion powder, sugar, and garlic powder in a small bowl using a spatula. Coat the meat with the seasoning mixture, bone side first, and turn to coat all the sides.
5. Insert an internal meat thermometer into the center of the meat. Bake for 22 minutes and 30 seconds, then turn off the heat and let the meat sit in the closed oven for 2 hours, allowing the residual oven heat to cook the meat all the way through. (At an oven temperature of 450°F/230°C, the meat needs to cook for 5 minutes per 1 pound/454g; for a 4½-pound/2kg prime rib, that's 22 minutes 30 seconds.)
6. Meanwhile, to make the cheese potato balls, place the potatoes in a large saucepan. Add salt, cover with water, and set over high heat. Cover and simmer for 20 minutes or until the potatoes are fork-tender. Uncover, drain the potatoes, and mash them in the pot with a potato masher. Line a baking sheet with parchment paper. Using a cookie scoop (I use a 1 tablespoon/20g scoop), scoop out a ball of potatoes and place it on the prepared baking sheet. Repeat with remaining mashed potatoes, placing the balls 2 inches (5cm) apart on the baking sheet.
7. Combine the cheddar, mozzarella, Parmigiano-Reggiano, and sugar in a medium bowl. Dip half of the potato balls in the cheese mixture, coating all sides generously with the cheese, and return them to the baking sheet. (The rest you'll leave uncoated.) Cover the balls with a tea towel and set aside.
8. When the internal temperature of the meat reaches the desired doneness, minus 7 degrees from the final temperature, remove the meat from the oven and transfer it to a piece of foil. Wrap the meat in the foil, seal tightly, and let rest for 30 minutes. (I like my meat rare, so I remove it from the oven when it reaches 115°F/45°C. The temperature of the meat will increase about 7 or 8 degrees as it rests.) Wait to remove the thermometer until the end of the resting time to prevent the juices from seeping out.
9. Heat the oven's broiler to 500°F (260°C).
10. Drizzle the uncoated potato balls with olive oil, place all of the potato balls in the oven, and broil for 10 to 15 minutes, until the cheese on the coated balls is melted and the edges are crisp and the plain potato balls are golden brown. Be careful not to let them burn because the oven will be very hot. Turn off the oven and let them sit inside to keep warm.

1 tsp (2g) lemon zest
½ tsp (0.5g) freshly ground black pepper

SPECIAL EQUIPMENT

Kitchen string
Potato masher
Cookie scooper (1 tbsp)
Ovenproof meat thermometer

11. To make the maple jus sauce, pour the wine into the roasting pan, set over medium-high heat, and deglaze the pan with a wooden spoon. Add the beef broth, maple syrup, Worcestershire sauce, and pepper, and simmer for 10 minutes. Strain the sauce through a fine-mesh sieve into a sauce dish. Discard any solids.

12. While the sauce is simmering, prepare the lemon butter sauce for the green beans. Add the butter, olive oil, shallot, and salt to a medium saucepan. Set over medium-high heat, and sauté for 3 minutes. Add the green beans, lemon juice, and maple syrup, and cook for 2 or 3 minutes, swirling the pan to coat the beans with the sauce. Remove from the heat, sprinkle with the lemon zest and pepper, cover, and set aside.

13. Unwrap the rested prime rib and place it on a cutting board. Remove the kitchen string and the thermometer, cut off the bones and separate them from the meat, and cut into four pieces. Place the meat on a large serving platter, arrange the potato balls and green beans together on the side of the platter, and serve with the maple jus sauce.

Steak with Pine Nut Sauce

PREP TIME: 1 hour • **COOK TIME:** 15 minutes • **SERVINGS:** 2 or 3

Rich in protein and healthy fats, pine nuts boost immunity and support heart health, making this steak dish as nutritious as it is flavorful. The toasted pine nuts and herb-infused cream sauce add a unique richness, transforming a classic steak into a memorable meal. When paired with velvety mashed potatoes and a robust red wine, this recipe delivers a dining experience that's both comforting and refined.

STEAK

12 oz (340g) beef steak (strip steak is perfect)
½ tsp (2.5g) kosher salt
⅛ tsp (0.5g) freshly ground black pepper
2 garlic cloves

PINE NUT CREAM SAUCE

1 cup (30g) dried mushrooms (any variety)
⅓ cup (50g) pine nuts
½ tsp (2.5g) kosher salt
⅛ tsp (0.5g) freshly ground black pepper
1 garlic clove
2 tbsp (30g) grated Parmesan cheese
1 cup (237ml) heavy cream
1 tbsp (7.5g) all-purpose flour

HERBED BUTTER

½ cup (115g) unsalted butter, room temperature
1 tbsp (5g) chopped fresh parsley
1 tsp (1.5g) chopped fresh sage
½ tsp (0.8g) chopped fresh thyme
½ tsp (0.8g) chopped fresh oregano

SPECIAL EQUIPMENT

Mortar and pestle
Meat thermometer

Notes

You can cook the steak to your preferred doneness. The 115°F to 125°F (45°C to 50°C) called for is rare; medium rare is 130°F to 135°F (54°C to 57°C), medium is 140°F to 145°F (60°C to 63°C), medium well is 150°F to 155°F (65°C to 68°C), and well is 160°F to 165°F (71°C to 74°C).

For a deeper, richer, tastier sauce, you can add 2 tablespoons (30ml) of cognac and 1 teaspoon (5g) of sugar to the cream sauce during Step 8.

1. Season the steak all over with salt and pepper, and place on a piece of parchment paper to rest at room temperature for 1 hour.
2. Place the mushrooms in a small bowl, fill with enough boiling water to cover, and let sit for 30 minutes to rehydrate. Gently squeeze out the excess water with your hands, and set aside the mushrooms.
3. To make the herbed butter, place the butter in a small bowl. Add the parsley, sage, thyme, and oregano, and mix well with a spatula.
4. Cut a 9 × 13-inch (23 × 33cm) piece of parchment paper. Fold it in half and then open it and place half of the herbed butter on one half of the parchment paper. Fold it closed over the butter, and press down evenly with a rolling pin to spread the butter into a thin layer. Roll out the butter slightly wider than the width of the steak. Fold out another 9 × 13-inch (23 × 33cm) piece of parchment paper and repeat with the other half of the butter. Place both slabs of butter in the freezer.
5. To make the pine nut cream sauce, using a mortar and pestle, crush the pine nuts, salt, pepper, and garlic. Add the Parmesan cheese and heavy cream, and mix well with a spatula. Set aside.
6. Pat the steak dry with paper towels. Remove the herbed butter from the freezer, peel it off the parchment paper, and place one slab of butter on each side of the meat.
7. Heat a medium cast-iron skillet over medium-high heat. When hot, add the steak, and cook for 1 minute per side. Add the garlic cloves. Cook for 3 or 4 more minutes, flip the steak, and cook 3 or 4 minutes more. When the steaks' internal temperature reaches 115°F to 125°F (45°C to 50°C), transfer it and the garlic to a sheet of parchment paper, roll them up in the paper, and let them rest for 15 minutes.
8. Meanwhile, place the cast-iron skillet with the remaining herbed butter over low heat. Sprinkle the flour evenly over the butter, and cook, stirring with a wooden spatula, for 3 minutes. Add the rehydrated mushrooms and the pine nut cream sauce, and cook until slightly simmered, 3 to 5 minutes.
9. Unwrap the rested steak, slice to your preferred thickness, and serve with the pine nut cream sauce.

Beef Tenderloins
with Diane Sauce

PREP TIME: 15 minutes plus 2 hours to rest • **COOK TIME:** 15 minutes • **SERVINGS:** 2

This recipe is inspired by the classic steak Diane, a dish created in the 1940s at the Drake Hotel in New York. The signature Diane sauce, named after the chef who created it, is a rich blend of cognac, Worcestershire sauce, mustard, and cream, which perfectly complements the tenderloin. The steak is seared to a beautiful golden brown and then enhanced with the flavorful sauce for a luxurious dining experience. Accompanying the dish are delicately blanched asparagus spears, tied together with green onions, and delicately smoky green peas and cherry tomatoes. This dish is ideal for a celebratory meal or when you want to indulge in a restaurant-quality dinner at home. It combines classic French technique with modern flair for a truly unforgettable meal.

BEEF TENDERLOINS

2 (1½-inch/3.75cm) beef tenderloins (each about ½ lb/225g)
4 stems of fresh thyme
2 stems of fresh rosemary
1 stem of fresh sage
1 tsp (5g) kosher salt
1 tsp (1g) freshly ground black pepper
3 tbsp (45ml) extra-virgin olive oil
5 garlic cloves
1 shallot, halved
2 tbsp (28g) unsalted butter

ASPARAGUS, GREEN PEAS, AND CHERRY TOMATOES

1 lb (454g) asparagus
1½ tsp (7.5g) kosher salt
9 strips of thin green onion or chives
½ cup (80g) fresh green peas, shelled
½ cup (114g) cherry tomatoes
1 tbsp (15ml) extra-virgin olive oil, plus ½ tbsp (7.5ml) for drizzling
1 tbsp (15ml) balsamic glaze
½ tsp (0.5g) freshly ground black pepper

DIANE SAUCE

½ cup (118ml) low-sodium beef broth
4 tsp (20ml) Worcestershire sauce
1 tbsp (10g) whole-grain Dijon mustard
2 tsp (13g) tomato paste
2 shallots, finely chopped
¼ cup (59ml) cognac or brandy
⅓ cup (79ml) heavy cream

SPECIAL EQUIPMENT

Kitchen string
Grill basket

1. Allow the tenderloin to sit at room temperature for about 2 hours. Meanwhile, tie together the thyme, rosemary, and sage stems with kitchen string to form a brush, and prepare an ice bath for the asparagus.
2. To make the asparagus, add 2 cups (473ml) of water to a saucepan that's at least as wide as the length of the asparagus, set over high heat, and bring to a boil. Add the asparagus and 1 teaspoon (5g) of salt, and blanch for 1 or 2 minutes. The asparagus will turn bright green. Remove from the water, plunge into the ice bath for about 10 seconds, and remove. Transfer to a paper towel–lined plate.
3. Add the green onions to the hot water for about 1 minute. When they bend slightly, transfer to a clean, paper-towel lined plate.
4. Divide the asparagus spears into thirds, and place one third of the spears on a cutting board. Trim off 2 or 3 inches from the tough root end. Tie together the bottom, middle, and top of the bundle using strips of the green onions, and cut the asparagus into thirds between the ties. Repeat with remaining asparagus. Set aside.
5. In a medium bowl, toss together the peas and tomatoes with the remaining ½ teaspoon (2.5g) of salt and 1 tablespoon (15ml) of olive oil. Transfer to a grill basket, and toast over medium heat, shaking the basket, for about 3 minutes. Set aside. (It can get messy on the stove, but you should definitely try it because the smoky flavor is amazing. Be sure to turn on the vent because the oil mixes with the heat and makes a lot of smoke.)
6. Tie the center of each tenderloin with kitchen string to hold the meat in a circle and sprinkle evenly all over with the salt and pepper.
7. Heat a cast-iron skillet over high heat. Add the olive oil. When it starts to smoke, add the tenderloins and sear until golden brown, 2 or 3 minutes. Flip and sear for another 2 or 3 minutes. Add the garlic, shallot, and butter, and use the herb brush to coat the meat with the butter. Cook the meat, flipping often, for another 2 minutes, or until your desired doneness. For rare: internal temperature of 115°F (46°C), for medium-rare: 125°F (52°C), for medium: 135°F (57°C), for medium-well: 145°F (63°C), for well done: 155°F (68°C). Note: Stop cooking the meat at 5°F (3°C) below your desired doneness temperature. The temperature of the meat will increase slightly as it rests.
8. Transfer the meat, roasted garlic, and shallots from the pan to a sheet of aluminum foil, close the foil around the meat, and let it rest for 5 to 10 minutes.
9. Meanwhile, to make the sauce, whisk together the beef broth, Worcestershire sauce, mustard, and tomato paste in a small bowl.

10. Set the cast-iron skillet over medium-high heat, add the shallots, and sauté until golden, about 3 minutes. Add the cognac or brandy and bring to a boil. Add the beef stock mixture, the cream, and the herb brush, and reduce the temperature to medium-low and simmer for 3 minutes.

11. Arrange the asparagus upright on one side of a serving platter, add the peas and cherry tomatoes, drizzle with olive oil and balsamic glaze, and season with pepper. Slice the tenderloins and set aside. Arrange the shallots and garlic on the other side of the platter, followed by the meat. Pour the sauce over the meat, and serve.

Corned Beef and Cabbage

PREP TIME: 20 minutes plus 5 days to cure • **COOK TIME:** 2 or 3 hours • **SERVINGS:** 8

Corned beef and cabbage is a traditional Irish dish often eaten on St. Patrick's Day. This brisket is cured for 5 days and then slowly cooked half-submerged in spiced water with all the vegetables. The meat is tender and delicious, and the spices and vegetables combine to add an incredible flavor. Enjoy with a beer, perhaps one that you dye green.

PICKLING SPICE BLEND

3 tbsp (25g) whole black peppercorns
2 tbsp (20g) mustard seeds
2 tbsp (10g) crushed hot red pepper
2 tbsp (10g) whole allspice
2 tbsp (10g) coriander seeds
1 tbsp (5g) whole cloves
4 bay leaves
1 cinnamon stick
1 tbsp (3g) ground mace
1 tbsp (5g) ground ginger

CURING BRINE

1¼ cups (300g) kosher salt
½ cup (100g) brown sugar, firmly packed
5 tsp (28g) pink curing salt
1 tsp (1g) garlic powder

BEEF AND CABBAGE

4 lb (1.8kg) beef brisket, trimmed
1 lb (454g) mini potatoes
4 medium carrots
3 small yellow onions, halved
½ medium head cabbage, cut in thirds (including the root)

HORSERADISH CREAM SAUCE

½ cup (118ml) heavy cream
½ cup (120g) sour cream
½ cup (120g) prepared horseradish
Juice of ½ lemon
½ tsp (2.5g) kosher salt
½ tsp (0.5g) freshly ground black pepper

SPECIAL EQUIPMENT

Mortar and pestle
Dutch oven
Ovenproof meat thermometer

1. To make the pickling spice blend, add the black peppercorns, mustard seeds, crushed red pepper, allspice, coriander seeds, cloves, bay leaves, and cinnamon stick to a small skillet over medium-high heat, and toast until fragrant, about 3 to 5 minutes.
2. Grind the cinnamon stick and bay leaves into small pieces using a mortar and pestle. Add the rest of the toasted spices, the mace, and the ginger, and mix well with a spoon. Set aside.
3. To make the curing brine, add the salt, brown sugar, pink curing salt, garlic powder, and 1 tablespoon (10g) of the pickling spice blend to a medium saucepan. Add 6⅓ cups (1.5 liters) of water, set over medium-high heat, bring to a boil, and cook until the sugar and salt dissolve, about 10 minutes.
4. Pour 9¾ cups (2.15 liters) of water into an 8½-quart (8-liter) heatproof container, add the curing brine, and set aside until completely cool.
5. Add the brisket to the cool curing brine, ensuring that the brisket is completely submerged. Cover and refrigerate for 5 days.
6. Preheat the oven to 300°F (150°C).
7. Wash the potatoes, carrots, onion, and cabbage under running water. Set aside in a colander.
8. Remove the brisket from the refrigerator, discard the brine, and wash the meat under running water. Place it in a large Dutch oven, and poke a heatproof meat thermometer into the thickest part of the meat.
9. Arrange the onions around the meat. Sprinkle 2 tablespoons (10g) of the pickling spice blend over the brisket, and pour 1 inch (2.5cm) of water into the Dutch oven. Set the Dutch oven over medium-high heat, and bring to a boil.
10. When the water starts to boil, cover the Dutch oven and transfer it to the oven. Bake until the internal temperature of the brisket reaches 140°F (60°C), open the lid, and add the potatoes, carrots, and cabbage. Cover and continue cooking until the brisket's internal temperature reaches 190°F (88°C) and the brisket is tender, about 2 to 3 hours from when the brisket first entered the oven.
11. Meanwhile, to make the horseradish cream sauce, pour the heavy cream into a medium bowl and whisk quickly until the cream doesn't bend when you lift the whisk. Add the sour cream, horseradish, lemon juice, salt, and pepper, and mix well. Set aside in the refrigerator.
12. Remove the Dutch oven from the oven. Transfer the vegetables to a plate and keep warm. Wrap the brisket in parchment paper, and let rest for 15 minutes.
13. Cut the brisket into slices ¼-inch (6mm) thick and serve with the horseradish cream sauce on top and roasted vegetables on the side.

Beef Bourguignon

PREP TIME: 15 minutes plus at least 12 hours to marinate • **COOK TIME:** 2 hours • **SERVINGS:** 8

Beef Bourguignon, the signature dish of the film Julie & Julia, became so meaningful for me after I watched the movie, like a recipe handed down from my grandmother, and the love and passion for cooking that I felt after watching the main character make the dish has stayed in my heart. After I got married, I tried this recipe in my own small kitchen. This recipe rekindles my passion for cooking and is the first thing I share with the people I love.

2 sprigs of rosemary
4 sprigs of thyme
1 sprig of sage
1 bay leaf
2 lb (1kg) beef shank, shoulder, or chuck stew meat, cut into 1-inch (2.5cm) pieces
1 medium red onion, chopped
1 shallot, sliced
3 garlic cloves, sliced
2 medium carrots, sliced into ⅜-inch (1cm) pieces
½ Preserved Lemon (page 14), chopped (optional)
1 tsp (5g) kosher salt
1 tsp (1g) freshly ground black pepper
2 cups (473ml) red wine, plus more to cover (I like to use pinot noir)
½ cup (60g) all-purpose flour
3 tbsp (45ml) extra-virgin olive oil
1 tsp (2g) whole cloves
1 tsp (2g) whole black peppercorns
1 cup (237ml) beef broth, divided
1 tbsp (14g) tomato paste
7 oz (200g) bacon, diced
1 shallot, finely diced
7 oz (200g) baby bella mushrooms, halved
1 tbsp (13g) brown sugar
1 tbsp (7g) cocoa powder

SPECIAL EQUIPMENT
Kitchen string
Dutch oven

Notes

You might need more than 2 cups (473ml) of wine. Use enough each time so that the ingredients are submerged.

Don't skip toasting the flour. That few minutes of toasting boosts the flavor of the whole dish.

1. Tie the rosemary thyme, sage, and bay leaf into a bundle using kitchen string. Set aside.
2. Add the beef, onion, sliced shallot, garlic, carrots, lemon (if using), salt, and pepper to a large bowl. Use your hands to mix well.
3. Pour in the wine until the ingredients are fully covered, and add the herb bouquet. Press the ingredients together to release any air. Cover with plastic wrap and refrigerate for 12 to 24 hours.
4. Place a fine-mesh strainer over a large bowl. Pour the beef mixture into the strainer to separate the liquid from the remaining ingredients. Do not discard.
5. Heat a small frying pan over medium heat. Add the flour and toast until it turns golden, about 5 minutes. Remove the pan from the heat.
6. Coat each piece of beef in the flour, shake off any excess, and place the coated beef on a clean plate.
7. Set a large Dutch oven over medium-high heat. Add the olive oil and then the beef, and cook for 5 to 7 minutes. Flip and cook 5 to 7 minutes more, until browned. Transfer the beef to a plate, and set aside.
8. Preheat the oven to 250°F (120°C).
9. Reduce the heat under the Dutch oven to medium. Add the marinated vegetables, and the herb bundle, cloves, black peppercorns, and ¼ cup (59ml) of the beef broth. Scrape the bottom of the pot with a wooden spoon to deglaze.
10. Add the beef, tomato paste, remaining beef broth, and enough reserved wine to cover the ingredients. Cover the pot, and bring to a boil.
11. Transfer the Dutch oven to the oven, and cook for 1 hour.
12. Heat a medium frying pan over medium-high heat. Add the bacon and diced shallot, and cook, stirring frequently, for 5 minutes.
13. Add the mushrooms and 2 tablespoons (30ml) of water. Use a wooden spoon to loosen up any browned bits and cook, stirring often, for 3 minutes.
14. Remove the Dutch oven from the oven. Add the mushroom mixture, brown sugar, and cocoa powder, and mix well. Return to the oven for 30 minutes, or until the meat is tender.
15. Remove the herb bundle, and serve. This goes perfectly with mashed potatoes. Bon appétit!

Bone Marrow Meatballs

PREP TIME: 15 minutes plus 6 hours to soak • **COOK TIME:** 1 hour 15 minutes • **SERVINGS:** 2 or 3

When I first tried making bone marrow meatballs, I was amazed by how the marrow added a rich depth of flavor to the beef. The meatballs are incredibly tender, and the combination of the creamy mashed potatoes and savory tomato sauce makes every bite a celebration. I love how the marrow melts right into the meat, creating a luxurious texture. This recipe was inspired by a long afternoon spent experimenting in the kitchen, where I wanted to blend the comfort of classic meatballs with a more indulgent twist. The fragrance of roasted marrow and fresh herbs will fill your kitchen, making it impossible to resist. I hope this dish brings as much warmth and happiness to your table as it has to mine!

MEATBALLS

4 (6-inch/15cm) frozen beef bones, split lengthwise
4¼ tsp (21.25g) kosher salt, divided
1 tbsp (15ml) extra-virgin olive oil
1 small white onion, finely chopped
1 celery stalk, finely chopped
1 small carrot, finely chopped
2 garlic cloves, minced
1 lb (454g) lean ground beef
1 tsp (1g) freshly ground black pepper
1 cup (60g) fresh breadcrumbs
1 tbsp (15ml) Worcestershire sauce
1 tbsp (16g) tomato paste
½ tbsp (2g) dried thyme
1 large egg
2 tsp (3.5g) crushed hot red pepper

CREAMY BAKED MASHED RED POTATOES

5 medium red potatoes, peeled and cubed
1 tbsp (5g) kosher salt
½ cup (118ml) heavy cream
¼ cup (58g) unsalted butter, cubed
½ tsp (0.5g) freshly ground black pepper

TOMATO SAUCE

¼ cup (59ml) low-sodium beef broth
1 cup (237ml) tomato pasta sauce
¼ cup (25g) grated Parmigiano-Reggiano, plus more for serving
½ tsp (0.5g) freshly ground black pepper

SPECIAL EQUIPMENT

Potato masher
Disposable kitchen gloves
Meat thermometer

1. Place the beef bones and 3 tsp (15g) of salt in a large container. Cover with cold water and set in the refrigerator for at least 6 hours.
2. Add the potatoes to a large pot. Cover with water, add the salt, and set over high heat. Bring to a boil and simmer for 30 minutes. Drain the water and leave the potatoes in the pot.
3. Pour the heavy cream in a heatproof bowl and microwave on high for 1 minute. Pour the cream over the potatoes, and mash with a potato masher.
4. Add the butter and pepper, and stir to combine. Transfer the mashed potatoes to a large pastry bag, and set aside. (A large ziplock bag will work if you don't have a pastry bag.)
5. Remove the beef bones from the refrigerator and place them cut sides up on a medium baking sheet. Lightly pat the tops dry with paper towels.
6. Preheat the oven to 450°F (230°C).
7. Sprinkle with ¼ teaspoon (1.25g) salt and roast for 20 minutes.
8. Transfer the marrow and any beef fat to a large bowl using a spoon. Set aside the bones.
9. Preheat the broiler to 500°F (260°C). Line a baking sheet with parchment paper.
10. Heat a medium skillet over medium heat and add the olive oil. Add the onion, celery, carrot, and garlic, and sauté for about 5 minutes. Transfer the vegetables to the large bowl with the marrow.
11. Don a pair of disposable kitchen gloves. Place the ground beef in another large bowl. Sprinkle with the remaining 1 teaspoon (5g) of salt and the pepper, and add the breadcrumbs, Worcestershire sauce, tomato paste, thyme, egg, and crushed red pepper.
12. Mix well using your gloved hands. Then, form golf-ball size balls (3 tablespoons or 45 grams). Set the finished meatballs on the prepared baking sheet.
13. Return the medium skillet to medium-high heat. Add the meatballs in batches, and cook, tossing frequently, until browned on the outside, about 8 minutes. Transfer the seared meatballs to the baking sheet, bake for about 7 minutes, or until the internal temperature reaches 165°F (75°C).
14. Meanwhile, squeeze the mashed potatoes into the bones where the marrow was, place in a clean medium baking dish, and add to the oven with the meatballs. Remove from the oven when you remove the meatballs.

15. Meanwhile, to make the tomato sauce, return the medium skillet to medium-high heat. Add the beef broth, and thoroughly deglaze the pan with a wooden spoon.

16. Add the tomato pasta sauce, and cook for 3 to 5 minutes. Turn off the heat, and add the Parmigiano-Reggiano and pepper, and stir to combine.

17. Place the baked potatoes on a plate, set three meatballs on top of each bone, drizzle with some tomato sauce, generously top with more Parmigiano-Reggiano, and serve immediately.

Sweet Soy-Marinated

Boneless Beef Short Ribs

PREP TIME: 1 hour 20 minutes plus at least 4 hours to marinate • **COOK TIME:** 35 minutes • **SERVINGS:** 4

These short ribs have always been a favorite at our family gatherings. I still remember the mouthwatering aroma of sizzling beef filling the house, making everyone eager to sit down and eat together. Traditionally, Korean galbi (갈비) is marinated with the bone in and grilled over an open flame, but this recipe takes a simpler approach, using thick, boneless short ribs—just as flavorful but easier to cook at home. The secret to this dish is in the marinade. A perfect blend of soy sauce, apple, and pineapple not only infuses the meat with incredible flavor but also makes it melt-in-your-mouth tender. Pair it with warm, fluffy rice and a fresh, slightly spicy salad, and you've got the perfect balance of savory, sweet, and tangy. Grab your chopsticks, and enjoy every bite!

SHORT RIBS

2 lb (1kg) boneless beef short ribs
1 tsp (5g) kosher salt
1 tsp (1g) freshly ground black pepper
1 tsp (3g) onion power
½ tsp (1.5g) garlic power
1 cup (240g) canned pineapple chunks, with juice
4 tbsp (60ml) olive oil

SWEET SOY SAUCE MARINADE

1¾ cups (414ml) warm water
1 cup (200g) dark brown sugar, firmly packed
1 cup (237ml) soy sauce
¼ cup (85g) light corn syrup
1 large Gala apple, pureed in a blender, or ½ cup (118ml) applesauce
2 tbsp (30ml) sesame oil (optional)
5 garlic cloves, or 1 tsp (3g) garlic powder
1 tsp (1g) freshly ground black pepper

RED PEPPER SALAD

½ lb (227g) red leaf lettuce
1 tbsp (15ml) white vinegar
½ medium sweet or red onion, thinly sliced
3 tbsp (45ml) extra-virgin olive oil
1 tbsp (15ml) soy sauce
1 tbsp (15ml) maple syrup
2 tsp (3g) cayenne, or 1 tbsp (6g) crushed hot red pepper
1 Thai red chile, thinly sliced (optional)

TO SERVE

2 cups (390g) short-grain rice
Crushed pine nuts (optional)

SPECIAL EQUIPMENT

Disposable kitchen gloves

Notes

The lettuce can wilt when seasoned, so do this just before cooking the meat.

For large cubed ribs, place the meat on a cutting board and slice it in half in a butterfly pattern, then flip the meat and slice each side again in a butterfly pattern to elongate the meat.

1. Pat the short ribs dry with a paper towel, and remove the fascia and thick fat. Cut the ribs in half lengthwise, and slice in half in a butterfly pattern to make them wider. Place the ribs horizontally on a cutting board. Holding a knife at a 45-degree angle, insert it just before the cut. Flip over the ribs and reinsert the knife so the angle of the blade is 90 degrees to the first cut. Be careful not to cut through the meat. Repeat with the remaining ribs. You should have a total of four flat, wide, pieces of meat.
2. Place the ribs side by side on the cutting board, and season with the salt, pepper, onion powder, and garlic powder.
3. Puree the pineapple with juice in a food processor. Coat the meat with ⅔ cup (160g) of the pureed pineapple, front and back. (Reserve the remaining ⅓ cup/80g pineapple puree for the marinade.) Transfer the ribs to a container, and refrigerate for 2 hours.
4. To make the marinade, whisk together the warm water and brown sugar in a medium bowl until the sugar is dissolved. Add the remaining ⅓ cup (80g) pineapple puree and the soy sauce, corn syrup, apple, sesame oil (if using), garlic, and pepper, and whisk to combine.
5. Remove the ribs from the refrigerator. Pour the marinade over the ribs, ¼ cup (59ml) at a time, and return the ribs to the refrigerator to marinate, at least 2 hours.
6. Place the rice in a medium bowl, add water to cover, and stir with your hands. If the water becomes cloudy, discard the water, add more water to submerge the rice again, and use your hands to stir. Repeat this process five or six times and then pour the rice into a colander and let drain for 30 minutes. Place the rice in a heavy, medium pot, and add 2⅓ cups (551ml) of water. Set over high heat, and bring to a boil for about 5 minutes. When most of the water has evaporated and the rice begins to bubble, reduce the heat to medium-low, cover, and simmer for 10 minutes. (Do not remove the lid.) Turn off the heat and let stand, covered, for 10 minutes. Using a wooden spoon, dig the rice from bottom and pull to the top to mix evenly. Cover and keep warm.

7. Place the lettuce in a large bowl, cover with water, and add the vinegar. Shake the lettuce gently and let sit for about 3 minutes. Remove each leaf and rinse under running water, place in a colander to drain, and let sit for 5 minutes.
8. Remove the ribs from the refrigerator and let them rest at room temperature for about 30 minutes.
9. To make the red pepper salad (see Note), don a pair of disposable kitchen gloves. Tear the lettuce into 2- or 3-inch (5 or 7.5cm) pieces with your hands and place in a large bowl. Add the onion and olive oil and use your hands to toss to coat evenly. Add the soy sauce, maple syrup, and cayenne, and toss again to coat. Add the Thai red chile (if using), and gently toss to combine. Cover with plastic wrap and set in the refrigerator.
10. Preheat a large skillet over medium-high heat (You can also grill the meat for a nice charred flavor, if you'd prefer). Add 1 tablespoon of the olive oil. Once glistening, add a batch of ribs, and cook for 2 or 3 minutes per side. Transfer the cooked ribs to a plate. While the pan is still hot, add about ½ cup (118ml) of water and use a wooden spoon to loosen any browned bits from the pan, remove from the heat, dump the water, and carefully wipe clean with a paper towel. Return the pan to the heat, add 1 tablespoon of olive oil, swirl to coat the pan, and cook the next batch of meat. Repeat until all ribs are cooked.
11. To serve, arrange the salad and rice on a platter, and set the meat on top of the rice. Garnish with crushed pine nuts (if using) and serve.

STAUB

Spicy Pork Ribs
with Melting Cheese

PREP TIME: 1 hour 5 minutes • **COOK TIME:** 1 hour 10 minutes • **SERVINGS:** 5 or 6

Get ready for a burst of sweet and spicy flavors! These tender pork ribs are marinated in a mix of garlic, ginger, and white wine for a deep, aromatic flavor. Then, they're roasted to a crispy golden brown and coated in a sweet, spicy sauce made with crushed red pepper, bringing out that signature heat. With each bite, the spicy kick from the crushed red pepper contrasts perfectly with the creamy melted cheese. Topped with a touch of cilantro for freshness, this dish delivers an ideal balance of heat and richness.

PORK RIBS

4 lb (1.8kg) pork back or side ribs
4 tsp (20g) kosher salt, divided
4 tsp (16g) sugar, divided
3 tbsp (45ml) white wine
5 garlic cloves, minced
½ tsp (1g) ground ginger powder
1 tsp (1g) freshly ground pepper
⅓ cup (43g) cornmeal
⅓ cup (43g) cornstarch
¼ cup (59ml) extra-virgin olive oil

SPICY STICKY SAUCE

¼ cup (59ml) extra-virgin olive oil
¼ cup (20g) crushed hot red pepper or cayenne (if you like it spicier)
2 tbsp (30ml) white wine
2 tbsp (30ml) soy sauce
2 tbsp (17g) minced garlic
1 tbsp (15ml) ketchup
2 tbsp (25g) sugar
¾ cup (260g) corn syrup
½ tsp (2.5g) kosher salt
1 tsp (1g) freshly ground black pepper, plus more for seasoning
1 tbsp (6g) chopped fresh cilantro (optional)

MELTING CHEESE

2 cups (225g) shredded mozzarella
3 tbsp (45ml) white wine
1 tsp (4g) sugar

Note

If you're craving something really spicy, add 3 or 4 thinly sliced Thai red chiles to the spicy sticky sauce. The heat will be offset by the cheese for a harmonious flavor.

1. Place the pork ribs on a cutting board, skin side up, and gently scrape the end of the fascia with a paper towel to grab it, pull it, and remove it. Hold the knife against the bone, and cut through the meat to divide the ribs into individual pieces.
2. Combine about 5 cups (1.2 liters) of water, 3 teaspoons (15g) of salt, and 3 teaspoons (12g) of sugar in a large bowl, stirring to dissolve the salt and sugar. Add the ribs to the bowl, adding more water to cover as needed. Let the ribs soak for about 30 minutes and then transfer them to a colander. Discard the water. Pat the ribs dry with paper towels.
3. Place the pork ribs in another large bowl, and add the remaining 1 teaspoon (4g) of sugar, 1 teaspoon (5g) of salt, and the white wine, garlic, ginger powder, and pepper, and toss, turning to coat evenly. Cover tightly with plastic wrap, and let marinate for 30 minutes.
4. Preheat the broiler to 500°F (260°C). Line two baking sheets with parchment paper.
5. Whisk together the cornmeal and cornstarch in a medium bowl. Add the ribs to the mixture one by one and lightly coat. Place the ribs on one of the prepared baking sheets, side by side. Drizzle with olive oil.
6. Place a baking sheet on the second rack from the bottom of the oven. Bake for 30 minutes. Remove the ribs from the oven, flip, and transfer them to the other prepared baking sheet. Bake for another 20 minutes, or until golden brown. Do not let the ribs burn.
7. When the ribs are almost done, make the spicy sticky sauce by combining all the ingredients except the cilantro (if using) in a large wok. Set over medium-high heat, and bring to a boil for about 5 minutes. Add the browned ribs when the sauce begins to simmer, and cook for about 10 minutes, tossing constantly to coat evenly.
8. Meanwhile, melt the mozzarella, white wine, and sugar in a large saucepan over low heat, about 10 minutes.
9. Place the ribs on the melted cheese, sprinkle with more pepper and the cilantro (if using), and serve.

Crispy Porchetta

PREP TIME: 20 minutes, plus 26 hours 30 minutes to dry and rest • **COOK TIME:** 2 hours 10 minutes • **SERVINGS:** 12

This porchetta recipe is a traditional Italian dish that's infused with love and care. The 24-hour drying process and slow roasting in the oven ensure that the flavors leave an unforgettable impression on your senses. This is the perfect recipe for preparing a feast for family and friends on special occasions.

2 tbsp (15g) fennel seeds
2 tbsp (12g) whole black peppercorns
4 tbsp (24g) lemon zest
3 tbsp (15g) finely chopped fresh sage
2 tbsp (10g) finely chopped fresh rosemary
1 tbsp (3g) crushed hot red pepper
10 garlic cloves, minced
6 lb (2.7kg) pork belly (skin on)
4 tbsp (60g) kosher salt, divided
2 tbsp (30ml) extra-virgin olive oil

SPECIAL EQUIPMENT

Spice grinder
Kitchen torch
Kitchen string
Ovenproof meat thermometer

Notes

This porchetta is delicious served with the Italian salsa verde sauce from the Porchetta Sandwiches (page 150). It's also great used in the Porchetta Sandwiches.

Store any leftover porchetta, wrapped tightly in plastic wrap, in the refrigerator for up to 3 days. To reheat, preheat the broiler to 450°F (230°C) with a rack in the center position and cook the porchetta for 3 to 5 minutes. Be careful not to let it burn.

1. Toast the fennel seeds and black peppercorns in a small pan over medium heat for 3 to 5 minutes or until fragrant. Set aside to cool for a few minutes, then transfer to a spice grinder, grind well, then transfer to a small bowl. Add the lemon zest, sage, rosemary, crushed red pepper, and garlic, and stir to combine. Set aside.
2. Place the pork belly on a work surface, skin side up, and burn off any excess hair with a kitchen torch or cut off with a razor. Poke the meat all over with a meat tenderizer or the tip of a knife. Starting on the long edge of the meat, make a cut across the meat almost to the other edge to butterfly it. Open the meat and flip skin-side down.
3. Season the meat all over with 3 tablespoons (45g) of salt and then sprinkle the red pepper seasoning blend over the top.
4. Roll the meat tightly from bottom to top, using kitchen string to tie the roll together at 1-inch (2.5cm) intervals. Place a wire rack on a baking tray, set the meat on top, and refrigerate, uncovered, for 24 to 48 hours to dry.
5. Remove the meat from the refrigerator and bring to room temperature, about 2 hours. Drizzle with the olive oil and sprinkle with the remaining 1 tablespoon (15g) of salt. Insert an ovenproof meat thermometer into the center of the meat.
6. Preheat the oven to 420°F (220°C).
7. Bake for 40 minutes. Reduce the oven temperature to 350°F (180°C), and cook for 40 more minutes. Reduce the oven temperature to 320°F (160°C), and cook for 40 to 50 minutes or until the internal temperature reaches 167°F (75°C).
8. Switch the oven to the broiler, and broil 2 or 3 minutes to completely crisp the skin. Watch carefully to avoid burning.
9. Remove from the oven, and let rest for 30 minutes. Cut into 1-inch (2.5cm) slices, and serve.

Notes

If the warmed cheesy potatoes do not stretch when you're ready to eat, reheat them over low heat or place them in an ovenproof bowl and warm them in the residual heat of the oven after it has been turned off.

For extra flavor, you can serve this dish with a drizzle of truffle oil or paste over the top.

Hamburger Steaks with Aligot

PREP TIME: 30 minutes • **COOK TIME:** 1 hour 30 minutes • **SERVINGS:** 6

Since I was young, hamburger steak has always held a special place in my heart. The rich aroma that fills the kitchen as the patties cook, and the way my mom would top them with her special sauce to serve alongside a warm bowl of rice—those memories are forever etched in my mind. This recipe is more than just a nostalgic taste; it's the result of countless attempts to create the perfect, comforting plate. The true star of this dish is the aligot, a French-style mashed potato loaded with creamy, stretchy, silky cheese. Top these juicy hamburger steaks with that heavenly cheese-laden aligot, add a drizzle of truffle oil, and you'll have the ultimate comfort food—warm, rich, and unforgettable.

ALIGOT (CHEESY POTATOES)

3 large russet potatoes, peeled and cut into large cubes
1 tsp (5g) kosher salt
⅓ cup (78g) unsalted butter, cubed
1 cup (237ml) warm heavy cream
1½ cups (150g) cheese curds, diced
⅔ cup (153g) shredded Swiss cheese
⅔ cup (153g) shredded Gruyère

HAMBURGER STEAKS

4 tbsp (60ml) extra-virgin olive oil
2 tbsp (28g) unsalted butter, cubed
1 medium white onion, chopped
1¾ tsp (8.75g) kosher salt
1½ lb (680g) ground beef
1 lb (454g) ground pork (optional; you can use all ground beef if you prefer)
1 tsp (2g) ground nutmeg
1 tsp (1g) freshly ground black pepper
1½ cups (225g) dry breadcrumbs
3 garlic cloves, minced
2 tbsp (30ml) Worcestershire sauce
2 tbsp (34g) ketchup
2 large eggs

MUSHROOM GRAVY

¼ cup (58g) unsalted butter
¼ cup (30g) all-purpose flour
1 medium sweet onion, chopped
1½ cups (234g) baby bella mushrooms, sliced
2 cups (473ml) beef broth
2 tbsp (12g) roughly chopped fresh parsley
1 tsp (1g) freshly ground black pepper

SPECIAL EQUIPMENT

Potato masher
Disposable kitchen gloves
Meat thermometer

1. To make the aligot (cheesy potatoes), place the potatoes and salt in a large pot and cover with enough water to submerge the potatoes. Set over medium-high heat, and cook until tender, about 30 minutes. Mash the potatoes with a potato masher or in a food mill.
2. Transfer the mashed potatoes to a large skillet set over low heat. Add the butter and heavy cream, and stir well with a wooden spatula. Cook until the butter is melted and incorporated in the cream.
3. Working with about ½ cup (100g) at a time, add the cheese curds, Swiss cheese, and Gruyère, stirring between each addition. Cook, stirring constantly, until all the cheese is melted and evenly distributed, about 10 to 15 minutes. Remove from the heat, and cover the skillet with foil to keep the potatoes warm and prevent them from drying out.
4. To make the hamburger steaks, add 2 tablespoons (30ml) of olive oil, the butter, onion, and ¼ teaspoon (1.25g) salt to a medium skillet. Set over medium heat, and sauté for about 5 minutes. Remove from the heat, and set aside to cool.
5. Don a pair of disposable kitchen gloves. Add the ground beef, ground pork (if using), the remaining salt, nutmeg, pepper, breadcrumbs, garlic, Worcestershire sauce, ketchup, eggs, and sautéed onion to a large bowl. Using gloved hands, mix well until all the ingredients are evenly distributed.
6. Divide the meat mixture into six equal portions. Use both hands to pinch the meat together to form a ball, then press and shape it into a 4-inch (10cm) disk. (The meat will puff up in the center as it cooks, so if you make a little puddle shape in the center of it, it will flatten out when it's done.) Repeat with the remaining five portions.
7. Preheat the oven to 375°F (190°C).
8. Heat a large skillet over medium-high heat. Add the remaining olive oil. Once shimmering, add the meat, and sear until golden brown, about 3 minutes per side. Transfer to a large baking dish.
9. To make the mushroom gravy, reduce the heat to medium-low, add the butter and flour to the pan with the drippings, and sauté for 2 minutes. Add the onion, mushrooms, and beef broth, and simmer for 5 minutes. Remove from the heat, add the parsley and pepper, stir to combine, and pour over the steaks.
10. Bake until the steaks reach an internal temperature of about 150°F (64°C) to 155°F (68°C), about 25 minutes.
11. Serve the steaks and gravy on a plate, with the cheesy potatoes on the side.

Herb-Marinated
Pork Shoulder Roast

PREP TIME: 40 minutes • **COOK TIME:** 3 hours • **SERVINGS:** 6 to 8

The richness of tender pork shoulder, the zesty kick of pickled red cabbage, and the savory goodness of roasted vegetables combine in this flavorful recipe. Infused with aromatic herbs and a hint of red wine vinegar, every bite is a taste sensation. The best part? The leftover veggies transform into a bold barbecue sauce that'll have you licking your plate clean. Perfect for gatherings or a comforting weekend dinner, this dish is a real crowd-pleaser.

PICKLED RED CABBAGE

1¼ cups (300g) sliced red cabbage
1 cup (125g) thinly sliced red onion
1 garlic clove, minced
1 tsp (1g) celery salt
⅓ cup (79 ml) maple syrup
½ cup (118ml) white vinegar
½ cup (118ml) boiling water

PORK SHOULDER AND HERB OIL

4 lb (1.8kg) pork shoulder
2 tsp (10g) kosher salt
½ tsp (0.5g) freshly ground black pepper
⅓ cup (79ml) extra-virgin olive oil
2 tbsp (30ml) red wine vinegar
2 tbsp (12g) chopped fresh parsley
½ tbsp (3g) chopped fresh oregano
½ tbsp (3g) chopped fresh thyme
½ tbsp (2.5g) crushed red pepper

BAKED VEGETABLES

3 medium russet potatoes, quartered
2 heads of garlic, top ½ inch (1.25cm) removed (keep the root)
2 medium carrots, cut into bite-size pieces
1 large white onion, quartered
1 (4-inch or 10cm) leek, white part only
1 tsp (5g) kosher salt
½ tsp (0.5g) freshly ground black pepper

BARBECUE SAUCE

½ cup (118ml) barbecue sauce
½ tsp (0.5g) freshly ground black pepper

SPECIAL EQUIPMENT

Dutch oven

1. To make the pickled red cabbage, combine the cabbage, onion, garlic, celery salt, maple syrup, and white vinegar in a medium bowl. Add the boiling water, and stir together with a wooden spoon. Cover the mixture with parchment paper or plastic wrap, pressing it tightly against the ingredients. Allow to cool to room temperature and then transfer to the refrigerator.
2. Preheat the oven or a grill to between 325°F (163°C) and 350°F (180°C).
3. Next, make the pork. Line a cutting board with paper towels. Place the pork shoulder on the prepared cutting board and pat dry with paper towels. With the fat side up, make ¼-inch (6mm) slits in the top in a grid pattern.
4. Sprinkle the pork all over with the salt and pepper, patting the seasonings to adhere. Set aside.
5. Whisk together olive oil, red wine vinegar, parsley, oregano, thyme, and crushed red pepper in a small bowl. Reserve 1 tablespoon (15ml) of the mixture, and brush the rest all over the pork.
6. To prepare the baked vegetables, add the potatoes, garlic, carrots, onion, and leek to a large Dutch oven. Toss with the salt and pepper, and the remaining 1 tablespoon (15ml) of the herb oil mixture, and spread into an even layer.
7. Place the pork, cut side up, on top of the vegetables, and cover with a lid.
8. Roast (or grill) for 1 hour. Remove the lid and add ¼ cup (59ml) of water if there is no moisture in the pan. Re-cover and return to the oven (or grill) and bake for 2 more hours.
9. Remove the pork from the Dutch oven, wrap it in parchment paper or foil, and let it rest for about 15 minutes.
10. Squeeze the garlic into a medium bowl, then add the baked vegetables. Add the barbecue sauce and pepper, and whisk to combine.
11. Slice the pork thinly, and arrange the slices on a large serving platter with the roasted carrots and potatoes on the side. Serve with the barbecue sauce and pickled red cabbage. Enjoy with tortillas, if you'd like.

Rack of Lamb Crown Roast

PREP TIME: 30 minutes • **COOK TIME:** 1 hour 10 minutes • **SERVINGS:** 8 to 10

This recipe is a showstopping centerpiece for any gathering, combining elegance with ease. Tender lamb is seasoned with a fragrant herbed salt and roasted to perfection alongside colorful vegetables. A fresh, vibrant salad with pomegranate seeds adds a bright contrast, both in flavor and presentation. Perfect for holidays or other special occasions, this is sure to impress your guests without keeping you in the kitchen for hours.

GREEN SALAD WITH POMEGRANATE

- 2 tbsp (30ml) white vinegar
- 1½ bunches of kale
- 1 head of iceberg lettuce
- 3 mini cucumbers
- 6 sprigs of fresh dill
- 3 tbsp (45ml) lemon juice
- 3 tbsp (45g) whole-grain Dijon mustard
- 2 tbsp (30ml) maple syrup
- 2 tbsp (30ml) pomegranate molasses (optional)
- 1 cup (175g) pomegranate seeds
- ½ tsp (2.5g) kosher salt
- 1 tsp (1g) freshly ground black pepper

HERBED SALT

- ¼ cup (60g) kosher salt
- 2 tbsp (14g) black peppercorns
- 2 tbsp (12g) chopped fresh rosemary
- 2 tbsp (12g) chopped fresh thyme
- 1 tbsp (15g) onion powder
- 1 tbsp (6g) lemon zest
- ½ tbsp (7.5g) garlic powder

LAMB CROWN ROAST

- 3 racks of lamb, at room temperature for 1 hour
- 5 tbsp (75g) herbed salt
- 3 tbsp (45ml) extra-virgin olive oil, plus more for drizzling
- 3 garlic heads
- 8 sprigs of fresh thyme
- 4 sprigs of fresh rosemary

ROASTED VEGETABLES

- 2 lb (907g) mini potatoes
- 1 lb (454g) multicolor carrots
- 1 fennel bulb
- 25 red pearl onions
- 3 tbsp (45g) herbed salt
- 3 tbsp (45ml) extra-virgin olive oil

SPECIAL EQUIPMENT

- Mortar and pestle
- Kitchen string
- Ovenproof meat thermometer

Note

If you have a cocktail smoker, try adding smoke to your salt to make a smoked seasoning.

1. To make the green salad with pomegranates, fill a large bowl with water and the vinegar. Add the kale, lettuce, cucumbers, and dill, and soak for 3 minutes. Rinse the vegetables under running water, being careful to remove any grit, and place on paper towels to absorb any excess water.
2. Tear the kale, lettuce, and dill into 1-inch (2.5cm) pieces by hand. Crush the cucumber in a mortar and pestle and then break it up into 2-inch (5cm) pieces by hand.
3. Whisk together the lemon juice, mustard, maple syrup, and pomegranate molasses (if using) in a large, wide bowl. Add all the vegetables, and toss to coat. Transfer to a serving dish, cover with plastic wrap, and set in the refrigerator.
4. Combine all the ingredients for the herbed salt in a small bowl, and set aside.
5. Next, make the lamb. Pat the lamb chops dry with paper towels, taking care to pat each bone dry, too. Grab the end of the fascia attached to the inner bone with a paper towel and pull to remove the fascia. You will be bending the three racks to form a crown, so cut slightly between the bones: place the removed fascia facing up, and cut a slit 1-inch (2.5cm) deep, leaning against the bone of the meaty side. (Don't cut too deep because the meat opens up and could dry out in the oven.) Sprinkle the racks evenly with the herbed salt and drizzle all over with olive oil.
6. To make the crown, arrange the three racks in a circle and cut the sides slightly flat. Set a round baking dish that will fit inside the racks in the center to help them hold their shape. Tie a piece of kitchen string around the bottom of the racks and then tie another piece of string around the middle.
7. Add the garlic, thyme, and rosemary to the baking dish, and drizzle with olive oil.
8. Preheat the oven to 400°F (200°C).
9. To make the roasted vegetables, cut the mini potatoes in half, and cut the carrots and fennel into 1-inch (2.5cm) pieces. Cut off the root of the onions and peel them. Transfer the vegetables to a large baking dish, sprinkle evenly with the herbed salt and olive oil, and toss to combine.
10. With the smaller round baking dish in the center of the lamb crown, place the lamb on top of the vegetables in the large baking dish, maintaining the crown shape. Insert an ovenproof instant-read thermometer into the center of the lamb.

11. Bake for 10 minutes. Reduce the temperature to 300°F (150°C), and bake for about 45 minutes, or until the lamb has an internal temperature of 125°F (52°C).
12. Remove everything from the oven. Transfer only the lamb to a serving platter, being careful to maintain the crown shape. Wrap the crown in foil or parchment paper, and let rest for 15 minutes.
13. While the meat rests, return the vegetables and the small round baking dish with the garlic and herbs to the oven, increase the temperature to 450°F (230°C), and roast for 15 minutes.
14. Remove the kitchen string from the middle of the lamb. Stuff the inside of the lamb (where the small round baking dish was) with the roasted vegetables, and arrange the salad around the outside of the lamb. Distribute the pomegranates evenly over the salad, and season with salt and pepper.
15. Remove the remaining kitchen string just before slicing and serving.

Rack of Lamb Cutlets

PREP TIME: 30 minutes plus 24 hours to pickle • **COOK TIME:** 15 minutes • **SERVINGS:** 2

This dish introduced me to the rich flavor of lamb. With its savory breadcrumb coating and crispy texture, the rack of lamb cutlet is perfectly complemented by tangy pickled radicchio and raspberries, and the zesty mint sour cream sauce adds a refreshing finish.

PICKLED RADICCHIO AND RASPBERRIES

1 head of radicchio

1⅓ cups (170g) raspberries

1 tbsp (15ml) plus 1 cup (237ml) white vinegar

1 cup (237ml) white wine

¼ tsp (1.25g) kosher salt

½ cup (100g) sugar

MINT SOUR CREAM SAUCE

2 tbsp (12g) finely chopped fresh mint leaves

1 clove of garlic, minced

1 cup (240g) sour cream

½ tsp (2.5g) kosher salt

½ tsp (0.5g) freshly ground black pepper

½ tsp (0.5g) crushed hot red pepper

Zest of ½ lemon

1 tbsp (15ml) fresh lemon juice

LAMB

2 qt (2 liters) canola oil, for frying

1 (17½ oz or 500g) rack of lamb

½ tsp (2.5g) kosher salt

½ tsp (0.5g) freshly ground black pepper

2 tbsp (15g) all-purpose flour

1 large egg

2 cups (120g) breadcrumbs

SPECIAL EQUIPMENT

Meat tenderizer

Deep-fry thermometer

Notes

When making the pickled radicchio and raspberries, you can substitute a sweet sparkling wine in place of the white wine for a sweeter pickle.

When seasoning the lamb chops, feel free to use herb salt for a boost of flavor.

1. Cut the radicchio into 6 equal pieces, leaving the root attached. Be sure the radicchio leaves don't fall apart.
2. Place the radicchio, raspberries, and mint in a large bowl. Cover with cold water, add 1 tablespoon (15ml) of white vinegar, and let sit for 5 minutes.
3. Rinse under running water and drain in a colander.
4. To make the radicchio pickles, combine the wine, the remaining 1 cup (237ml) white vinegar, salt, and the sugar in a medium saucepan over medium heat. Cook, stirring, until the sugar dissolves, about 5 minutes. Remove from the heat and cool to room temperature.
5. Transfer the radicchio and raspberries to a 1-quart (1-liter) jar, pour in the vinegar mixture, and press down on the ingredients to submerge them in the vinegar mixture. Cover and refrigerate for 24 hours.
6. To make the mint sauce, add the mint, garlic, sour cream, salt, black pepper, crushed red pepper, lemon zest, and lemon juice to a medium bowl, and mix with a spoon. Cover with plastic wrap and refrigerate.
7. Attach a deep-fry thermometer to the side of a large skillet. Add the canola oil to the pot and heat to 350°F (180°C) over medium heat.
8. Meanwhile, line a cutting board with paper towels, place the rack of lamb on the towels, and pat dry with another towel.
9. On the inside of the rack, use a paper towel to pull away the skin from the ends and then trim off any excess fat. Lean the knife against one bone, and cut down to separate the cutlet completely. Do the same with the remaining bones and cutlets. Pound each cutlet over the entire surface with a meat tenderizer to tenderize and increase the size of the meat. Season with salt and pepper on both sides and then evenly dust with flour to coat.
10. Beat the egg on a medium plate. Add the breadcrumbs to another plate. Line a baking sheet with paper towels. Dip each cutlet in the egg, immediately coat in the breadcrumbs, and place on the prepared baking sheet.
11. Working in batches of three, carefully add the cutlets to the oil and fry until golden brown, about 5 minutes, maintaining an oil temperature of 340°F (170°C) to 350°F (180°C). Transfer the cooked lamb to a wire rack to cool slightly, and repeat with the remaining cutlets.
12. Arrange the pickled radicchio and raspberries on a serving platter, and serve the lamb on top and mint sour cream sauce on the side.

Lamb Chop Birria Tacos

PREP TIME: 45 minutes • **COOK TIME:** 3 hours • **MAKES:** 20 tacos

Lamb is not only delicious but also loaded with protein, iron, and omega-3s, making it both tasty and good for you! These lamb chop birria tacos highlight everything great about lamb. The meat is tender, flavorful, and cooked to perfection in a bold birria sauce. Stuffed into warm tortillas with gooey cheese and finished with fresh toppings, every bite is packed with excitement. Don't skip the birria sauce for dipping; it's what makes these tacos truly irresistible. Perfect for taco nights or impressing guests, this recipe is all about celebrating the magic of lamb.

CHILI OIL

1½ cups (355ml) vegetable oil
3 garlic cloves, sliced
3 green onions, chopped
1 tsp (2.5g) whole black peppercorns
½ inch (1.25cm, or 14g) ginger, sliced
¼ cup (20g) crushed hot red pepper

TACOS

2 lb (1kg) lamb chops
1 tsp (5g) kosher salt
½ tsp (0.5g) freshly ground black pepper
4 cups (400g) shredded mozzarella
½ medium white onion, diced
½ bunch of fresh cilantro, chopped
2 limes, cut into wedges

BIRRIA

6 dried guajillo chiles
4 dried morita chiles
2 dried ancho chiles
2 cups (474 ml) boiling water
2 tbsp (30ml) vegetable oil
1 Roma tomato
1 medium white onion
5 garlic cloves, peeled
2 bay leaves
1 tsp (2g) dried oregano
½ tsp (1g) ground cumin
1 tsp (2.5g) whole black peppercorns
½ tsp (2g) whole cloves
2 tsp (10g) kosher salt
2 tbsp (30ml) white vinegar

CORN TORTILLAS

2 cups (240g) corn flour (I like MASECA corn flour)
2 cups (473ml) warm water

SPECIAL EQUIPMENT

Spice grinder
Tortilla press
Food processor

Note

This recipe works best if you use a tortilla press. If you don't have one, you can roll out the dough between two sheets of parchment paper with a rolling pin.

1. Combine all ingredients for the chili oil in a small saucepan. Set over low heat, and cook for about 10 minutes. Turn off the heat and let stand.
2. Pat the lamb dry with paper towels and then sprinkle with salt and pepper. Set aside.
3. Begin making the birria by wiping the guajillo, morita, and ancho chiles with paper towels and removing the stems. Wash them under running water and place them in a large bowl. Cover the chiles with the boiling water and let them steep for 10 minutes to soften.
4. Meanwhile, heat a large skillet over medium-high heat. Add the vegetable oil, and when it begins to smoke, add the lamb, tomato, onion, and garlic, and cook, tossing the meat and vegetables back and forth, until golden brown, about 3 minutes. Transfer the lamb to a large saucepan. Add 1 cup (237ml) of the chile soaking water to the skillet, and deglaze for about 1 minute.
5. Finely grind the bay leaves, oregano, cumin, black peppercorns, cloves, and salt in a spice grinder, and transfer to a blender.
6. Add the tomatoes, onions, garlic and their juices to the food processor, along with the soaked chiles, and the vinegar, and blend until smooth. If it seems like there isn't enough moisture, add about ½ cup (118ml) more of the chile soaking water.
7. Pour the chile mixture into the saucepan with the lamb. Add the remaining chile soaking water to the food processor, shake well, and pour over the lamb.
8. Strain the chili oil through a fine-mesh sieve and add to the saucepan. Set the pan over medium-high heat, and cook for 1 hour. Reduce the heat to low and cook for 30 minutes. Stir and cook for 30 more minutes or until the lamb is tender.
9. Meanwhile, make the corn tortillas. Add the corn flour and warm water to a large bowl, and knead for about 3 minutes. Cover with a tea towel and let rest for 10 minutes.
10. Preheat a large skillet over medium-high heat. Cut a sheet of parchment paper or plastic wrap 2 inches (5cm) larger than your tortilla press.
11. Weigh the tortilla dough on a scale, and divide the total weight by 20. Using your hands, shape 1⁄20 of the dough into a ball. Place a sheet of parchment paper on the tortilla press, set the dough ball on the parchment paper, cover the dough with another sheet of parchment paper, and press to form a 4- or 5-inch (10 to 12.5cm) tortilla.

12. Add the tortilla to the preheated skillet, and cook for 1 minute 30 seconds on each side. Move to a plate and cover with a tea towel to prevent drying. Repeat with the remaining 19 dough balls.
13. Transfer the lamb from the saucepan to a plate, de-bone it, and shred it. Pour some of the birria sauce over the lamb, cover it with foil, and place it in a warm oven to keep it warm.
14. Heat a large griddle over medium-high heat. Dip both sides of a tortilla in the chili oil from the birria, set on the griddle, and top with about 2 tablespoons (30g) of the lamb and 3 tablespoons (20g) of the mozzarella, and let cook for about 3 minutes. Fold the tortilla in half, and transfer to a warm serving platter. Repeat with the remaining tortillas, lamb, and mozzarella.
15. Pour the birria sauce into a small bowl, and add the diced onion and cilantro to separate small bowls. While the tacos are still warm, open them, add as much onion and cilantro as you like on top of the lamb, squeeze some lime juice over the top, and dip in the birria sauce.

CHAPTER 4

Poultry

Balsamic Glaze-Marinated Roasted Chicken Legs

with Olives and Potatoes

PREP TIME: 40 minutes plus 2 hours 30 minutes to marinate • **COOK TIME:** 1 hour • **SERVINGS:** 3 or 4

This dish is the perfect comfort food, combining rich, savory flavors with a touch of sweetness from a balsamic glaze. Marinating the chicken legs allows the spices to deeply penetrate the meat, ensuring every bite is packed with flavor. The roasted garlic and green olives bring a delightful contrast to the richness of the chicken, while the tender red potatoes soak up all the delicious juices. Green olives are packed with heart-healthy fats, antioxidants, and vitamins, making this dish flavorful and nourishing. Don't rush the marinating process—it's worth the wait! When serving, be sure to scoop up a little bit of everything in one bite—the crispy chicken skin, juicy meat, olives, and garlic make for a heavenly combination.

ROASTED CHICKEN LEGS

4 chicken legs, back attached (3 lb/1.4kg)
¼ cup (59ml) balsamic glaze, divided
½ tsp (2.5g) kosher salt
½ tsp (0.5g) freshly ground black pepper
1 tsp (2g) dried thyme
½ tsp (0.5g) garlic powder
1 tbsp (15ml) extra-virgin olive oil

GREEN OLIVES AND RED POTATOES

4 medium red potatoes
¾ tsp (4g) kosher salt
20 garlic cloves, peeled
1 cup (230g) green olives
¼ cup (40g) bico or red paprika chile
1 tbsp (15ml) balsamic glaze
1 tsp (2g) dried thyme
½ tsp (0.5g) freshly ground black pepper

SPECIAL EQUIPMENT

Meat thermometer

1. To prepare the chicken legs, remove the giblets from the inside of the chicken, and pat the chicken dry with a paper towel. Brush the chicken with 2 tablespoons (30ml) of the balsamic glaze.
2. Whisk together the salt, pepper, thyme, and garlic powder in a small bowl, and sprinkle evenly over the chicken. Drizzle with the olive oil, place in a bowl, cover tightly with plastic wrap, and set in the refrigerator to marinate for 2 hours.
3. Let marinate at room temperature for 30 more minutes.
4. Preheat the oven to 400°F (200°C). Line a rimmed baking sheet with parchment paper.
5. Place the chicken, cut side down, on the prepared baking sheet. Bake for 30 minutes.
6. Meanwhile, peel the potatoes, cut into quarters, and place in a large saucepan. Cover with water and season with ½ teaspoon (2.5g) of the salt. Set over medium-high heat, and cook until fork-tender, 20 to 25 minutes. Remove from the heat, and set aside.
7. Add the remaining balsamic glaze to a heatproof bowl. Microwave on high for 10 seconds. Use a pastry brush to brush the warm glaze back and forth over the surface of the chicken. After 5 minutes, brush the chicken again with the balsamic glaze. Repeat 2 more times at 5-minute intervals.
8. Meanwhile, place a medium ovenproof dish in the oven to preheat. When the internal temperature of the chicken legs reaches 175°F (80°C) and they are deeply browned, remove the ovenproof dish from the oven, add the chicken legs to the preheated ovenpoof dish, and cover the dish with foil to keep the chicken legs warm.
9. Add the potatoes, garlic, olives, and bico chile to the baking sheet with the chicken juices. Drizzle with the balsamic glaze and season with the remaining ¼ teaspoon (1.25g) of salt, and the thyme and pepper. Grab the ends of the parchment paper and lift up, rolling the ingredients to coat them in the chicken juices. Gently pull back and forth to roll until evenly coated. Return the parchment to the baking sheet (it should be flat again) and smooth the ingredients into an even layer. Roast for 15 minutes.
10. Lift the parchment paper from the baking sheet, pour the roasted vegetables over the chicken legs in the baking dish, and serve.

Chicken Breast Rolls

PREP TIME: 10 minutes • **COOK TIME:** 1 hour and 5 minutes • **SERVINGS:** 3

Grilled vegetables and meats have a flavor unlike what you can achieve with any other cooking method. Add a rich and luscious butter sauce, which goes well with the cheesy stuffed chicken breast and beetatoes (aka, beets and potatoes) in this recipe, and you have an instant favorite. Let's have a wonderful dinner.

CHICKEN

2 (14 oz/400g) boneless, skin-on chicken breasts
½ tsp (2.5g) kosher salt
½ tsp (0.5g) freshly ground black pepper
¼ cup (56g) crumbled blue cheese
¼ cup (55g) bocconcini or mini mozzarella
2 tsp (2g) dried basil, sage, thyme, or your favorite herb
1 tsp (5ml) extra-virgin olive oil
2 tbsp (28g) unsalted butter

VEGETABLES

2 leeks
1 head of radicchio, halved
1 tbsp (15ml) white vinegar
2 king oyster mushrooms
2 medium beets
2 medium yellow potatoes
1¼ tsp (6.25g) kosher salt
¾ tsp (0.7g) freshly ground black pepper
2 tbsp (30ml) extra-virgin olive oil, divided
1 tbsp (14g) unsalted butter

BUTTER SAUCE

¼ cup (58g) unsalted butter
2 tbsp (15g) nonpareil capers
1 garlic clove, minced
Juice of ½ lemon
1 tbsp (6g) chopped fresh parsley
¼ tsp (1.25g) kosher salt
⅛ tsp (0.1g) freshly ground black pepper

SPECIAL EQUIPMENT

Kitchen string
Grill basket
Meat thermometer

1. Remove the chicken breasts from the refrigerator and let sit at room temperature, no longer than 2 hours.
2. Preheat a pizza oven or grill to 360°F (180°C). To prepare the vegetables, cut the leeks into 3-inch (7.5cm) pieces and then slice each piece into thin strips.
3. Add the radicchio and leeks to a medium bowl, pour in enough water to cover, add the vinegar, and let soak for about 3 minutes. Using a strainer, drain the water from the vegetables and rinse them twice under running water. Put the leeks in a small bowl, and cover with fresh water to soak. (This removes the sharp taste from the leek.) Set the radicchio aside.
4. Use a paper towel to remove any grit from the mushrooms.
5. Remove the stems from the beets and poke them all over with the tip of a knife. Halve the beets. Poke and halve the potatoes.
6. Place the radicchio, mushrooms, beets, and potatoes in a 9 × 13-inch (23 × 33cm) baking dish. Season all over with ½ teaspoon (2.5g) salt and ¼ teaspoon (0.2g) pepper, and drizzle with 1 tablespoon (15ml) of olive oil. Set aside.
7. Place a chicken breast on a cutting board, skin side up. Butterfly the breast by cutting horizontally into the thickest part, about a third up the height of the breast. Do not cut all the way through; leave about ¼ inch (6mm) intact at the side. Open the cut breast, and press it flat. Cut horizontally into the thick side again so the breast can be spread flat out, without cutting through to the side. The chicken breast should be a consistent thickness throughout but now three times the width of the original breast. Repeat with the second breast. Season the chicken with salt and pepper, evenly distribute the blue cheese and bocconcini over the top, and season with the basil, sage, or thyme.
8. Start rolling the breasts over the cheese from the inside of the breast (the part you cut), so the rolled breast can be wrapped in the chicken skin. Roll it tightly so the cheese cannot come out. Smooth the skin.
9. Cut 10 pieces of kitchen string long enough to tie the chicken breasts together. Roll up the chicken and secure each breast with five pieces of string. Use a pastry brush to coat the skin with the olive oil. Transfer the chicken rolls to a separate 9 × 13-inch (23 × 33cm) baking dish.
10. Add the vegetables and chicken to the pizza oven. Cook until the chicken reaches an internal temperature of 165°F (75°C), about 30 to 35 minutes. Remove the chicken and transfer it to a sheet of aluminum foil. Add the butter on the top of the chicken and then wrap in the foil. Remove the potatoes and beets from the oven when they are fork-tender, about 1 hour total.
11. Drain the water from the leeks and pat dry with a paper towel. Drizzle the remaining 1 tablespoon (15ml) of olive oil over the top, sprinkle with half of the remaining salt and pepper, and toss to coat. Place the leeks, mushrooms, and radicchio in a grill basket, and cook for 3 to 5 minutes (see Note). Don't let the vegetables burn, and only cook the mushrooms until tender and juicy. Remove the vegetables from the pizza oven and keep warm.

12. Transfer the cooked potatoes and beets to a food processor along with the remaining salt, pepper, and butter, and process until smooth.
13. To make the butter sauce, add the butter to a small heatproof bowl. Microwave on high until bubbling, about 30 to 45 seconds. Stir in the capers, garlic, lemon juice, parsley, salt, and pepper.
14. Cut the chicken into ¼-inch (6mm) slices. Using scissors, cut the mushrooms at the base and pull them apart using tongs.
15. Spread the mashed beets and potatoes ("beetatoes") on a serving plate, and add the vegetables and chicken breasts on top. Pour the butter sauce over all, and serve.

Note

If you'd prefer, you can broil the vegetables. To broil, preheat the broiler with a rack in the center position. Add the vegetables to a baking sheet and cook until lightly charred, 3 to 5 minutes.

Creamy Chicken
with Green Pasta

PREP TIME: 40 minutes plus 30 minutes to rest • **COOK TIME:** 15 minutes • **SERVINGS:** 2 or 3

This recipe is a feast for your eyes as well as for your taste buds. The pasta is colored green using fresh spinach, which is rich in nutrients such as vitamins, iron, and fiber. Accompanying the pasta is moist and tender chicken—which is a good source of protein—and a rich and creamy sauce coats both. The fresh spinach pasta dough takes a few steps to make, but one bite of this dish will convince you it's worth it.

SPINACH PASTA DOUGH

1 cup (30g) spinach
1 large egg
2 tsp (10 ml) extra-virgin olive oil
½ tsp (2.5g) kosher salt
1 cup (120g) all-purpose flour

CREAMY CHICKEN SAUCE

2 tbsp (30ml) extra-virgin olive oil
5 garlic cloves, sliced
½ cup (50g) chopped white onion
1 (7 to 9 oz/200–250g) boneless, skinless chicken breast, sliced
1 cup (237ml) whole milk
1 cup (237ml) heavy cream
2 tbsp (7g) sun-dried tomatoes
1½ tsp (7.5g) kosher salt
1 tsp (1g) freshly ground black pepper
¼ cup (22g) grated Parmesan cheese
1 tsp (1g) chicken-flavor instant bouillon
1 tsp (1g) crushed hot red pepper

SPECIAL EQUIPMENT

Pasta roller
4-inch (10cm) round fluted cookie cutter
Fluted pasta wheel

1. To make the pasta dough, process the spinach, egg, olive oil, and salt in a food processor until smooth.
2. Add the flour and spinach puree to a medium bowl, and mix well with a wooden spoon until just a few lumps remain. Turn out the dough onto a work surface and knead for 10 minutes.
3. Wrap the dough in plastic wrap, and place in the refrigerator for 30 minutes.
4. Turn out the dough onto a floured work surface, and roll it to a thickness of ¼ inch (6mm). Using a pasta roller, roll to a thickness of 1⁄16 inch (about 1mm).
5. Place the dough on the work surface, and cut using a 4-inch (10cm) round fluted cookie cutter. Using a fluted pasta wheel, cut the circle into halves and then quarters. Place a dough quarter in the palm of your hand, and use your fingertip to rub some water across the quarter about a third of the way up from the point to the outside edge. Then use your fingers to pinch together the quarter to form a mini bouquet. (The water helps the dough stick together at the pinch point.) Set aside and repeat with the remaining quarters.
6. To make the pasta sauce, heat a large skillet over medium heat. Add the olive oil, garlic, and onion, and cook, stirring, for 3 minutes. Add the chicken, and cook for 3 minutes. Add the milk, cream, sun-dried tomatoes, ½ teaspoon (2.5g) of the salt, and the pepper. Reduce the heat to low, and simmer until the cream sauce thickens, about 5 minutes.
7. Bring 4 cups (948ml) of water to a boil in a medium saucepan over medium-high heat. Add the bouquet-shaped pasta and the remaining 1 teaspoon (5g) of salt, and cook for 5 minutes. Drain and add to the skillet.
8. Add the Parmesan cheese and bouillon to the skillet, and stir well.
9. Garnish with crushed red pepper, and serve.

Lollipop Drumsticks

with Sweet Chili Oil Sauce and Jalapeño Coleslaw

PREP TIME: 10 minutes plus 2 hours to marinate • **COOK TIME:** 1 hour 20 minutes • **SERVINGS:** 5

These grab-and-go lollipop-style drumsticks are prepared so you can hold the bone like a lollipop while enjoying the juicy, tender meat. Coated in a sweet, spicy, and seriously addictive chili oil sauce, each bite has crispy skin and deep flavor. The taste and texture will keep you coming back for more.

SWEET CHILI OIL SAUCE

¼ cup (59ml) extra-virgin olive oil
4 garlic cloves, minced
½ medium white onion, finely diced
¼ cup (25g) crushed hot red pepper
¾ cup (177ml) corn syrup
⅓ cup (79ml) ketchup
2 tbsp (30ml) soy sauce
2 tbsp (30ml) Worcestershire sauce
½ tsp (0.5g) ground cinnamon
2 tsp (4g) smoked paprika (optional)

JALAPEÑO COLESLAW

1 lb (454g) head of cabbage
2 jalapeños
2 small Gala apples
1 small carrot, thickly grated
1 tbsp (15ml) white vinegar
½ tsp (2g) baking soda
1 medium lemon
2 tbsp (30ml) maple syrup or sugar
½ cup (115g) mayonnaise
2 tbsp (22g) whole-grain Dijon mustard seeds
½ tsp (2.5g) kosher salt
½ tsp (0.5g) freshly ground black pepper

CHICKEN AND MARINADE

1 tsp (2g) onion powder
1 tsp (5g) kosher salt
1 tsp (1g) freshly ground black pepper
½ tsp (1g) garlic powder
¼ tsp (0.25g) ground cinnamon
1 tsp (2g) smoked paprika (optional)
3½ lb (1.6kg) chicken drumsticks
1 tbsp (15ml) extra-virgin olive oil

1. To make the sweet chili oil sauce, add the olive oil, garlic, and onion to a medium saucepan, and set over low heat. Cook, stirring frequently, until fragrant, about 5 minutes. Add the crushed red pepper, and cook, stirring frequently, for 3 to 5 minutes.
2. Add the corn syrup, ketchup, soy sauce, Worcestershire sauce, cinnamon, and paprika (if using), and increase the heat to medium-high. Simmer, stirring often, for 15 minutes. (The sauce will bubble up as it cooks, so be careful not to burn your hands as you stir.) Remove from the heat. (The sauce will not look thick while simmering, but it will thicken when it's completely cooled.)
3. To make the jalapeño coleslaw, place the cabbage, jalapeños, apples, carrot, and lemon in a large bowl. Cover with water, add the vinegar, and let sit for 5 minutes. Rub the lemon all over with the baking soda and then rinse under running water. Rinse the rest of the vegetables.
4. Cut the cabbage into ¼-inch (0.5cm) slices, cut again into 1-inch (2.5cm) pieces, and place in a large bowl. Slice the apples into the same size pieces as the cabbage, and add to the bowl. Cut the jalapeño in half, slice very thinly, and add the pepper and the seeds to the bowl. Grate the carrot using the thickest holes of a grater until you have ½ cup (45g), and add to the bowl. Zest and juice the lemon, and add to the bowl. (You will need 1 tablespoon [6g] lemon zest and 3 tablespoons [45ml] lemon juice.) Add the maple syrup, mayonnaise, mustard seeds, salt, and pepper to the bowl, and toss well to combine. Cover with plastic wrap, and place the slaw in the refrigerator until ready to serve.
5. To make the marinade, combine the onion powder, salt, pepper, garlic powder, cinnamon, and paprika (if using) in a small bowl. Set aside.
6. Place the chicken drumsticks on a cutting board, and using a rotating motion with a knife, slice through the skin and tendons on the foot side within 1 inch (2.5cm) of the bone. Grab the 1-inch (2.5cm) section of skin with a paper towel, flip it over, pull it away, and peel it off, leaving a clean bone. If you look inside the cut meat, you'll see a needle-like bone, which you can break off with your thumb and forefinger. Push the meat back onto the bone, forming it into a lollipop. Repeat with the rest of the drumsticks.
7. Sprinkle the seasoning blend evenly on the meat side only, drizzle with the olive oil, place in a container, cover, and set in the refrigerator to marinate for at least 2 hours.
8. Preheat the oven to 375°F (190°C).
9. Place the legs in a baking dish, bone side up, and roast in the oven for 1 hour or until the bones and skin are golden brown.
10. Remove from the oven, and dip the drumsticks in the sweet chili oil sauce to coat. Serve immediately with the jalapeño coleslaw and extra sauce on the side.

Chicken Soup

with Spicy Green Onion Soy Sauce

PREP TIME: 35 minutes • **COOK TIME:** 1 hour 35 minutes • **SERVINGS:** 6

This soup is a comforting winter dish my mom would make to boost our immune system. Filled with a generous amount of garlic, it's perfect for when you're feeling under the weather. One bowl of this rich broth, and you can feel your energy returning. I've changed this version to be a lighter, chicken broth–style soup instead of a thick porridge like my mother made, but it still pairs wonderfully with steamed rice. It's the kind of meal that wraps you up in warmth and nourishment, perfect for chilly winter days.

CHICKEN SOUP

1 cup (195g) short-grain rice or sweet rice
1 bunch green onions (about ¼ lb/113g)
1 (4 lb or 1.8kg) whole chicken
2 garlic heads, peeled
1 tbsp (6g) black peppercorns
2 bay leaves
Kosher salt and freshly ground black pepper, for serving

SPICY GREEN ONION SOY SAUCE

2 tbsp (30ml) soy sauce
2 tbsp (30ml) warm water
1 tbsp (12g) sugar
2 Thai red chiles, thinly sliced (optional)
½ cup (50g) chopped green onion
1 garlic clove, minced
1 tbsp (6g) cayenne or chili powder
1 tsp (1g) freshly ground black pepper
2 tbsp (18g) toasted sesame seeds
2 tbsp (30ml) toasted sesame oil

SPECIAL EQUIPMENT

Kitchen string
Disposable kitchen gloves
Tea bags

Note

If you don't have a tea bag to hold the peppercorns and bay leaves, simply add them to the pot loosely. After the chicken is cooked, remove and discard the peppercorns and bay leaves.

1. Place the rice in a small bowl, cover with water, and rub the rice with one hand five or six times. Immediately discard the water and any residue in the bowl. Repeat this process five or six times until the water is lightly colored. Set aside the rice on a strainer to drain for 30 minutes.
2. Wash the green onions thoroughly under running water, cut them in half lengthwise to separate the white root end from the tender green end, and tie the root ends together with kitchen string. Reserve the green parts.
3. Line a cutting board with a paper towel, place the chicken on the paper towel, and pat the chicken dry inside and out.
4. Set the chicken neck-side down on the cutting board. Place half of the garlic cloves inside the chicken and then add the rice, and then the green parts of the onions. Twist the chicken legs and tie them together with kitchen string, making sure no rice falls out. Flip over the chicken, and fill the remaining space in the neck with the rest of the garlic. Set the chicken in a large pot.
5. Place the peppercorns and bay leaves in a tea bag or a piece of cheesecloth secured with kitchen string, and add them to the pot along with the white parts of the onions. If you have any leftover rice that wouldn't fit in the chicken, put it in another tea bag and add to the pot.
6. Add 13 cups (3 liters) of water, and set over high heat. Bring to a boil and cook over high heat for 15 minutes. Reduce the heat to low, cover, and simmer for 1 hour 15 minutes. Uncover and skim off any chicken fat that rises to the top three or four times about halfway through the cook time.
7. Meanwhile, to make the spicy green onion soy sauce, combine the soy sauce, water, and sugar in a small bowl, stirring with a spoon until the sugar is dissolved. Add the chiles (if using), green onions, garlic, cayenne, black pepper, sesame seeds, and sesame oil, and mix with a spoon. Set aside.
8. When the chicken is cooked to the point that the legs are wiggly, transfer it to a plate and let it cool slightly. Don a pair of disposable kitchen gloves and remove and discard the skin and bones. Cut the meat into bite-sized pieces and return it to the broth in the pot.
9. Discard the green parts of the green onions from inside the chicken. Add the cooked rice to the soup. Mash the garlic in a small bowl with a fork and then add it to the soup, too. (Only the rice, garlic, and chicken should be in the soup.) Increase the heat to high, and simmer, uncovered, for about 5 minutes.
10. Ladle into bowls, and serve hot with salt, pepper, and the spicy green onion soy sauce to taste.

Turkey Breast

with Orange Sauce

PREP TIME: 10 minutes • **COOK TIME:** 40 minutes • **SERVINGS:** 4

This dish is created by perfectly sautéing turkey breast with a rich orange sauce made with oranges and carrots—a combination that, perhaps surprisingly, goes very well together. The flavor combination tastes like spring in my mouth! The orange sauce also goes well with chicken or duck.

TURKEY

1 (28 oz/800g) skin-on turkey breast
1½ tsp (7.5g) kosher salt
1½ tsp (1.5g) freshly ground black pepper
6 tbsp (90ml) extra-virgin olive oil
2 sprigs of rosemary
2 sprigs of oregano
2 sprigs of thyme
1 medium grapefruit
1 tsp (4.7 g) sugar

ORANGE SAUCE

1 cup (240g) baby carrots
1¼ cups (296ml) orange juice
½ tsp (2.5g) kosher salt
¼ cup (57g) unsalted butter

SPECIAL EQUIPMENT

Kitchen string
Kitchen torch
Meat thermometer

Note

Use any fresh herbs you'd like. Tarragon and sage work well for this turkey recipe and can be used in place of (or in addition to) the rosemary, oregano, and thyme.

1. Score the skin side of the turkey breast to a depth of about ½ inch (1cm). Season both sides of the turkey with the salt and pepper and then rub all over with 2 tablespoons of the olive oil. Set aside.
2. Tie the rosemary, oregano, and thyme into a bundle using kitchen string (see Note). Set aside.
3. To make the orange sauce, add the carrots to a medium saucepan and cover with water. Set over high heat, and cook until the carrots are tender-crisp, about 10 minutes. Drain the water from the pan, leaving only the carrots.
4. Add the orange juice and salt to the pan with the carrots, and simmer over medium-high heat for about 15 minutes.
5. Add the butter, and simmer, undisturbed, for 5 minutes more. Remove the pan from the heat, and set aside.
6. Line a baking sheet with a sheet of aluminum foil large enough to encase the turkey.
7. Heat a large skillet over medium-high heat, and add the remaining 4 tablespoons olive oil. Add the turkey breast, skin-side down, and cook until the skin is yellowish and crispy, about 4 to 6 minutes. Flip over the turkey, and add the herb bundle to the pan. Cook, continuously spooning the hot herb oil over the skin side of the breast, for 4 to 6 minutes. When the internal temperature of the turkey breast reaches 165°F (75°C), transfer it to the foil-lined baking sheet, top with the herb bundle, and fold the foil over the turkey breast to enclose. Allow the turkey to rest for at least 15 minutes.
8. Peel the grapefruit, cut the segments into small cubes, and add them to a small baking dish. Sprinkle the sugar over the grapefruit, and caramelize the sugar with a kitchen torch. (Or set the oven to broil with a rack as close to the heat source as possible and cook 2 or 3 minutes.)
9. Unwrap the turkey, discard the herb bundle, and thinly slice the turkey. Arrange the slices on a serving platter, and add the carrots to the side. Drizzle the orange sauce over the sliced turkey breast and sprinkle the caramelized grapefruit cubes over the turkey. Serve warm.

Roasted Turkey

with Stuffing and Candied Lemon Peel Cranberry Sauce

PREP TIME: 2 hours • **COOK TIME:** 3 hours 50 minutes • **SERVINGS:** 8 to 10

This is a dish that brings warmth and comfort, not only for festive occasions but also for any day you crave something truly special. The succulent roasted turkey, with its perfectly golden and crispy skin, is paired with stuffing made from freshly baked whole-wheat bread and seasoned with rich herbs and vegetables to bring out deep, savory flavors. The candied lemon peel cranberry sauce adds a delightful sweet and tangy contrast, while the rich gravy ties everything together. It's a meal that nourishes the body and warms the soul.

ROASTED TURKEY

- 1 (12 lb or 5.5kg) whole turkey
- 2 stems of fresh sage
- 2 stems of fresh rosemary
- 4 stems of fresh thyme
- 3 small yellow onions, halved
- 6 shallots, halved
- 4 long celery stalks, cut into 4- or 5-inch (10 or 12.5cm) pieces
- ½ cup (120g) kosher salt
- 2 tbsp (12g) freshly ground black pepper
- ¼ cup (59ml) extra-virgin olive oil
- 1 large orange, cut into 6 wedges

STUFFING

- 13 slices (480g) of fresh whole-wheat bread, cut into 1-inch (2.5cm) cubes
- 1 cup (227g) unsalted butter
- 2 cups (240g) diced sweet onion
- 1½ cups (150g) diced celery
- 2 tbsp (11g) poultry seasoning
- ¾ tsp (3.75g) kosher salt
- 2 tsp (2g) freshly ground black pepper

CANDIED LEMON PEEL AND CRANBERRY SAUCE

- 12oz (340g) fresh whole cranberries
- 1 cup (237ml) candied lemon syrup (left over from the White Chocolate–Coated Candied Lemon Peels; see page 218), or maple syrup
- ¼ cup (20g) Candied Lemon Peels (page 218)
- 1 cinnamon stick
- 1 whole star anise
- ⅛ tsp (0.6g) kosher salt

GRAVY

- 3 tbsp (42g) unsalted butter
- 1 (.88 oz or 25g) packet instant turkey gravy
- 1 tsp (2.5g) all-purpose flour
- 1 tsp (1g) freshly ground black pepper
- 3 cups (710ml) boiling water

SPECIAL EQUIPMENT

- Kitchen string
- Disposable kitchen gloves
- Two ovenproof meat thermometers

1. To make the turkey, remove it from the refrigerator and let it sit at room temperature for about 1½ hours. Tie the sage, rosemary, and thyme stems into a bunch using kitchen string. Add the onions, shallots, and celery to a roasting pan.
2. Place a paper towel on a cutting board, and set the turkey on top. Remove the neck and giblets, and add them to the roasting pan. Pat the turkey dry inside and out with paper towels.
3. Whisk together the salt and pepper in a small bowl. With the turkey breast-side down, season it evenly from front to back and then drizzle with the olive oil. Turn the turkey over and coat the breast, legs, and wings evenly with the seasoning and then drizzle with the olive oil.
4. Place the turkey breast-side down in the roasting pan with the vegetables (you can use a rack if you like), and tuck the wingtips behind the neck. This will keep the turkey secure and prevent it from spreading apart.
5. Preheat the oven to 400°F (200°C).
6. To make the stuffing, place the bread in a large bowl and set aside.
7. Melt the butter in a large skillet over medium heat. Add the onion, celery, poultry seasoning, salt, and pepper, and sauté for about 10 minutes or until the onion is soft. Pour the butter and vegetables over the bread, and use gloved hands or two wooden spatulas to mix well to coat the bread. Stuff the turkey with the stuffing.
8. Juice half of the orange (you'll need ¼ cup/59ml), and set aside. (This will be used later for the cranberry sauce.) Cover the stuffing with the peels of half the orange, and use to press the stuffing into the turkey. (If you have leftover stuffing, place it in an ovenproof dish, cover with foil, and set aside.) Insert two meat thermometers in the turkey, one in the breast and one in the thigh. Pour about 2 cups (473ml) of water in the bottom of the roasting pan.
9. Roast for 25 minutes. Rotate the turkey 180 degrees on its side in the pan (do not flip), and roast for 20 minutes. Reduce the oven temperature to 350°F (177°C), and roast for an additional 45 minutes.
10. Remove the turkey from the oven and brush the skin with the juices from the bottom of the roasting pan using the herb brush. Return to the oven and roast for 45 minutes.

11. Remove the turkey from the oven again. Using a large slotted spoon, scoop out the stuffing and transfer it to an ovenproof dish. Cover the dish with foil and set aside. Brush the turkey skin with the pan juices again. (If you had leftover stuffing earlier, you can add it to the turkey at this point.) Reduce the oven temperature to 300°F (149°C), and roast the turkey for about 45 minutes more, or until the thickest part of the breast reads 158°F (70°C) on the thermometer and the thickest part of the thigh reads 150°F (66°C). If there is a large temperature difference, cover only the breasts with heavy foil so they don't overcook. Do not let the internal temperature of the breast exceed 170°F (77°C). When the thighs reach 150°F (66°C), transfer the turkey to a cutting board, and let it rest for 30 to 40 minutes. During this time, the thigh temperature will increase. When the thigh temperature reaches 165°F (74°C), you can start carving. (See step 15.) Turn off the oven, and keep the stuffing warm inside the closed oven.

12. To make the candied lemon peel cranberry sauce, add the cranberries, lemon syrup, candied lemon peels, orange juice from step 8, cinnamon stick, star anise, and salt to a small saucepan. Set over medium-high heat, and simmer for 10 to 15 minutes. Transfer the sauce to an ovenproof dish, and set aside.

13. To make the gravy, set the roasting pan with the roasted vegetables, neck, and giblets over high heat. Add the used herb brush and the boiling water, and simmer for 10 minutes, deglazing the pan as needed. Strain the vegetable stock over a bowl using a fine-mesh sieve and discard the solids.

14. Add the butter, turkey gravy mix, flour, and pepper to a medium saucepan. Set over medium-low heat, stir with a wooden spatula to combine, and cook for 3 minutes. Add the boiling water, increase the heat to medium, and simmer for 10 minutes. Reduce the heat to low and simmer for 5 minutes. Transfer to a gravy boat and keep warm in the turned-off oven.

15. Once the turkey has rested, break apart the legs with your hands and cut them off with a knife. Separate the wings by running a knife along the bone. Cut the breast across the breastbone in the center of the turkey and then slice to your desired thickness.

16. Arrange the meat on a large serving platter, drizzle with warm gravy, and serve with cranberry sauce and warm stuffing.

CHAPTER 5

Breads

No Butter, No Egg
Sandwich Bread

PREP TIME: 20 minutes plus 12 hours to ferment and 4 hours to rise • **COOK TIME:** 1 hour • **MAKES:** 1 loaf

Although this bread contains no butter and no eggs, it more than compensates with its delightful simplicity, boasting a flavor that never gets boring, thanks to just water, flour, yeast, and salt. The slow fermentation process through the poolish method results in a light loaf with a pleasantly chewy texture. (A poolish is a fermentation starter, or mother dough.) This sandwich bread is a wholesome choice, perfect for those seeking a healthy alternative without sacrificing taste. It pairs beautifully with various fillings, making it an excellent base for sandwiches or hearty breakfasts. Plus, any leftovers can be frozen, ensuring you have fresh, homemade bread whenever you like.

POOLISH

1 cup (237ml) warm water
⅓ tsp (1g) active dry yeast
240g bread flour

DOUGH

1½ cups (355ml) warm water
⅓ tsp (1g) active dry yeast
600g bread flour, plus more for dusting
2 tsp (10g) kosher salt

SPECIAL EQUIPMENT

13×4×4-inch (33×10×10cm) loaf pan with cover

Note

If your loaf pan doesn't have a lid, you can put a baking sheet over the pan and top it with something heavy to prevent the dough from pushing up the baking sheet as it rises. The lid, or baking sheet, will help shape the top of the bread.

1. To make the poolish, combine the warm water and yeast in a large, deep bowl. Add the flour, and mix well using a spatula. Cover with plastic wrap, and let ferment at room temperature for 12 hours. (I recommend doing this in the evening for an overnight ferment.)
2. To make the dough, whisk together the warm water and yeast in another large bowl. Add the poolish and then the flour and salt, and mix with a spatula until just combined and the flour does not clump. Cover with a towel, and let rest for 30 minutes.
3. Add some warm water to a small bowl, and dip both hands in the water. (This helps keep the dough from sticking to your hands.) With wet hands, grab the dough on the side of the bowl, lift it, stretch it, and place it on top of the other side of the dough. Repeat this three more times, rotating the bowl 90 degrees each time. Cover with a tea towel, and let rest for 30 minutes. (This is the first fold.) Repeat the lifting, stretching, and folding a second time. (The second fold.) Repeat a third and fourth time, letting the dough rest 30 minutes after each fold.
4. Turn out the dough onto a floured surface. Gently press down on it with your hands to release the gas, and roll from the top to the bottom like a log, pinching the dough to close it. Place the dough seam side down in a nonstick 13½×4×12-inch (34×10×30.5cm) baking pan, and lightly press to flatten. Cover with a tea towel, and let rise until the dough has risen to ¼ inch (0.5cm) below the rim of the pan, about 1 hour 30 minutes. Cover with a lid (see Note).
5. When the dough is at least halfway risen in the loaf pan, preheat the oven to 375°F (190°C).
6. Bake for 50 minutes to 1 hour, until golden brown. (You can check the color of the top by lifting the lid.)
7. Remove from the oven, uncover, and lightly tap the pan on a work surface to loosen the bread. Transfer the bread to a wire rack to cool completely before serving. Store in an airtight plastic bag at room temperature for up to 3 days, or slice and freeze in a container for up to 1 month.

Hotel Bread

PREP TIME: 35 minutes plus 1 hour 45 minutes to rise • **COOK TIME:** 50 minutes • **MAKES:** 1 loaf

This white bread is very soft and sweet, yet it uses a very small amount of butter. Once you take it out of the oven and start eating it, don't be surprised if you finish the whole loaf! The origins of the name "hotel bread" aren't clear, but it tastes like something you'd find in a fancy hotel.

DOUGH

1 cup (237ml) warm water
¼ cup (50g) granulated sugar
2¼ tsp (7g) active dry yeast
390g bread flour
1 tsp (5g) kosher salt
1 medium egg
2 tbsp (28g) unsalted butter

MAPLE BROWN BUTTER SPREAD

½ cup (113g) unsalted butter
¼ cup (59ml) maple syrup
½ tbsp (4g) ground cinnamon
¼ tsp (1.25g) kosher salt

TOPPING

1 tbsp unsalted butter, at room temperature
1 tbsp granulated sugar

SPECIAL EQUIPMENT

8 × 4-inch (20 × 10cm) loaf pan

1. To make the dough, pour the warm water, sugar, and yeast into a small bowl, cover with a tea towel, and let stand until foamy, about 10 minutes.
2. Whisk together the flour and salt in a large bowl. Add the yeast mixture and egg, and mix well with a wooden spoon.
3. Turn out the dough onto a work surface. Add the butter and knead for about 10 minutes.
4. When the dough looks smooth and doesn't stick to your hands, roll it into a ball and pinch the bottom. Return the dough to the bowl, cover with a tea towel, and let it rise until doubled in size, about 1 hour.
5. Dust a work surface lightly with flour and turn out the dough. Press the dough to remove the gas and then evenly divide it into three pieces. Roll each piece into a ball, cover with a tea towel, and let rest for 15 minutes.
6. Preheat the oven to 340°F (170°C). Line an 8 × 4-inch (20 × 10cm) loaf pan with parchment paper.
7. Place one ball of dough on a lightly floured work surface. Roll out the dough into a circle ½ inch thick. Fold over the top third of the dough to the center, and fold up the bottom third over the top third. Turn the dough 90 degrees. Starting from the short end, roll the dough from the top to the bottom, and pinch the end to seal the roll. Repeat with the remaining two dough pieces.
8. Place the three pieces of rolled dough in the prepared loaf pan and press down lightly. Cover with a tea towel, and let rise until the dough is ½ inch (1.25cm) from the top of the pan, about 30 minutes.
9. Meanwhile, to make the maple brown butter spread, heat a medium saucepan over medium heat. Add the butter, and cook until lightly browned, about 5 minutes. Continue to cook, swirling the pan, until the butter bubbles almost disappear, about 5 minutes. The butter will brown – be careful not to burn it.
10. Add ice water to a medium bowl and set a small bowl on top of the ice. Pour the brown butter into the small bowl and whisk as fast as you can. When the brown butter turns to a creamy texture, after about 5 minutes, remove the bowl from the ice water. Add the maple syrup, cinnamon, and salt, and whisk again as fast as you can, about 3 minutes. Set aside.
11. Uncover the dough, and make a cut ¼-inch (6mm) deep down the center of the long side of the dough. Place the 1 tablespoon butter for the topping in a plastic bag, snip off the corner of the bag, and squeeze the butter into the cut. Sprinkle the sugar over the butter.
12. Bake for 35 minutes, or until golden brown.
13. Immediately remove from the pan – the bread is very soft and fluffy, so you'll need to grab the parchment paper and gently pull it out – and place on a wire rack to cool.
14. Slice and serve with the delicious maple brown butter spread. Store any leftovers in an airtight container at room temperature for up to 3 days or freeze and then thaw to room temperature before serving.

Pide Bread
with Kaymak

PREP TIME: 1 hour 20 minutes plus 5 hours to rest and 1 to 3 days to age • **COOK TIME:** 3 hours • **MAKES:** 1 loaf of bread and 3 kaymak rolls

In this recipe, soft, savory pide bread and creamy kaymak create a perfect harmony and capture the essence of Turkish flavors. The preparation takes time—about 1 hour and 20 minutes, and the kaymak requires 5 hours of resting time and between 1 and 3 days of refrigeration—but the results are worth it. The magic of kaymak begins with the careful simmering of milk and cream, which results in a thick, captivating foam. The kaymak and the warm pide bread, drizzled with honey and topped with pistachios, pair perfectly with Turkish black tea. Black cumin seeds further enhance the dish.

KAYMAK

4 cups (945ml) whole milk
5 cups (1185ml) heavy cream

PIDE (TURKISH BREAD)

2 cups (473ml) warm water, divided
3 tsp (9g) active dry yeast
1 tbsp (12.5g) sugar
480g bread flour, divided, plus more for dusting
2 tsp (10g) kosher salt

EGG WASH AND TOPPINGS

¼ cup (59ml) warm water
30g bread flour
1 egg yolk
1 tbsp (9g) sesame seeds
1 tbsp (9g) raw black cumin seeds (Kalonji, Nigella Sativa)
1 tbsp (21g) honey
¼ cup (25g) pistachios, shelled and chopped

SPECIAL EQUIPMENT

Disposable kitchen gloves
12½-inch (32cm) round pizza pan

Note

Don't skip the black cumin seeds in the topping. Their distinctive flavor gives all the other ingredients a nice kick.

1. Warm the milk and heavy cream in a large saucepan over high heat for 10 to 15 minutes. Dip a whisk halfway into the milk and cream mixture, and shake vigorously from side to side in the center to create a thick foam. (This process separates the fats while creating a foam. The better the fat is separated, the thicker the kaymak you will get.)
2. When the milk has bubbled up to at least one and a half times the original amount of milk and a thick layer of foam has formed, reduce the heat to medium, and use a ladle to continuously scoop up and pour the milk back into the saucepan from a height of 12 to 16 inches (30.5 to 40cm). Simmer for about 30 minutes more, scooping and pouring the milk, until the amount of milk is reduced by about one third. If too much of the foam has disappeared, create more foam by whisking. The milk should boil just below the foam.
3. Reduce the heat to the lowest setting and keep warm for about 2 hours. The milk should not boil and break through the foam layer during this time, and the foam layer should remain dry and form a film on top. If the milk boils and tries to break through the foam layer despite the lowest heat, turn off the heat for a while and then set to low again.
4. After 2 hours, a film should have formed on the surface of the foam. Turn off the heat. Wrap a towel around the inside of the pan's lid, and tie the ends of the towel up around the lid's handle. (This ensures that any moisture in the pot is absorbed by the towel and doesn't affect the foam.) Cover the pan, and leave the kaymak to cool at room temperature for at least 5 hours. Replace the towel if it gets too wet.
5. Transfer the kaymak to the refrigerator to age for at least 1 day and up to 3 days.
6. The surface of the milk will be rough with a dried film of foam that has subsided and will feel coarse to the touch. Use a knife to trim the edges of the kaymak around the pan, and cut it into three long strips. Put on kitchen gloves, and roll each strip so the dried surface remains on the outside of the roll. Place the rolls in a container, and store them in the refrigerator. (You can use the leftover milk mixture in any baking that requires milk.)
7. To make the pide bread, whisk together 1 cup (237ml) of warm water, and the yeast, sugar, and 120g of flour in a large bowl. Cover with a tea towel and let rise until doubled in size, 15 to 20 minutes.
8. Stir the yeast mixture once with a wooden spoon. Add the remaining 1 cup (237ml) of warm water, the remaining 360g of flour, and salt, and stir until no flour is visible. Cover with a tea towel, and let rise for about 30 minutes.
9. Dust a work surface with flour. Turn out the dough onto the surface and dust the dough generously with a little more flour. Fold the dough from the outsides in, pressing down to form a smooth ball.
10. Dust a 12½-inch (32cm) round pizza pan with flour. Place the dough on the pan, and press down with the palm of your hand to stretch the dough to fill the pan.

Cover with a towel and let rise for 30 to 40 minutes or until the dough is ¼ inch (6mm) over the top of the pan.

11. Preheat the oven to 450°F (230°C).
12. To make the egg wash, whisk together the warm water, flour, and egg yolk in a small bowl. Combine the sesame seeds and black cumin seeds in another small bowl.
13. Brush the dough twice with the egg wash. Using your fingers (not your thumb), press a circle 1 inch (2.5cm) in from the edge all around the dough. Then press again, this time making a 1½-inch (3.75cm) grid inside the pressed circle. Sprinkle the seed blend over the dough.
14. Bake for 15 to 20 minutes, until golden on top. Transfer the pide bread to a wire rack to cool slightly.
15. Remove the kaymak from the refrigerator, and place on a plate. Drizzle with the honey, and sprinkle with the pistachios. Serve with the sliced pide bread and some Turkish black tea on the side.

Braided Cinnamon Loaf

PREP TIME: 15 minutes plus 1 hour 45 minutes to rise • **COOK TIME:** 30 minutes • **SERVINGS:** 6 to 8

My daughters ask me to style their hair every morning before school, so the word braid reminds me of my daughters' hair designs. It also reminds me of this loaf, which is made by filling the dough with a sweet cinnamon paste, twisting it into a beautiful braid, and allowing it to rise perfectly. The triple flavor combination of cinnamon, cream cheese, and butter makes this bread exquisite.

DOUGH

1 cup (237ml) warm whole milk
¼ cup (58g) melted unsalted butter
¼ cup (50g) granulated sugar
2¼ tsp (7g) active dry yeast
300g bread flour, plus more for dusting
½ tsp (2.5g) kosher salt
½ tsp (2.5g) baking powder
2 egg yolks

CINNAMON PASTE

½ cup (113g) unsalted butter, at room temperature
⅓ cup (71g) brown sugar, firmly packed
2 tsp (5g) ground cinnamon

CREAM CHEESE ICING

4 oz (113g) cream cheese
¼ cup (58g) unsalted butter
1½ cups (173g) confectioners' sugar
½ cup (120g) sour cream
1 tsp (5ml) vanilla extract

SPECIAL EQUIPMENT

Stand mixer fitted with a dough hook

1. To make the dough, add the warm milk, melted butter, sugar, and yeast to a small bowl, and mix well. Cover with a tea towel and let sit until foamy, about 10 minutes.
2. Whisk together the flour, salt, and baking powder in a large bowl.
3. Add the yeast mixture to the flour mixture and knead by hand for 10 minutes. (You also can use a stand mixer, fitted with a dough hook, on medium for 7 or 8 minutes.) Cover with a tea towel and let sit until the dough has doubled in size, about 1 hour.
4. Meanwhile, make the cinnamon paste by mixing together all the ingredients in a medium bowl.
5. Turn out the dough onto a floured work surface, and roll it out into a rectangle about ½ inch (1.25cm) thick. Use a spatula to spread the cinnamon paste evenly over the dough.
6. Fold both long sides of the dough to the center and then fold one half over the other. You should have a total of four layers. Use a sharp knife to cut the dough lengthwise into three equal strips.
7. Line a baking sheet with parchment paper. Place the dough strips on the prepared baking sheet. Twist each strip, pinch the strips together at one end, and then braid the strips together. Cover the dough with a clean towel and let rise for 45 minutes.
8. Preheat the oven to 365°F (185°C).
9. Make the cream cheese icing by combining all the ingredients in a medium bowl. (I prefer to use a hand mixer on medium to mix the cream cheese icing.) Set aside.
10. Whisk the egg yolks in a small bowl. Use a pastry brush to spread the egg wash over the risen dough braid twice. Bake for 30 minutes.
11. Remove from the oven and let cool for 5 minutes. Spread the cream cheese icing over the warm cinnamon loaf and serve. Store in an airtight container at room temperature for up to 3 days, or cut into thick slices, freeze, and then thaw to room temperature before serving.

Pumpernickel Bread

PREP TIME: 10 minutes plus 13 hours to rise and 1 hour to cool • **COOK TIME:** 55 minutes • **MAKES:** 1 loaf

Pumpernickel bread is more than just a deep, dark loaf—it's a wholesome powerhouse packed with fiber, minerals, and natural energy. The combination of rye and whole-wheat flour gives it a rich, earthy flavor, while molasses and cocoa powder add depth without extra sugar. The slow fermentation process not only enhances the taste but also makes the bread easier to digest. With heart-healthy seeds and whole grains, this loaf is as nourishing as it is delicious. Toast a slice, spread on some butter, and enjoy a bread that's good for both your body and soul.

360g rye flour
60g whole-wheat flour, plus more for dusting
¼ cup (29g) cornmeal
2 tsp (10g) kosher salt
1 tsp (5ml) instant coffee
2 tbsp (28g) unsweetened cocoa powder
2 cups (473ml) warm water
2 tbsp (40g) molasses
½ tsp (1.4g) active dry yeast
1¼ cup (100g) old-fashioned oats
½ cup (60g) pumpkin seeds, divided
½ cup (60g) sunflower seeds, divided
2 cups (500g) ice cubes

SPECIAL EQUIPMENT

Baking stone or large cast-iron skillet

1. Combine the rye flour, whole-wheat flour, cornmeal, salt, coffee, and cocoa powder in a large bowl, and mix well by hand.
2. Whisk together the warm water, molasses, and yeast in a medium bowl until the yeast is dissolved. Pour into the flour mixture, and stir with a wooden spatula to combine.
3. Add 1 cup (80g) of oats, ¼ cup (30g) of pumpkin seeds, and ¼ cup (30g) of sunflower seeds to the dough, and stir to incorporate evenly. Shape the dough into a ball, cover with plastic wrap, and let rest at room temperature for 12 hours. (You may want to do this the day before.)
4. Turn out the dough onto a floured work surface, and press down with your hands to deflate slightly. Fold both sides into the middle, and roll the dough from top to bottom.
5. Spread the remaining ¼ cup (30g) of oats, ¼ cup (30g) of pumpkin seeds, and ¼ cup (30g) of sunflower seeds on a work surface. Spray the dough with cooking spray, and roll the moistened portion over the seeds to adhere them to the dough.
6. Line an oval basket with a towel, place the dough seed side down on the towel, and gently press down on the top to flatten. Cover the dough with a towel, and let ferment until doubled in size, about 1 hour.
7. About 30 minutes before the end of fermentation, place a baking stone or large cast-iron skillet set on an empty baking sheet on the bottom rack of the oven, and preheat the oven to 450°F (230°C). Line another baking sheet with parchment paper.
8. Remove the towel from the dough basket, invert the basket onto the prepared baking sheet and remove the basket and other towel. Holding a knife at a 45-degree angle, cut a slit ¼ inch (0.5cm) deep across the long side of the dough. Set the dough on the hot baking stone or place in the hot skillet.
9. Add the ice cubes to a baking pan, and set it on the bottom rack of the oven. Close the door quickly and steam for 15 minutes. Do not open the oven door while the bread is steaming.
10. Reduce the oven temperature to 420°F (215°C), and bake for 40 minutes, or until the bread smells nutty and is golden brown. The bread is done when the internal temperature is about 210°F (100°C).
11. Remove from the oven, transfer to a wire rack, and allow to cool to room temperature, at least 1 hour, before slicing, toasting, and serving with butter.

Herbed Flatbread
with Beet Hummus

PREP TIME: 2 hours 30 minutes plus 12 hours to ferment • **COOK TIME:** 25 minutes • **SERVINGS:** 4 or 5

This freshly baked herbed flatbread topped with creamy beet hummus, fresh salad, and smooth burrata is a nourishing, feel-good meal. The flatbread dough, slowly fermented with herbs and citrus zest, develops a rich flavor while the bread bakes to a crispy outside and soft, chewy inside. With the nutty hummus, crunchy veggies, and creamy burrata coming together in perfect harmony, each bite feels like a little moment of happiness. The flatbread is perfect for tearing and sharing, naturally bringing people together and making the time spent around the table even warmer.

POOLISH

1 cup (237ml) warm water

¼ tsp (1g) active dry yeast

240g bread flour

HERBED FLATBREAD DOUGH

570g bread flour, plus more for dusting

1 tbsp (6g) finely chopped fresh flat-leaf parsley

1 tbsp (6g) finely chopped fresh rosemary

1 tbsp (6g) finely chopped fresh sage

1 tbsp (6g) lemon zest

1 tbsp (6g) orange zest

2 tsp (4g) onion powder

1½ tsp (7.5g) kosher salt

1 tsp (1g) freshly ground black pepper

1 tsp (2g) garlic powder

½ tsp (1g) mustard powder

¼ tsp (1g) active dry yeast

1⅔ cups (393ml) warm water

¼ cup (30g) cornmeal, for dusting

BEET HUMMUS

1 small beet

½ tsp (2.5g) kosher salt

2 cups (328g) chickpeas, drained and rinsed

⅓ cup (79ml) tahini

2 tbsp (30ml) fresh lemon juice

1 garlic clove

2 tbsp (30ml) maple syrup

BASIL OLIVE OIL BURRATA SALAD

¼ cup (59ml) extra-virgin olive oil

3 tbsp (18g) finely chopped fresh basil leaves, plus 1 stem of basil, for garnish

1 tbsp (6g) lemon zest

1 (8 oz/225g) ball of burrata

¼ cup (60g) baby arugula

1 cup (40g) radicchio

¼ cup (60g) oak lettuce or baby lettuce leaves

½ cup (75g) cherry tomatoes, halved

¼ cup (60g) fresh mini mozzarella balls or bocconcini

1 tbsp (15ml) balsamic glaze

¼ tsp (1.25g) kosher salt

1 tsp (1g) freshly ground black pepper

SPECIAL EQUIPMENT

Pizza oven or baking stone

Food processor

1. To make the poolish, add the warm water and yeast to a large bowl. When the yeast is dissolved, stir in the flour with a wooden spatula. Cover with a towel, and let sit at room temperature for 12 hours.
2. To make the flatbread dough, add the flour, parsley, rosemary, sage, lemon zest, orange zest, onion powder, salt, pepper, garlic powder, and mustard powder to a medium bowl, and mix, using your hands, until evenly combined.
3. Dissolve the yeast in the warm water in a small bowl. Dip your hands in the mixture to moisten them, and press down on the edges of the poolish to separate it from the bowl. Pour the yeast water around the edges of the bowl. Add the flour mixture, and knead with your hands until the dough comes together. Cover with a tea towel, and let rest for 30 minutes.
4. Fold the dough into the center on all sides and place top down in the bowl. Cover and let rest for another 30 minutes. Repeat this process two more times, for a total resting time of 2 hours.
5. Preheat a pizza oven, or an oven with a baking stone inside, to 550°F (288°C).
6. Turn out the dough on a work surface generously dusted with flour. Divide the dough into three parts using a scraper. Roll the dough into three balls. Set one ball on a work surface generously dusted with cornmeal, and store the remaining two dough balls in an airtight container in the refrigerator for up to 3 days.
7. Press your fingers into the edges of the dough, 1 inch (2.5cm) in from the edge, and press your palm into the center of the dough. Stretch and press with all 10 fingers to form the dough into a 12-inch (30.5cm) circle.
8. Lift the dough with a pizza peel or large spatula, and place in the oven to bake for 3 to 5 minutes or when the edges of the bread are puffed, golden, and crisp,. Transfer to a wire rack to cool.
9. To make the beet hummus, wrap the beet in wet parchment paper and microwave for 4 minutes. Peel and quarter the beet, and place in a small bowl. Cover with water, add the salt, and cook over medium-high heat for 15 minutes. Transfer the beet and ⅓ cup (79ml) of its cooking water to a food processor.

10. Add the chickpeas, tahini, lemon juice, garlic, and maple syrup to the food processor, and process until smooth, about 3 minutes. Set aside.
11. To make the basil olive oil burrata salad, whisk together the olive oil, basil, and lemon zest in a medium bowl. Use scissors to carefully cut open the top of the burrata, like a lid. Add 1 tablespoon (15ml) of the basil oil, toss with the filling inside, and close the "lid." Garnish with a basil stem.
12. Toss the remaining oil, baby arugula, radicchio, and lettuce in a medium bowl until evenly coated with the basil oil. Set aside.
13. To serve, place the flatbread on a serving platter, spread the beet hummus evenly over the flatbread, and top with the salad. Spread the halved cherry tomatoes and mini mozzarella balls evenly over the salad, and tuck the filled burrata in the center. Drizzle balsamic glaze over the top, season with salt and pepper, and serve.

Sweet Garlic Butter Leaves Bread

PREP TIME: 25 minutes plus 12 hours to ferment and 2 hours 10 minutes to rise • **COOK TIME:** 30 minutes • **MAKES:** 4 loaves

This bread offers a delightful combination of crisp and tender textures with rich, savory flavors. The process is a bit time-consuming due to the slow fermentation with the poolish (a fermentation starter or mother dough), but the results are well worth the wait. Fresh from the oven, the warm bread melts with sweet garlic butter, and a sprinkle of Parmesan adds an extra layer of flavor, making it a perfect choice for special occasions. For the holiday season, it can be shaped like a Christmas tree for a festive touch, and you can experiment with different shapes and flavors at other times of the year. Add your favorite cheese for a unique twist!

POOLISH

½ cup (118ml) warm water
⅓ tsp (1g) active dry yeast
100g bread flour

DOUGH

1½ cups (355ml) warm water
2¼ tsp (7g) active dry yeast
500g bread flour, plus more for dusting
2 tsp (10g) kosher salt
¼ cup (30g) grated Parmigiano-Reggiano
2 cups (500g) of ice cubes

SWEET GARLIC BUTTER

1 (14 oz/300g) can sweetened condensed milk
1¼ cups (295g) unsalted butter, at room temperature
1 head of garlic, cloves separated and finely minced
¼ cup (24g) chopped fresh parsley
½ tsp (2.5g) kosher salt

SPECIAL EQUIPMENT

Stand mixer fitted with a dough hook
Kitchen scissors

Notes

When you cut the dough with the scissors, you can make more cuts for smaller leaves or fewer cuts for larger leaves. Or make the loaves in the shape of leaves and serve them as holiday bread!

You also can top the butter with mozzarella instead of the Parmigiano-Reggiano.

1. To make the poolish, whisk together the warm water and yeast in a large bowl. Add the flour, and mix well using a spatula. Cover with plastic wrap, and let ferment at room temperature for 12 hours. (I recommend doing this in the evening for an overnight ferment.)
2. To make the dough, combine the warm water and yeast in a small cup. Cover with a tea towel, and let sit until foamy, about 10 minutes. Add the flour, salt, and yeast mixture to the poolish, and mix with a spatula until no flour is visible and the dough is lumpy. Turn out the dough onto a work surface, and knead by hand for 10 minutes. (You also can use a stand mixer fitted with a dough hook.)
3. Return the dough to the bowl, cover with a towel, and let it rise until triple in size, about 1 hour 30 minutes.
4. Meanwhile, to make the sweet garlic butter, add the condensed milk to a medium saucepan. Set over low heat, and cook, stirring often, until warmed through, about 5 minutes. Remove from the heat and add the butter in two batches, whisking to combine after each addition. Add the garlic, parsley, and salt, and stir to combine. Allow to cool and then transfer to a pastry bag and set aside.
5. Turn out the dough onto a floured work surface and divide in half. Fold the dough of one half inward on all sides, and flip it over. You should end up with a 7 × 8-inch (17.75 × 20cm) rectangle. Cover with a tea towel. Repeat with the remaining dough. Let rest for 15 minutes.
6. Place one piece of dough on a generously floured work surface, and use a scraper to cut it lengthwise into two long, equal pieces. Place the dough with the cut side up (the cut side will make the dough sticky). Dust your hands with flour, and begin to fold the dough in 1-inch (5cm) increments, starting on the left side and moving to the right, pressing down with the palm of your hand. Do this once or twice to form a log and then pinch the ends of the dough together. Using both hands, roll and press from the center of the log to the ends to form a 14-inch (35.5cm) loaf.
7. Transfer the loaf to a parchment paper–lined baking sheet. Repeat with the rest of the dough, placing only two loaves of dough per baking sheet, leaving space between each. Cover with a tea towel, and let rise for 40 to 50 minutes.
8. Place an empty baking sheet on the lowest rack of the oven and preheat the oven to 480°F (250°C).
9. After the dough rises, it will be about 2½ inches (6.25cm) wide. Carefully turn over the dough so it is seam side up, and pinch the top and bottom ends together in the middle to reduce the width. The dough will be reduced to about 2 inches (5cm) wide. Place the dough seam side down again.
10. Holding clean kitchen scissors at a 45-degree angle, cut off the ends of the dough, leaving ¼ inches (0.5cm) intact. (Don't cut all the way through.) Make seven or eight cuts, 1 or 2 inches (2.5 or 5cm) wide, rotating each cut 45 degrees from the previous

cut, and then place the dough on its side. It should look like a branch with leaves. Repeat with the remaining loaves.

11. Place all the loaves in the preheated oven. Add the ice cubes to the preheated baking sheet, and quickly close the oven. Turn off the oven, and let the bread steam for 10 minutes.
12. Heat the oven to 450°F (230°C), and bake the bread for about 10 minutes, or until golden brown. Remove from the oven and allow to cool slightly on a wire rack.
13. Reduce the oven temperature to 400°F (200°C).
14. Using a small knife, cut a slit about 1 inch (2.5cm) deep in the center of each leaf. Open the slits, squeeze in the sweet garlic butter, and sprinkle the Parmigiano-Reggiano over the top.
15. Return to the oven for about 5 minutes, or until the cheese is melted. Serve warm.

Cheesy Caramelized Onion Bread

PREP TIME: 40 minutes plus 1 hour 15 minutes to rise • **COOK TIME:** 1 hour • **SERVINGS:** 4 to 6

Imagine the aroma of a freshly baked bread that's loaded with caramelized onions and an irresistible blend of cheeses. Inspired by a love of all things cheesy, this recipe combines the comfort of homemade bread with the savory goodness of an onion bagel. Topped with a sprinkle of everything bagel seasoning, it's the perfect fusion of flavors. One bite, and you'll be hooked!

CARAMELIZED ONIONS

2 tbsp (30ml) extra-virgin olive oil
3 large white onions, thinly sliced
½ tsp (2.5g) kosher salt

DOUGH

⅔ cup (158ml) warm water
2¼ tsp (7g) active dry yeast
¼ cup (50g) sugar
400g bread flour, plus more for dusting
1 tsp (5g) kosher salt
1 tbsp (6g) finely chopped fresh flat-leaf parsley
½ cup (80g) caramelized onions
2 large eggs, beaten

TOPPING

2 cups (225g) shredded cheddar
1 egg yolk
1 tbsp (9g) everything bagel seasoning
1 tbsp (15ml) mayonnaise
2 cups (225g) shredded mozzarella
1 cup (160g) caramelized onions
1 cup (113g) shredded Havarti cheese
½ tbsp (3g) finely chopped fresh flat-leaf parsley
¼ tsp (0.25g) crushed hot red pepper

SPECIAL EQUIPMENT

12½ × 18 inch (32 × 46cm) baking sheet

1. To make the caramelized onions, heat the olive oil, onions, and salt in a large skillet over medium-high heat. Cook, stirring constantly, until deep brown in color, 25 to 30 minutes. You may need to add a little water to the pan to help the caramel release some of its goodness. Transfer the onions to a plate, and set aside.
2. To make the dough, pour the warm water into a small bowl, and add the yeast and sugar. Cover with a tea towel, and let sit for 10 minutes.
3. Using your hands, combine the flour, salt, parsley, and caramelized onions in a large bowl. Pour the yeast mixture into the flour, add the beaten eggs, and mix with a wooden spoon.
4. Turn out the dough onto a work surface and knead for 15 minutes. When the dough is smooth and no longer sticks to your hands, return it to the bowl, cover with a tea towel, and let it rise until it has more than doubled in size, about 1 hour.
5. Turn out the dough onto a floured work surface, and punch it down to release the gas. Divide the dough in half, and shape each piece into a ball. Cover with a tea towel, and let the dough rest for 15 minutes.
6. Preheat the oven to 400°F (200°C). Line a 12½ × 18 inch (32 × 46cm) baking sheet with parchment paper.
7. Place 1 ball of dough on a floured work surface, and use a rolling pin to roll out to a 9-inch (23cm) circle. Place the dough on the prepared baking sheet. Leaving a ½-inch (1.25cm) edge around the outside of the dough, use half of the cheddar to make a ring about 1 inch (2.5cm) thick around the outer edge of the dough, leaving the center of the dough clear from the cheese. Pull the uncovered outer edge of the dough over the cheese, and push down to seal. (Think of this like a stuffed-crust pizza, where the cheese is sealed in the outer edge of the crust.) Brush the cheese-filled dough with the egg yolk and sprinkle with half of the everything bagel seasoning.
8. Spread ½ tablespoon (7.5ml) of mayonnaise on the middle of the dough, sprinkle with half of the mozzarella, and add half of the caramelized onions in an even layer. Top with half of the Havarti and sprinkle with half of the parsley and half of the crushed red pepper. Repeat with the remaining dough and topping ingredients.
9. Bake for 30 minutes.
10. Transfer to a serving dish and serve with a salad and a cold drink.

Monkey Bread

PREP TIME: 40 minutes plus 1 hour 30 minutes to rise • **COOK TIME:** 40 minutes • **MAKES:** 1 (10-inch [25.5cm]) loaf

If you've never had monkey bread, you're in for a treat. Round pastries are dipped in butter, coated with cinnamon and sugar, baked in a Bundt pan, and then torn apart one by one to eat. This bread, originally from Hungary, is a special pastry I give to my favorite people on special days. It's especially good drizzled with cream cheese frosting (from the Braided Cinnamon Loaf recipe, page 107).

1 cup (237ml) warm whole milk
⅓ cup (79ml) warm water
4 tbsp (58g), divided, plus ½ cup (113g) unsalted butter, melted
2¼ tsp (7g) active dry yeast
¼ cup (50g) granulated sugar
450g bread flour, plus more for dusting
2 tsp (10g) kosher salt
1 tbsp (8g) ground cinnamon
1 cup (200g) brown sugar, firmly packed

SPECIAL EQUIPMENT

10-inch (25.5cm) round Bundt cake pan
Pizza cutter

1. Combine the milk, water, 2 tablespoons (28g) of the melted butter, the yeast, and the granulated sugar in a small bowl. Cover with a tea towel, and let sit until foamy, about 10 minutes.
2. Meanwhile, add the flour and salt to a large bowl and mix well using your hands or a wooden spoon.
3. Add the yeast mixture to the flour and stir with a wooden spoon until no dry flour remains.
4. Turn out the dough onto a lightly floured work surface and knead until the dough forms a neat ball, about 10 minutes. Cover with a towel, and set in a warm spot to rise until double in size, about 1 hour.
5. Mix the cinnamon and brown sugar in a small bowl, and add the ½ cup (113g) of melted butter to a separate small bowl. Set aside both.
6. Coat a 10-inch (25.5cm) round Bundt cake pan with the remaining 2 tablespoons (28g) of melted butter.
7. Turn out the dough onto a lightly floured work surface, press down with your hands to deflate the dough, and roll out to 1-inch (2.5cm) thickness using a rolling pin. Using a pizza cutter, cut the dough into strips 1 inch (2.5cm) wide. Pull 1-inch (2.5cm) pieces from each strip and roll them in the palm of your hand. Repeat with the remaining dough, making about 57 equal-sized balls.
8. Dip 1 ball of dough in the melted butter, roll it in the cinnamon sugar, and place it in the Bundt pan. Repeat with the remaining dough balls. Cover the pan with a tea towel, and let the dough rise about ½ inch (1.25cm), about 30 to 40 minutes.
9. Preheat the oven to 350°F (180°C). Bake for 40 minutes.
10. Remove from the oven, immediately cover the pan with a cake stand or wide plate, and turn over both to separate the monkey bread from the Bundt pan. Serve warm.

Raspberry Babka

PREP TIME: 30 minutes plus 1 hour 30 minutes to rise • **COOK TIME:** 45 minutes • **MAKES:** 1 (12-inch [30.5cm]) babka wreath

Indulge in the beautiful harmony of tart raspberries and rich chocolate in this babka. The swirls of Nutella, Oreo cookie crumbs, and fresh raspberries create a luscious filling that's complemented by the raspberry-infused dough. Each bite is a delightful balance of tangy and sweet, making it a treat you won't forget.

DOUGH

½ cup (118ml) warm milk (whole or 2%)

½ cup (118ml) warm water

¼ cup (50g) sugar

2¼ tsp (7g) active dry yeast

500g bread flour, plus more for dusting

1 tsp (1g) freshly grated nutmeg

½ tsp (0.5g) ground cinnamon

¼ cup (24g) freeze-fried raspberry powder

1 tsp (5g) kosher salt

2 large eggs

1 tsp (5ml) vanilla extract

¼ cup (58g) unsalted butter, at room temperature

FILLING

½ cup (140g) Nutella

1 cup (120g) Oreo cookies, cut into small pieces

1 cup (125g) fresh raspberries

RASPBERRY SYRUP

10 raspberries

¼ cup (50g) sugar

1 tsp (5ml) lemon or lime juice

SPECIAL EQUIPMENT

Stand mixer fitted with a dough hook

1. To make the dough, add the milk, water, sugar, and yeast to a cup, and stir well. Cover with a tea towel, and let sit until foamy, about 10 minutes.
2. Add the flour, nutmeg, cinnamon, raspberry powder, and salt to a large bowl, and mix well with your hands or a whisk until the raspberry powder is evenly incorporated and the mixture is slightly pink in color.
3. Beat together the eggs and vanilla extract in a small bowl. Set aside.
4. Add the yeast mixture to the flour mixture, followed by the egg mixture, and mix with a wooden spoon until the dough comes together.
5. Turn out the dough onto a floured work surface, add the butter in two or three batches, and knead for 10 to 15 minutes. (If using a stand mixer, this will take about 8 minutes.) Return the dough to the bowl, cover with a tea towel, and let rise until doubled in size, about 1 hour.
6. Turn out the dough onto a floured work surface, and roll with a rolling pin into a rectangle about 18 inches (46 cm) long, 14 inches (35.5cm) wide, and ⅛ inch (3mm) thick.
7. Evenly spread a thin layer of Nutella over the dough and then sprinkle the Oreos and raspberries evenly over the top.
8. Roll the dough up and over the filling from the bottom. Invert the dough so the ends are on bottom. Cut the dough in half lengthwise, turn the cut sides up, and twist the two rows of dough, starting in the middle. Curve the twisted dough into a wreath shape, and pinch the ends of the dough together to seal. The wreath will be about 9 inches (23cm) in diameter.
9. Using a wide spatula, transfer the wreath to a large baking sheet lined with parchment paper, cover with a tea towel, and let rise for 30 to 40 minutes.
10. Preheat the oven to 350°F (180°C). Bake for 35 minutes.
11. Meanwhile, to make the raspberry syrup, combine the raspberries, sugar, ¼ cup (59ml) of water, and the lemon or lime juice in a small saucepan over medium heat. Simmer until thickened, 10 to 15 minutes. Remove from the heat, and set aside.
12. Lift the babka from the baking sheet using the parchment paper, and transfer to a wire rack. Brush with the syrup and allow to cool before cutting and serving.

Chocolate Bread
with Pearl Sugar

PREP TIME: 20 minutes plus 2 hours 15 minutes to rest and rise • **COOK TIME:** 25 minutes • **MAKES:** 2 small loaves

This delightful bread combines the rich, sweet flavors of chocolate with the unique crunch of pearl sugar. Sweet chocolate chips and a hint of cinnamon create a deliciously aromatic bread, and the pearl sugar topping brings a surprising textural contrast that makes every bite exciting. Enjoy it as a special breakfast treat or a sweet afternoon snack.

½ cup (118ml) warm water
½ cup (118ml) warm milk (whole or 2%)
2 tbsp (24g) granulated sugar
1⅛ tsp (4g) active dry yeast
360g bread flour, plus more for dusting
¼ cup (25g) unsweetened Dutch-processed cocoa
1 tsp (2.5g) ground cinnamon
1 tsp (5g) kosher salt
½ cup (85g) semisweet chocolate chips
1 large egg, beaten
3 tbsp (42g) unsalted butter, divided, at room temperature
1 egg yolk, beaten
¼ cup (50g) pearl sugar

SPECIAL EQUIPMENT

Two 8 × 4½ × 4½-inch (20 × 11.5 × 11.5cm) loaf pans
Bread scoring tool or sharp knife

1. Combine the water, milk, granulated sugar, and yeast in a large cup, and stir with a wooden spoon. Cover with a towel, and let sit until the yeast is foamy, about 10 minutes.
2. Combine the flour, cocoa powder, cinnamon, salt, and chocolate chips in a large bowl. Add the yeast mixture and the egg and stir with a wooden spoon until a dough forms.
3. Turn out the dough onto a work surface, add 2 tablespoons (28g) of the butter, and knead for about 10 minutes.
4. Return the dough to the bowl, cover with a tea towel, and let rise until doubled in size, about 1 hour to 1½ hours.
5. Line two 8 × 4½ × 4½-inch (20 × 11.5 × 11.5cm) loaf pans with parchment paper. Set aside.
6. Turn out the dough onto a lightly floured work surface. Divide the dough into two pieces, press down to let out the air, and shape into balls. Cover with a tea towel and let rest for 15 minutes.
7. Using a rolling pin, roll the dough out into a rectangle about ½ inch (1.25cm) thick. Then roll the dough from top to bottom into a log, and pinch the ends to seal well. Place the rolled dough in one of the prepared pans, and press down lightly. Repeat with the remaining piece of dough. Cover both pans with a towel, and let the dough rise until ½ inch (1.25cm) from the top edge of the pan, 40 minutes to 1 hour.
8. Preheat the oven to 340°F (170°C).
9. Brush the risen dough with the egg yolk. Use a bread scoring tool or sharp knife to make a long, ⅛-inch (3mm) deep cut down the center of each loaf.
10. Squeeze ½ tablespoon (7g) of butter into the cut in each loaf, and sprinkle each loaf with half of the pearl sugar.
11. Bake for 20 to 25 minutes or when it smells like finished bread and has an internal temperature of 190°F (88°C).
12. Remove from the oven. Let cool on a wire rack for a few minutes before slicing and serving.

Candied Orange Peel

Chocolate Babkas

PREP TIME: 40 minutes plus 1 hour 40 minutes to rise • **COOK TIME:** 30 minutes • **MAKES:** 2 loaves

This babka recipe brings together the classic combination of chocolate and orange, creating a sweet, comforting dessert bread. The candied orange peel adds a delightful contrasting texture to this sweet and soft loaf.

DOUGH

½ cup (118ml) 2% milk

2 tbsp (28g) sugar

2¼ tsp (7g) active dry yeast

400g bread flour, plus more for dusting

1 cup (225g) candied orange peel, diced

½ cup (85g) semisweet chocolate chips

¼ cup (28g) unsweetened Dutch-processed cocoa

1 tsp (1g) grated nutmeg

1 tsp (5g) kosher salt

2 large eggs, beaten

¼ cup (58g) unsalted butter, at room temperature

FILLING

½ cup (85g) semisweet chocolate chips, melted

⅓ cup (50g) dark brown sugar, firmly packed

2 tbsp (15g) unsweetened Dutch-processed cocoa

⅓ cup (76g) unsalted butter, at room temperature

SPECIAL EQUIPMENT

Two pound cake pans

1. In a small, heatproof bowl, microwave ½ cup (118ml) water and the milk on high for 20 seconds, being careful not to heat the liquids above 100°F (38°C) to prevent the yeast from dying when it's added. Add the sugar and yeast, cover with a tea towel, and let sit for 10 minutes.
2. Meanwhile, using your hands, mix the flour, candied orange peel, chocolate chips, Dutch-processed cocoa, nutmeg, and salt in a large bowl until well combined. Add the yeast mixture and eggs to the flour mixture, and mix well with a wooden spoon until no dry flour is visible.
3. Turn out the dough onto a work surface, and knead, adding the softened butter in two or three batches, until the dough is smooth and no longer sticky, about 15 minutes. (If using a mixer with a dough hook, this will take about 10 minutes.) Return the dough to the bowl, cover with a tea towel, and let rise until doubled in size, about 1 hour.
4. Meanwhile, to make the filling, melt the chocolate chips in a small bowl in a double boiler over medium heat. When the chocolate reaches 80°F (27°C), turn the heat off, remove the bowl from the heat and add the brown sugar, Dutch cocoa, and butter, and stir with a spoon until well combined. Return to the double boiler (keeping the heat off).
5. Turn out the dough onto a floured work surface, and use a rolling pin to roll the dough into a 13 × 16-inch (33 × 40cm) rectangle. Using a spatula, evenly spread the chocolate filling over the dough, leaving a ¼-inch (6mm) border around the edges.
6. Starting on one of the longer sides, roll the dough over the filling, putting the ends of the dough at the bottom of the loaf. Cut the dough in half and cover 1 loaf with a tea towel.
7. Place the other loaf on a work surface, and cut it in half lengthwise. Turn the cut sides up, and gently pull the dough with your hands to form two 15-inch (38cm) strips of dough. Twist the dough by crossing the two strips in the middle. Keeping the cut sides up will show the chocolate in the finished loaf. Place the twisted dough in a pound cake pan lined with parchment paper. Repeat with the remaining loaf. Cover both loaves with a tea towel, and let them rise to ¼ inch (6mm) above the edge of the pan, 40 to 50 minutes.
8. When the dough reaches the edge of the pan, preheat the oven to 350°F (180°C). Bake for 30 minutes.
9. Remove the babkas from the pan, peel off the parchment paper, and transfer to a wire rack to cool. When completely cooled, cut a slice and serve with milk, if you'd like.

CHAPTER 6

Buns

Crunchy Cinnamon Balloon Buns

PREP TIME: 20 minutes plus 30 minutes to rest • **COOK TIME:** 15 minutes • **MAKES:** 12 buns

With their hollow center, these Crunchy Cinnamon Balloon Buns are the perfect April Fool's Day treat, surprising everyone with their playful twist. Each crunchy bite reveals a delightful burst of cinnamon-sugar goodness, making them a fun and delicious "prank." These buns are sure to bring smiles and laughter to any gathering.

DOUGH

400g bread flour, plus more for dusting

2 tbsp (14g) black sesame seeds

1 tsp (5g) kosher salt

1 tbsp (15ml) vegetable oil

1½ tbsp (20g) unsalted butter, at room temperature

CINNAMON SUGAR FILLING

½ cup (100g) dark brown sugar, firmly packed

2 tbsp (15g) bread flour

2 tbsp (25g) granulated sugar

1 tsp (1g) ground cinnamon

Note

When baking the buns, if the cinnamon sugar filling leaks from any of the buns, remove the offending buns from the oven when the filling stops boiling. You can enjoy the broken buns with a spoon or with your fingers.

1. Combine the flour, black sesame seeds, and salt in a medium bowl using your hands. Add 1 cup (237ml) of water and the oil, and mix with a wooden spoon until the dough comes together.
2. Turn the dough out onto a work surface, add the softened butter, and knead by hand for about 10 minutes. Wrap the dough in plastic wrap, and place in the refrigerator for 30 minutes.
3. Meanwhile, to make the cinnamon sugar filling, combine the brown sugar, flour, granulated sugar, and cinnamon in a small bowl. Set aside.
4. Turn the dough out onto a floured work surface, and press down with your hands to form an 8-inch (20cm) circle. Using a scraper, cut the dough into 12 equal portions. Using your hands, round the portions into balls, and cover them with a tea towel to keep them from drying out.
5. Preheat the oven to 450°F (230°C). Line two baking sheets with parchment paper.
6. Place one ball of dough on a floured work surface, and roll it out to a 4-inch (10cm) circle using a rolling pin.
7. Place the dough circle in your hand, add 1 tablespoon (12.5g) of the cinnamon sugar filling to the center, and pull and pinch the ends of the dough toward the center to seal completely and keep the cinnamon sugar filling inside. Hold the filled dough with both hands, place your thumbs in the center of the dough, and squeeze and rotate the dough to distribute the cinnamon sugar filling evenly throughout the bun and increase the size of the dough.
8. Set the filled dough on a floured work surface, and roll it out evenly to a 5-inch (12.5cm) circle. Place the dough on one of the prepared baking sheets (each sheet should hold 6 buns), and repeat with the remaining dough and filling.
9. Bake for 13 to 15 minutes.
10. Transfer the buns to a wire rack to completely cool before serving.

Butter Eye Buns

PREP TIME: 30 minutes plus 2 hours to rise • **COOK TIME:** 15 minutes • **MAKES:** 8 buns

Cardamom has many advantages—it contains chemicals that can kill some bacteria, reduce swelling, and help the immune system. It also smells wonderful and is used in many spice blends and baked goods for its warmth and earthy flavor. In this soft bread, it shines with the sweet "butter eye."

1 cup (237ml) warm whole milk
¼ cup (50g) plus 8 tsp (33g) granulated sugar
2¼ tsp (7g) active dry yeast
400g bread flour
1 tsp (5g) kosher salt
3 tsp (3g) ground cardamom
1 large egg, beaten
½ cup (113g) unsalted butter, in chunks, plus 4 tbsp (58g) unsalted butter, cut into 8 pieces
2 egg yolks
⅓ cup (52g) pearl sugar

SPECIAL EQUIPMENT

Stand mixer fitted with a dough hook

1. Combine the warm milk, ¼ cup (50g) of sugar, and yeast in a small bowl. Cover with a tea towel, and let sit for 10 minutes.
2. Whisk together the flour, salt, and cardamom in a large bowl. Add the yeast mixture and the beaten egg, and mix well using a wooden spoon.
3. Form the dough into a ball and turn it out onto a work surface. Add the ½ cup (113g) of butter in chunks, and knead by hand until the dough doesn't stick to your work surface or hands, about 15 minutes. (You also can use a stand mixer, fitted with a dough hook, on medium for 8 minutes.)
4. Cover with a tea towel and let rise in a warm place until over double in size, about 1½ hours.
5. Line a baking sheet with parchment paper.
6. Turn the dough out onto a floured work surface and divide it into 8 equal pieces. Place a piece of dough in one hand and roll it with the other to form a ball and then pinch the bottom.
7. Place the dough on the prepared baking sheet, cover with a tea towel, and let rise until doubled in size, about 30 minutes.
8. Preheat the oven to 360°F (180°C).
9. Using your fingers, poke a hole in the center of the each dough ball. Add 1 piece of butter in each hole, and press it down gently. This is the "butter eye."
10. Whisk the egg yolks in a small bowl. Brush each dough ball twice with the egg.
11. Spoon 1 teaspoon (4g) of sugar over each piece of butter and then sprinkle the dough ball tops with pearl sugar.
12. Bake for 15 minutes or until golden brown.
13. Remove from the oven, let cool for 5 minutes, and serve. Store in an airtight container at room temperature for up to 3 days, reheating in the microwave for about 15 to 20 seconds to soften, or freeze and then thaw to room temperature before serving.

Pretzels

with Smoked Paprika Cheese Sauce

PREP TIME: 30 minutes plus 1 hour 30 minutes to rest and rise • **COOK TIME:** 20 minutes • **MAKES:** 8 pretzels and 1⅔ cups (400g) sauce

Get ready to twist and dip your way to snack heaven with these pretzels and smoked paprika cheese sauce. The soft, warm pretzels have a perfect balance of chewy texture and salty goodness, thanks to a quick bath in caustic soda water. But the real party starts when you dunk them into the smoky, creamy cheddar sauce. It's a playful, savory treat that's sure to please your taste buds.

DOUGH

⅔ cup (158ml) warm water
⅔ cup (158ml) whole milk
1 tsp (4g) sugar
2¼ tsp (7g) active dry yeast
500g bread flour
2 tsp (10g) salt
2 tbsp (28g) unsalted butter
2 tbsp (20g) food-grade sodium hydroxide (lye, caustic soda)

SMOKED PAPRIKA CHEESE SAUCE

2 tbsp (28g) unsalted butter
2 tbsp (15g) all-purpose flour
1 cup (237ml) whole milk
1 cup (125g) shredded cheddar
1 tsp (2g) smoked paprika
¼ tsp (1.25g) kosher salt
¼ tsp (0.25g) freshly ground black pepper

SPECIAL EQUIPMENT

Pizza cutter
Stand mixer fitted with a dough hook
Disposable kitchen gloves

Note

Instead of using caustic soda, you can substitute baking soda, using 3 tablespoons (50g) baking soda per 2 cups (473ml) hot water. However, caustic soda is best for flavor and color.

1. To make the dough, combine the water, milk, sugar, and yeast in a small bowl, stirring well with a wooden spoon. Cover with a tea towel and let sit until the yeast dissolves and bubbles form, about 10 minutes.
2. Meanwhile, add the flour and salt to a large bowl, and mix by hand. Add the yeast mixture to the flour, and mix with a wooden spoon until the dough comes together in a lump.
3. Turn out the dough onto a work surface, add the butter, and knead for about 15 minutes. (If using a stand mixer, knead until the dough does not stick to the sides of the bowl, 8 to 10 minutes.) Return the dough to the bowl, cover with a tea towel, and let rise in a warm place until at least doubled in size, about 1 hour.
4. After 1 hour, shape the dough into a circle, and press down to release the gas. Use a pizza cutter to cut across the dough, creating 8 wedge-shaped slices. Place one piece on your work surface with the pointed end up. Using a rolling pin, roll the dough in all directions to release the gas while maintaining the triangular shape. Then roll the dough from top to bottom, shaping it into a thin oblong shape. The center will be wider than the ends, and the dough will be about the length of your hand after you finish rolling it. Repeat with the remaining dough, and cover with a tea towel to rest for 15 minutes.
5. Preheat the oven to 425°F (220°C). Line two large baking sheets with parchment paper.
6. Place one piece of dough lengthwise on your work surface, and press the rolling pin against the top, bottom, and sides to release the gas. Then roll the dough tightly from top to bottom, and pinch the ends together. Using both hands, roll the dough from the center to the ends, except for the center of the dough, and stretch it out to 22 inches (56cm). Leave the dough convex in the center. Cross the ends of the dough, twist them together, and place them on top of the convex center in the shape of a pretzel. Press down lightly to seal. Transfer to a prepared baking sheet and repeat with the remaining pieces of dough (placing 4 pretzels on each sheet). Cover with a tea towel and let rest for 15 minutes.
7. Meanwhile, to prepare the caustic soda water, don silicone gloves and open a door or window for ventilation. Add the caustic soda to 2 cups of (473ml) water, and stir gently with a spoon to dissolve. Using gloved hands, pick up each pretzel, coat it completely in the caustic soda water, and return it to the baking sheet.
8. Bake for at least 15 minutes, or until the pretzels are dark brown.
9. While the pretzels are baking, begin making the cheese sauce by melting the butter in a medium saucepan over low heat. Whisk in the flour, stirring to combine, and bring to a boil. Add the milk in two or three batches, whisking to incorporate after each addition.
10. Increase the heat to medium-high, and add the cheddar, smoked paprika, salt, and pepper. Cook, stirring constantly, until the mixture thickens, about 5 minutes. Remove from the heat, and set aside. (The sauce will keep at room temperature for no more than 2 hours. Refrigerate any leftovers, and reheat in the microwave when serving.)
11. Remove the pretzels from the oven, allow them to cool for a bit, and then serve with the warm cheese sauce for dipping.

Brioche
with Lemon Whipped Cream

PREP TIME: 30 minutes plus 2 hours 40 minutes to rise • **COOK TIME:** 25 minutes • **MAKES:** 8 buns

There's nothing quite like the soft, buttery richness of freshly baked brioche. Pair it with a light and zesty lemon whipped cream, and you've got a dessert that feels fancy but is surprisingly easy to make. The dough takes a bit of patience to rise, but the pillowy texture and golden crust are well worth the wait. Whether you're serving these at brunch or as a sweet treat after dinner, they're sure to impress. Plus, any leftovers make the perfect next-day indulgence. Trust me, this is the kind of recipe you'll want to make again and again!

DOUGH

⅓ cup (79ml) warm whole milk
3 tbsp (38g) granulated sugar
2¼ tsp (7g) active dry yeast
300g bread flour
1 tsp (5g) kosher salt
4 large eggs, beaten
½ cup (115g) unsalted butter, at room temperature, plus more for greasing
2 egg yolks, for egg wash
¼ cup (50g) pearl sugar

LEMON WHIPPED CREAM

2 cups (473ml) heavy cream
½ cup (50g) confectioners' sugar
1 tbsp (6g) lemon zest
1 tbsp (15ml) fresh lemon juice
¼ tsp (1g) kosher salt

SPECIAL EQUIPMENT

Stand mixer fitted with a dough hook
Kitchen scale
Brioche molds or large muffin tin

1. To make the dough, combine the milk, granulated sugar, and yeast in a small bowl. Cover with a tea towel, and let sit for 10 minutes.
2. Whisk together the flour and salt by hand, either in a large bowl and using a whisk or in the bowl of a stand mixer and using the mixer's dough hook. (Use the dough hook by hand, too, not in the mixer yet.) Add the yeast mixture and the eggs, and mix again by hand. Add the butter, fit the dough hook into the mixer, and mix on medium for 10 minutes.
3. Remove the dough from the bowl, shape it into a ball using floured hands, and return it to the bowl. Cover with plastic wrap, and let rise until tripled in size, about 1½ to 2 hours.
4. Turn out the dough onto a floured surface and press down with both hands to release the gas. Weigh the dough on a scale, and divide into 8 equal portions. Take 10 grams of dough from one portion, shape it into a ball, and then make another ball with the remaining dough from that portion. These two balls will become one brioche. Do the same with the remaining 7 portions. Cover the balls with a towel, and let rest for 10 minutes.
5. Butter 8 brioche molds or a large muffin tin. Working with one pair of dough balls, place a large ball in the mold, pressing it down to fill the ridges, and then poke a floured finger into the center to create a space. Roll one end of the smaller ball between your hands to make a point, and put the pointed end into the space where you poked the larger ball. Repeat with the remaining pairs of dough balls.
6. Cover with a tea towel or large container, and let rise until the dough has risen to about ¼ inch (0.5cm) from the top edge of the pan, about 1 hour.
7. Meanwhile, to make the lemon whipped cream, whisk together all the ingredients in a large bowl until stiff peaks form. Cover with plastic wrap, and place in the refrigerator.
8. Preheat the oven to 375°F (190°C).
9. Whisk the egg yolks in a small bowl. Brush each brioche twice with the egg wash, and sprinkle with the pearl sugar.
10. Bake for 10 minutes. Reduce the oven temperature to 350°F (180°C), and bake for an additional 10 to 15 minutes, until golden brown on top.
11. Remove from the oven, and allow the brioche to rest in the pan for 10 minutes. If the egg wash has run off and stuck to the sides of the pan, use a knife to gently scrape and loosen it. Transfer the brioche to a wire rack to cool.
12. Serve the cooled lemon whipped cream with the brioche. Store any leftover brioche in an airtight container at room temperature for up to 3 days. Store any leftover lemon whipped cream in an airtight container in the refrigerator for up to 3 days.

Meringue Cinnamon Rolls

PREP TIME: 35 minutes plus 1 hour 30 minutes to rise • **COOK TIME:** 30 minutes • **MAKES:** 12 rolls

When something delicious is added to something else delicious, the result is often an amazing combination. In this recipe, sweet and soft cinnamon rolls are topped with caramelized sticky sauce and a lightly toasted Italian meringue for a delicious way to start a happy day. Enjoy with a cup of coffee.

DOUGH

1 cup (237ml) warm milk

¼ cup (57g) unsalted butter, melted

¼ cup (50g) granulated sugar

2¼ tsp (7g) active dry yeast

300g bread flour

½ tsp (2.5g) kosher salt

½ tsp (2.5g) baking powder

CINNAMON PASTE

½ cup (113g) unsalted butter, at room temperature

½ cup (85g) brown sugar, firmly packed

1 tbsp (8g) ground cinnamon

STICKY SAUCE

12 tbsp (156g) brown sugar

¼ cup (57g) salted butter, cut into 12 pieces

ITALIAN MERINGUE

2 egg whites

2 tsp (10ml) vanilla extract

⅓ cup (79ml) water

¾ cup (150g) granulated sugar

SPECIAL EQUIPMENT

Stand mixer fitted with a dough hook

12-cup muffin pan

Kitchen string

Ice-cream scoop

Kitchen blowtorch

Thermometer

1. To make the dough, add the warm milk, melted butter, granulated sugar, and yeast to a small bowl, and mix well. Cover with a tea towel and let stand until foamy, about 10 minutes.
2. Whisk together the flour, salt, and baking powder in a large bowl. Add the yeast mixture, and mix with a wooden spoon.
3. When the dough forms a ball, turn it out onto a work surface and knead for 10 minutes. (You also can use a stand mixer, fitted with a dough hook, on medium for 7 or 8 minutes.) Roll the dough into a ball, and pinch the bottom. Return the dough to the bowl, cover with a tea towel, and let rise until doubled in size, about 1 hour.
4. Meanwhile, to make the cinnamon paste, mix the butter, brown sugar, and cinnamon in a small bowl. Set aside.
5. Preheat the broiler to 500°F (260°C).
6. Make the sticky sauce directly in a 12-cup muffin pan. Place 1 tablespoon (13g) of brown sugar, ½ tablespoon (7ml) of water, and 1 piece of butter in each of the 12 cups. Broil on the center rack until boiling, about 5 minutes. Remove from the oven, and set aside.
7. Turn out the dough onto a floured work surface, and roll out to a rectangle approximately 13 × 10 inches (33 × 25.5cm).
8. Spread the cinnamon paste evenly over the dough, leaving about ⅜ inch (1cm) uncovered along one long edge of the dough. Starting at the side opposite the uncovered long edge, begin rolling the dough tightly over the cinnamon paste filling. Before you reach the uncovered edge, use a finger to apply water to the uncovered area. (The water helps the dough stick together.) Finish rolling the dough over the filling.
9. Mark the rolled dough into 12 equal parts and place a 10-inch (25.5cm) piece of kitchen string under the dough and bring up and over and pull tightly to cut the rolls. You also can use a knife to cut the rolls. Place each roll in a muffin cup and let rise until about ¼ inch (6mm) from the top edge of the pan, about 30 minutes.
10. Meanwhile, preheat the oven to 360°F (180°C).
11. Bake the rolls for 30 minutes. When the cinnamon rolls are golden brown, remove them from the oven and immediately turn over the pan onto a cooling rack sitting on a baking sheet to let the gooey sauce run down over the rolls. Allow to cool slightly.
12. While the rolls are baking, make the Italian meringue. Place the egg whites and vanilla extract in a clean stand mixer bowl and set aside. Combine the water and sugar in a small saucepan over high heat and bring to a boil. When the sugar water reaches about 210°F (100°C), turn the stand mixer on medium-low and begin beating the egg whites and vanilla, gradually increasing to high. When the sugar water reaches 250°F (120°C), remove from the heat and slowly pour down the sides of the bowl. Beat the meringue until stiff peaks form.
13. Using an ice-cream scoop, scoop the meringue onto the cinnamon buns and toast with a blowtorch until golden brown. Do not place them too close together to avoid burning.
14. Serve warm. Store any leftovers in an airtight container at room temperature for up to 3 days, or freeze and then thaw to room temperature. You can store the meringue in an airtight container in the refrigerator for up to 4 days.

Butter Crumble Buns
with Strawberry Cream

PREP TIME: 30 minutes plus 1 hour 45 minutes to rise • **COOK TIME:** 15 minutes • **MAKES:** 12 buns

This is my family bun. It's a delightful treat that's become a birthday favorite in our family, replacing the traditional cake. The bun boasts a soft, buttery dough, is topped with a rich crumble, and is paired with a luscious strawberry whipped cream. The combination of sweet, creamy, and fruity flavors makes it an irresistible choice for special occasions. Each bite delivers a burst of flavor and a touch of homemade warmth that's sure to make any day feel extraordinary.

DOUGH

1 cup (237ml) warm water
¼ cup (50g) granulated sugar
2¼ tsp (7g) active dry yeast
450g bread flour, plus more for dusting
1 tsp (5g) kosher salt
2 tbsp (16g) powdered milk
1 large egg, beaten
⅓ cup (76g) unsalted butter

STRAWBERRY WHIPPED CREAM

8 strawberries
1 tsp white vinegar
2 cups (473ml) cold heavy cream
½ cup (50g) confectioners' sugar
⅛ tsp (0.6g) kosher salt

BUTTER CRUMBLE

⅓ cup (76g) unsalted butter, at room temperature
2 tbsp (32g) peanut butter
½ cup (50g) granulated sugar
¼ tsp (1.25g) kosher salt
1 large egg
180g all-purpose flour
1 tbsp (14g) powdered milk
1 tsp (5g) baking powder

1. To make the dough, combine the warm water, granulated sugar, and yeast in a small bowl, cover with a tea towel, and let sit for 10 minutes.
2. Meanwhile, mix the bread flour, salt, and powdered milk in a large bowl. Add the yeast mixture and egg to the flour mixture, and mix with a wooden spoon.
3. Turn out the dough onto a work surface and knead by hand, adding the butter in two or three batches. Continue kneading until the dough stops sticking to your hands, 10 to 15 minutes. Return the dough to the bowl, cover with a tea towel, and let sit until doubled in size, about 1 hour.
4. To make the strawberry whipped cream, place the strawberries in a small bowl, cover with water, and add the vinegar. Let sit for a few minutes. Wash the strawberries under running water, gently pat dry with a paper towel, and chop into small cubes.
5. In a medium bowl, whisk together the cream, confectioners' sugar, and salt. Add the diced strawberries, and mix well. Cover with plastic wrap, and set in the refrigerator.
6. To make the butter crumble, whisk together the softened butter, peanut butter, and granulated sugar in a small bowl.
7. In a clean small bowl, whisk together the salt and egg. Add this to the creamed butter in two or three batches, beating to combine after each addition.
8. Sift the all-purpose flour, powdered milk, and baking powder into a medium baking pan. Add the butter mixture, and cut and mix with a dough scraper. If the flour is clumpy, use the scraper to break it into small, pea-sized pieces. Divide the crumble into 12 portions, and set aside.
9. Turn out the dough onto a floured surface, and lightly punch it down to release the gas. Divide the dough into 12 equal pieces, shape into balls, cover with a tea towel, and let rest for 15 minutes.
10. Line a baking sheet with parchment paper. Add ½ cup (118ml) of water to a small bowl. Place 1 portion of the crumble in a 4-inch (10cm) circle on your work surface. Dip 1 piece of dough in the water, place it on the crumble, and press with the palm of your hand to flatten into a 4-inch (10cm) circle. Place the coated dough crumble-side up on the prepared baking sheet. Repeat with the remaining dough and crumble. Cover with a tea towel and let sit at room temperature until doubled in size, 30 to 40 minutes.
11. Preheat the oven to 360°F (185°C). Bake for 15 minutes.
12. Transfer to a wire rack to cool completely. Slice the cool buns in half in the middle, fill with strawberry cream, and serve.

Cardamom Butter Buns

PREP TIME: 40 minutes plus 1 hour 30 minutes to rise • **COOK TIME:** 20 minutes • **MAKES:** 9 buns

You'll love the enchanting aroma of these Cardamom Butter Buns as the smell of the warm, buttery dough combines with the exotic scent of the cardamom. Each bite is a delight, too, with a rich, melt-in-your-mouth filling of dark brown sugar and black cocoa. These buns are perfect for making any moment extraordinary.

DOUGH

1 cup (237ml) warm 2% milk

¼ cup (50g) granulated sugar

2¼ tsp (7g) active dry yeast

400g bread flour, plus more for dusting

1 tsp (5g) kosher salt

1 tsp (2g) ground cardamom

1 large egg, beaten

⅓ cup (76g) unsalted butter, at room temperature

CARDAMOM PASTE FILLING

½ cup (50g) dark brown sugar, firmly packed

⅓ cup (76g) unsalted butter, at room temperature

2 tsp (4g) ground cardamom

1 tsp (2.5g) black cocoa powder

TOPPING

1 egg yolk

¼ cup (50g) pearl sugar

1. Combine the warm milk, granulated sugar, and yeast in a small bowl. Cover with a tea towel, and let sit for 10 minutes.
2. Mix the flour, salt, and cardamom in a large bowl. Add the yeast mixture and the egg, and stir with a wooden spoon.
3. Turn out the dough on a work surface, and knead, adding the butter in two or three batches, until the dough is smooth and does not stick to your hands, about 15 minutes. Return the dough to the bowl, cover with a towel, and let rise until it has more than doubled in size, about 1 hour.
4. Meanwhile, to make the cardamom paste filling, mix together the brown sugar, softened butter, ground cardamom, and black cocoa powder in a medium bowl. Set aside.
5. Turn out the dough onto a floured work surface, and press down with your hands to release the gas. Using a rolling pin, flatten the dough into a 14 × 20-inch (35.5 × 50cm) square. Use a spatula to evenly spread the cardamom paste over the dough.
6. Fold the left third of the dough to the center and then fold the right third to the center, over the left side. Gently press the dough flat with your hands to make it 7 inches (17.75cm) wide. Cut the dough lengthwise into strips ¾ inch (2cm) wide. You should have 9 strips.
7. Line a baking sheet with parchment paper. Grab both ends of one strip of dough, and twist them together. Then roll the twisted dough into a spiral and pinch the ends together to prevent unraveling. Place the bun in the prepared baking sheet. Repeat with the remaining strips. Cover with a tea towel, and let rise until doubled in size, about 30 minutes.
8. Preheat the oven to 350°F (180°C).
9. Brush the buns with the egg yolk, sprinkle with pearl sugar, and bake for 20 minutes.
10. Transfer to a wire rack to cool. Serve warm with milk, if you'd like.

Anchovy Grilled Naan

PREP TIME: 30 minutes plus 30 minutes to rise • **COOK TIME:** 20 minutes • **MAKES:** 10 pieces

Naan was once a royal favorite, baked in the tandoor ovens of Indian palaces. Now we're giving this classic bread a zesty upgrade with our Anchovy Grilled Naan, blending the rich flavors of anchovies, savory butter, and tangy capers. Perfectly grilled, it's a bite of history with a modern twist.

DOUGH

½ cup (118ml) warm water
½ cup (118ml) warm milk
1 tsp (3g) active dry yeast
1 tsp (5g) sugar
400g all-purpose flour, plus more for dusting
1 tsp (5g) kosher salt
1 tsp (5g) baking powder
3 tbsp (45g) plain yogurt

SAVORY BUTTER SAUCE

6 anchovies
2 garlic cloves
1 tbsp (6g) lemon zest
1 tbsp (15ml) fresh lemon juice
2 tbsp (18g) nonpareil capers, divided
½ tbsp (2.5g) crushed hot red pepper
½ cup (115g) unsalted butter, boiled to 210°F (100°C)

FINAL TOUCH SAUCE

½ tbsp (2.5g) crushed hot red pepper
2 tbsp (18g) nonpareil capers
3 or 4 anchovies
½ cup (118ml) extra-virgin olive oil, heated to 350°F (180°C)

TOPPING

1 tbsp (5g) grated Parmesan cheese
1 tbsp (5g) chopped fresh parsley

SPECIAL EQUIPMENT

Mortar and pestle

Note

Grilling this bread imparts a wonderful flavor, but you also could cook it on a stovetop in a heavy skillet over medium-high heat for 2 or 3 minutes per side for similar results.

1. To make the dough, pour the warm water and warm milk in a small bowl. Add the yeast and sugar, and stir. Cover with a tea towel and let sit for 10 minutes or until foamy.
2. Whisk together the flour, salt, and baking powder in a large bowl.
3. Add the yogurt and yeast mixture to the flour mixture, and knead for 10 minutes. Cover the bowl with a tea towel, and let the dough rest for 30 minutes.
4. Meanwhile, to prepare the savory butter sauce, finely grind the anchovies, garlic, lemon zest, lemon juice, and 1 tablespoon of capers using a mortar and pestle, or finely chop them with a knife.
5. In a small heatproof bowl, combine the anchovy mixture, the crushed red pepper, and remaining 1 tablespoon of capers. Pour the boiling butter into the bowl, and mix well. Set aside.
6. Preheat a grill to 350°F (180°C).
7. Turn out the dough onto a floured work surface. Divide the dough into 10 equal pieces, shape into rounds, and cover with a tea towel to prevent it from drying out.
8. Place one of the dough pieces on a floured work surface. Using a rolling pin, roll out the dough to a 5-inch (12.5cm) circle. Repeat with the remaining dough pieces, covering with a towel between rollings.
9. Brush the butter sauce on one side of a piece of dough, place the dough butter side down on the hot grill, and brush the top of the dough with the butter sauce. Cook for 2 or 3 minutes, flip, and cook for 2 or 3 minutes more or until the naan puffs up and turns golden brown.
10. Transfer the cooked naan to a serving plate, cover with a towel to keep warm, and repeat with the remaining dough.
11. To make the final touch sauce, combine the remaining butter sauce with the crushed red pepper, capers, and anchovies in a heatproof bowl. Add the hot extra-virgin olive oil, and stir well.
12. Pour the final touch sauce over the naan, sprinkle with cheese and parsley, and serve. Store any leftovers at room temperature for up to 3 days. Reheat in the microwave for 20 to 30 seconds.

Olive Fougasse

PREP TIME: 25 minutes plus 2 hours 50 minutes to rise • **COOK TIME:** 15 minutes • **MAKES:** 6 pieces

This bread is packed with the flavors of herbs and olives, making it an ideal addition to Mediterranean-style meals. Fragrant rosemary, basil, thyme, and sage blend beautifully with Gouda cheese, cherry peppers, and capers to create a rich and savory loaf. The inclusion of olives provides heart-healthy monounsaturated fats that help lower bad cholesterol levels. Baked in an attractive leaf shape, this bread features a golden, crispy crust while remaining soft and moist inside. Serve it with balsamic vinegar and olive oil for a healthy, delicious bread.

½ cup (80g) forage Gouda cheese, cubed
¼ cup (50g) pickled cherry peppers or halved cherry tomatoes
¼ cup (45g) green olives, halved
¼ cup (45g) pitted kalamata olives
2 tbsp (15g) nonpareil capers
1 tbsp (6g) lemon zest
2 cups (473ml) warm water
2¼ tsp (7g) active dry yeast
2 tbsp (30ml) extra-virgin olive oil, plus more for serving
1 tbsp (15ml) maple syrup
480g bread flour, plus more for dusting
¼ cup (24g) finely chopped rosemary, basil, thyme, and sage
1 tsp (5g) kosher salt
Balsamic vinegar, for serving

Note

You can substitute 4 teaspoons (8g) dried herb mix for the finely chopped fresh herbs. Using fresh herbs makes for a more flavorful fougasse, but you can use any dried herb mix you have on hand.

1. Combine the Gouda, cherry peppers or cherry tomatoes, green olives, kalamata olives, capers, and lemon zest in a medium bowl.
2. Whisk together the warm water, yeast, olive oil, and maple syrup in a small bowl. Cover with a towel, and let sit for 10 minutes.
3. Combine the flour, herbs, and salt in a large bowl. Add the Gouda and olive mixture, and toss to coat.
4. Add the yeast mixture, and mix with a wooden spoon until a shaggy dough forms. Cover with a tea towel and let rise for 30 minutes.
5. Add some warm water to a small bowl, and dip both hands in the water. (This helps keep the dough from sticking to your hands.) With wet hands, pull the bottom of the dough up and over the top of the dough. Turn the bowl 90 degrees, and repeat pulling up and over three times. (This is the first fold.) Turn the dough so the top is down, cover with a tea towel, and let rest for 30 minutes. Repeat this process two more times (the second and third folds). After the third fold, cover and let rest for 1 hour.
6. Turn out the dough onto a generously floured work surface, and sprinkle a generous amount of flour on top of the dough. Press down on the dough with your hands to deflate the mixture slightly, and use a scraper to divide into 6 equal pieces. Pick up one piece, and use both hands to fold the dough into the center, seam side down. Be sure to fold gently to prevent too much gas from escaping. Repeat with the remaining five pieces of dough. Cover with a tea towel, and let rest for 20 minutes.
7. Preheat the oven to 450°F (230°C). Line a baking sheet with parchment paper.
8. Place one piece of dough on a floured work surface, flatten the dough slightly, and pull it out at three points to make a triangle. Using the edge of a small (1½ inches/2.75cm) stainless-steel spatula dipped in flour, punch seven lines into the triangle around one of the points: one hole 1½ inches (2.75cm) long that's ½ inch (1.25cm) below the top point of the triangle and then three evenly spaced 45-degree holes on both sides. (You're making a leaf shape, so these lines represent the veins of the leaf radiating out from the center spine.) Stretch the dough into a 7-inch (17.75cm) triangle by inserting your fingers into the holes and gently pulling. Transfer the dough to the prepared baking sheet.
9. Bake for 15 to 20 minutes, until golden brown on top and then transfer to a wire rack to cool. Serve with olive oil and balsamic vinegar.

Apple and Cream Cheese Filled Buns

PREP TIME: 45 minutes plus 2 hours to rise • **COOK TIME:** 45 minutes • **MAKES:** 16 buns

Perfect for special occasions, these sweet buns invite you to create cherished memories with friends and family. The homey scent of apples and the richness of cream cheese fill each bite, making these buns a delightful way to celebrate warm moments with loved ones.

APPLE AND CREAM CHEESE FILLING

2 or 3 (400g) large apples, any variety (Ambrosia, Honeycrisp, Gala, or Jazz all work well)

1 lemon

1 tbsp (15ml) white vinegar

½ cup (100g) sugar, divided

¼ tsp (1.25g) kosher salt

2 cups (450g) cream cheese, at room temperature

DOUGH

1½ cups (355ml) warm milk

¼ cup (50g) sugar

2¼ tsp (7g) active dry yeast

3 tbsp (20g) red yeast rice, or ½ tsp (3g) red food coloring

450g bread flour, plus more for dusting

½ tsp (2.5g) kosher salt

¼ cup (58g) unsalted butter, at room temperature

16 thin breadsticks, cut into pieces 1½ inch (3.75cm) long

1 tbsp (14g) unsalted butter, melted

SPECIAL EQUIPMENT

Mortar and pestle or spice grinder

Stand mixer fitted with a dough hook

1. To make the apple and cream cheese filling, place the apples and the lemon in a medium bowl, and add enough water to cover. Pour in the vinegar, and let sit for 5 minutes. Scrub the fruit to clean the surface and then rinse under running water.
2. Slice the apples from top to bottom, avoiding the core, and then dice the slices small (leaving the skin on). Place the apples in a medium saucepan.
3. Add ¼ cup (50g) of sugar, the salt, 1 tablespoon (6g) lemon zest, and 1 tablespoon (15ml) fresh lemon juice to the pan, and set over medium-low heat. Cook, stirring occasionally, until no moisture remains in the pan, about 15 to 20 minutes. Remove from the heat, and allow to cool to room temperature, about 15 minutes.
4. Add the cream cheese to the cooled apples in two or three batches, mixing well with a spatula after each addition. Add the remaining ¼ cup (50g) of sugar and mix well. Line a baking sheet with parchment paper. Using an ice-cream scoop, scoop the apple and cream cheese filling into 16 balls and place on the prepared baking sheet. Set in the refrigerator until ready to use.
5. To make the dough, combine the warm milk, sugar, and yeast in a large bowl. Cover with a tea towel, and let sit for 10 minutes.
6. Using a mortar and pestle or spice grinder, finely grind the red yeast rice. Add it to the yeast mixture and stir to combine. Add the flour and salt and use a wooden spatula to incorporate.
7. Turn out the dough onto a work surface, add the butter in two or three batches, and knead by hand until the dough stops sticking to your hands, about 15 minutes. (A stand mixer with a dough hook is handy for this process.)
8. Return the dough to the bowl, cover with a tea towel, and let rise until doubled in size, about 1 hour.
9. Turn out the dough onto a floured surface, and press down with your hands to release the gas. Cut the dough into 16 pieces (like a pie). Form each piece into a ball, cover with a tea towel, and let rest for 15 minutes.
10. Stretch one piece of dough between your fingers to form a disk about 4 inches (10cm) across. Remove the filling from the refrigerator, and place one ball, flat-side up, on the dough disk and pull the dough up and around the filling to seal. Using both hands, roll the dough into a ball and place seam side down in a muffin tin. Repeat with the remaining dough and filling.
11. Insert one breadstick in the center of each filled dough ball to resemble an apple stem. Cover with a towel, and let rise until the dough has doubled in size, about 45 minutes.
12. Preheat the oven to 300°F (150°C).
13. Bake the buns for 20 to 25 minutes. Remove them from the oven, brush with melted butter, and place on a wire rack to cool slightly before serving.

CHAPTER 7

Sandwiches

Tamago Sandwiches
with Wasabi Mayonnaise

PREP TIME: 10 minutes • **COOK TIME:** 15 minutes • **SERVINGS:** 3 or 4

During my time as a sushi chef, I learned the art of making traditional Japanese tamago, which is delightful on its own. However, when transformed into a sandwich, tamago offers a whole new world of flavors. This fluffy, sweet egg dish pairs beautifully with soft, homemade bread, creating a harmonious blend that melts in your mouth. The wasabi mayonnaise takes it a step further, uniting the tamago's sweetness with the bread's tenderness and adding a unique depth of flavor. This recipe is a lovely way to enjoy traditional Japanese flavors in a modern context.

WASABI MAYONNAISE

6 tbsp (90g) mayonnaise
2 tsp (10g) wasabi powder
2 tbsp (30ml) maple syrup
⅛ tsp (0.6g) kosher salt

TAMAGO

10 large eggs
½ tsp (2.5ml) tsuyu soy sauce
½ tsp (2.5g) kosher salt
3 tbsp (37.5g) sugar

ASSEMBLY

¼ cup (59ml) extra-virgin olive oil
4 thick slices of sandwich bread (see Note)

SPECIAL EQUIPMENT

Tamago skillet

Note

The tamago pairs well with soft-textured breads. A soft brioche bun, Texas sandwich bread, or the Hotel Bread (page 103) would work well.

1. To make the wasabi mayonnaise, whisk together the mayonnaise, wasabi powder, maple syrup, and salt in a small bowl. Cover with plastic wrap, and place in the refrigerator.
2. Next, make the tamago. Whisk together the eggs, ½ cup (118ml) water, and the soy sauce, salt, and sugar in a medium bowl. Set aside.
3. Pour the olive oil into a small bowl and place a palm-sized piece of paper towel, folded into a 2-inch (5cm) square, in the oil.
4. Preheat a square tamago skillet over medium-high heat and coat the inside of the skillet with the oiled paper towel.
5. When the skillet is hot and sizzling, use a ⅓ cup measuring cup to add ⅔ cup (180g) of the egg mixture, lifting and tilting the skillet to distribute the egg mixture evenly across the pan. When the egg is 70 to 80 percent cooked, fold it in half from top to bottom by inserting a spatula under the upper right corner.
6. Move the folded cooked egg to one side of the pan and brush the empty side of the skillet with the oiled paper towel.
7. Pour another ⅓ cup (90g) of the egg mixture onto the empty part of the skillet, lifting the folded cooked egg and moving the pan so the egg mixture is evenly distributed underneath. After the eggs have cooked for 1 or 2 minutes, shake the pan and fold the cooked egg in half. Repeat steps 6 and 7 until all the egg mixture is used.
8. Invert a wide plate over the pan to cover the finished egg mixture and, holding the pan and plate together, flip and transfer the egg mixture to the plate. Allow to cool briefly.
9. Meanwhile, toast the bread. Remove the wasabi mayonnaise from the refrigerator, and spread it on one side of each slice of bread.
10. Cut the tamago in half and divide between two slices of wasabi mayonnaise–covered bread. Top with the remaining slices of bread, slice the sandwiches in half, and serve.

Porchetta Sandwiches

PREP TIME: 30 minutes plus 13 hours to rise • **COOK TIME:** 15 minutes • **SERVINGS:** 4

In this authentic Italian sandwich, crispy porchetta, tangy pickles, and rich salsa verde are nestled in ciabatta buns. Each bite evokes the vibrant streets of Italy. The preparation takes some time, but the anticipation that builds during the process makes the flavors even more special. Serve this sandwich at cherished gatherings with friends or on a special occasion, or enjoy it during a cozy evening at home.

PICKLED RED ONIONS

½ cup (118ml) white vinegar
½ cup (100g) sugar
½ tsp (2.5g) kosher salt
2 small red onions, thinly sliced
1 tsp (3g) black peppercorns
2 garlic cloves, crushed
1 tbsp (11g) whole-grain Dijon mustard

CIABATTA BUNS

1¾ cups (415ml) warm water
½ tsp (1.5g) active dry yeast
500g bread flour, plus more for dusting
2 tsp (10g) kosher salt

ITALIAN SALSA VERDE SAUCE

½ cup (18g) fresh Italian parsley
¼ cup (59ml) extra-virgin olive oil
1 tbsp (7.5g) nonpareil capers
1 garlic clove
½ tbsp (3g) lemon zest
1 tbsp (15ml) lemon juice
¼ tsp (1.25g) kosher salt

SANDWICHES

21 oz (600g) porchetta from the Crispy Porchetta recipe (page 70)
¼ tsp (1.25g) kosher salt
¼ tsp (0.25g) freshly ground pepper

SPECIAL EQUIPMENT

10-ounce (295ml) glass jar
Mortar and pestle or food processor

1. To make the pickled onions, add the vinegar, ½ cup (118ml) of water, sugar, and salt to a small saucepan. Set over low heat, and cook, stirring, until the sugar dissolves, about 5 minutes.
2. Place the onions, peppercorns, garlic, and mustard in a 10-ounce (295ml) glass jar, pour the warm vinegar over the onions, and press down the ingredients to submerge in the vinegar mixture. Add the lid, and turn the jar upside down. Allow to cool to room temperature, then flip the jar right-side up and place it in the refrigerator.
3. To make the ciabatta buns, combine the warm water and yeast in a 9 × 13-inch (23 × 33cm) baking dish. Add the flour and salt, and stir with a spatula until no flour is visible. Spread the dough flat in the bottom of the baking dish. Cover with plastic wrap, and let rise at room temperature for 12 hours. (I recommend making these in the evening for an overnight rise.)
4. Wet your hands with water, and gently push the sides of the dough down the baking dish. Generously dust the top of the dough and a work surface with flour. Turn the baking dish upside down over the work surface to let the dough drop. Fold the outer third of the dough to the center on both sides. Turn the dough 90 degrees, and fold the outer thirds to the center again. Press and gently pull to form a 9 × 12-inch (23 × 30cm) rectangle of dough. Cover with a towel, and let rise for 20 minutes.
5. Line a baking sheet with parchment paper. Using a scraper, divide the dough into quarters. Transfer the dough to the prepared baking sheet, cover with a tea towel, and let rise for 40 minutes.
6. Preheat the oven to 450°F (230°C). Bake for 10 minutes. Transfer to a cooling rack.
7. To make the Italian salsa verde sauce, crush the parsley, olive oil, capers, garlic, lemon zest, lemon juice, and salt in a mortar and pestle or food processor. Transfer to a bowl, and set aside.
8. Remove the crispy skin from the porchetta, and cut the skin into small pieces. Then cut the meat into thin slices and sprinkle with salt and pepper. Divide both the meat and skin into four portions.
9. Slice the buns in half, and place the meat and crispy skin on the bottom halves. Top with the pickled onions, and drizzle the salsa verde sauce over the top. Cover with the other half of the buns, and serve.

Rack of Lamb Sandwiches

PREP TIME: 30 minutes plus 10 minutes to rest • **COOK TIME:** 15 minutes • **SERVINGS:** 2

This sandwich is an excellent choice for meat lovers seeking a flavorful treat. The tender lamb, cooked to a golden brown, is enhanced by aromatic herbs and a drizzle of maple syrup that elevate its natural richness. Combined with roasted Brussels sprouts, fresh cherry tomatoes, crunchy pistachios, and a spicy mustard sauce, this sandwich offers a vibrant medley of colors, textures, and flavors. Enjoy it as a hearty lunch or a gourmet dinner option that is sure to impress.

SPICY MUSTARD SAUCE

3 tbsp (45g) mayonnaise
1 tbsp (15g) Dijon mustard
1 tbsp (15g) sweet relish
1 tsp (4g) sugar
½ tsp (0.5g) crushed hot red pepper
¼ tsp (0.25g) freshly ground black pepper

SANDWICHES

20 oz (565g) rack of lamb (9 oz/250g of meat, without the bones)
1 tsp (5g) kosher salt, divided
1 tsp (1g) freshly ground black pepper, divided
5 tbsp (75ml) extra-virgin olive oil, divided
1 tbsp (5g) chopped fresh oregano
1 tbsp (5g) chopped fresh thyme
6 oz (170g) Brussels sprouts
1 tbsp (15ml) white vinegar
1 tbsp (14g) unsalted butter
4 thick slices artisan bread
1 tbsp (15ml) maple syrup
2 tbsp (20g) pistachios, shelled and crushed
¼ pint (85g) cherry tomatoes, halved

SPECIAL EQUIPMENT

Meat thermometer

1. Preheat the oven to 450°F (230°C).
2. To make the spicy mustard sauce, whisk together the mayonnaise, mustard, relish, sugar, crushed red pepper, and black pepper in a small bowl. Cover with plastic wrap, and place in the refrigerator.
3. To make the sandwiches, separate the lamb meat from the ribs, and remove the fat and fascia. Season the meat with ¾ teaspoon (4g) of salt and ½ teaspoon (0.5g) of pepper. Drizzle with 1 tablespoon (15ml) of olive oil, and coat with the oregano and thyme. Set aside.
4. Place the Brussels sprouts in a medium bowl with enough water to cover. Add the vinegar, and let sit for 3 minutes. Drain the sprouts in a colander, rinse under running water, and shake the colander to drain.
5. Dry the sprouts on a towel. Pull off 4 or 5 leaves from each sprout. Cut off the bottom of the stem with a knife, cut each sprout in half, and place in a medium bowl. Add the remaining ¼ teaspoon (1g) of salt, the remaining ½ teaspoon (0.5g) of pepper, and 2 tablespoons (30ml) of olive oil, and toss to coat. Evenly spread the sprouts on a baking sheet, and broil for 3 to 5 minutes or until golden brown. Turn off the oven and leave the sprouts in the oven.
6. Heat a medium skillet over medium-high heat. Add the remaining 2 tablespoons (30ml) of olive oil, and heat until lightly smoking. Add the lamb to the skillet, and cook, turning, until golden brown on all sides, 6 or 7 minutes. When the internal temperature reaches 125°F (50°C), transfer the lamb to a sheet of parchment paper. Add the butter on top of the lamb, wrap the lamb in the parchment paper, and let rest for 10 minutes.
7. Meanwhile, toast the bread on a grill pan or in a toaster. Let cool slightly and then spread the spicy mustard sauce on one side of each slice. Set aside.
8. Open the parchment paper, and drizzle the lamb with maple syrup to coat. Spread the pistachios evenly on a plate and then roll the lamb in the pistachios to coat. Transfer any meat juices and maple syrup remaining on the parchment paper to a small bowl and set aside.
9. Cut the meat into ¼-inch (0.5cm) slices and divide between two slices of bread. Top with the Brussels sprouts and cherry tomatoes, drizzle with remaining meat juices, cover with remaining slices of bread, and serve.

Black Ciabatta Egg Sandwich

PREP TIME: 30 minutes plus 2 hours 30 minutes to rise • **COOK TIME:** 15 minutes • **SERVINGS:** 6

This egg sandwich is made with black ciabatta bread that is colored with squid ink. It looks very dramatic, and it tastes lovely, too, with the softness of the egg filling and the scent of the sea from the squid ink. It reminds me of the song "Puttin' on the Ritz."

CIABATTA DOUGH

1¾ cups (415ml) warm water

¼ tsp (1g) sugar

2¼ tsp (7g) active dry yeast

2 tbsp (30ml) extra-virgin olive oil, plus more for topping

500g bread flour, plus more for dusting

1 tsp (5g) kosher salt

2 tsp (16g) squid ink

8 cheddar and mozzarella string cheese sticks, chopped

CREAMY EGG FILLING

6 hard-boiled eggs, peeled

2 cups (440g) mayonnaise

⅓ cup (79ml) heavy cream

1 tbsp (15g) sugar

½ tsp (2.5g) kosher salt

½ tsp (0.5g) freshly ground black pepper, plus more for topping

TOPPINGS

Honey mustard

Arugula leaves

Grated Parmesan cheese

EQUIPMENT

9 × 13-inch (23 × 33cm) baking dish

Canvas cloth

1. Combine the warm water, sugar, and yeast in a large bowl. Cover with a tea towel, and let sit until foamy, about 10 minutes.
2. Add the olive oil, flour, and salt, and mix with a wooden spoon or spatula.
3. Dust a work surface with flour, and turn out the dough. Make a well in the dough, add the squid ink, and knead with your hands for 8 minutes. Form the dough into a ball, cover with a tea towel, and let sit for 1 hour.
4. Line a 9 × 13-inch (23 × 33cm) baking dish with parchment paper, and sprinkle the paper with flour. Add the dough and press down with your hands to stretch it into a rectangle that fills the dish.
5. Sprinkle half of the cheese evenly across the center width of the dough, and fold over one-third of the dough to cover the cheese. Sprinkle the remaining cheese over the folded dough, and fold the remaining third of the dough over the cheese to cover. Turn the dough 90 degrees and press it down with your hands to fill the dish again. Cover with a tea towel, and let rise until tripled in size, about 1 hour.
6. Meanwhile, make the egg filling. Add all the ingredients to a medium bowl. Using a fork, break the eggs into small pieces and mix until well combined. Cover with plastic wrap or a lid and refrigerate until ready to use.
7. At the end of the rising time, turn the pan upside down on a work surface and remove the parchment paper. Dust the dough with flour, and quarter it using a knife or bench scraper.
8. Spread out a canvas cloth on your work surface. Carefully transfer the dough pieces to the canvas cloth, placing them 2 inches (5cm) from the edges of the cloth and spacing them about 2 inches (5cm) apart. Fold the canvas to create walls 2 inches (5cm) high between the loaves. (This will help the dough rise up, not out.) Cover the dough completely with a tea towel to prevent drying out and let rise until doubled in size, about 30 minutes.
9. Preheat the oven to 445°F (230°C). Line a baking sheet with parchment paper.
10. Remove the tea towel. Using a wide bench scraper or spatula that can accommodate a whole loaf, lift the canvas cloth and flip over each loaf onto the scraper. Transfer the loaves to the prepared baking sheet, and bake for 15 minutes, then transfer the loaves to a rack to cool for 5 minutes.
11. Slice each loaf in half, and spread one half of each with honey mustard. Top each bottom half with ¼ of the creamy egg filling, followed by ¼ of the arugula and Parmesan. Drizzle some olive oil over the top, and season with more freshly ground black pepper. Add the top half of the loaves, and serve.

Reuben Sandwiches
with Spicy Garlicky Sauerkraut

PREP TIME: 40 minutes plus 7 days to ferment • **COOK TIME:** 2 minutes • **MAKES:** 2 sandwiches

Who can resist a good Reuben sandwich? This version brings the classic up a notch with a tangy, spicy, garlicky sauerkraut that packs a punch and a creamy homemade Russian dressing that ties it all together. The sauerkraut does require a bit of patience with its fermentation time, but trust me, it's worth it. Pair it with toasted rye bread, corned beef, and melted Swiss cheese, and you've got a mouthwatering bite that's perfect for any meal. A little messy, a lot delicious—just the way a Reuben should be!

SPICY GARLICKY SAUERKRAUT

1 medium head of cabbage
2 tbsp (30ml) white vinegar
8 garlic cloves, thinly sliced
5 Thai red chiles, thinly sliced
½ tsp (2.5g) caraway seeds
2 tbsp (14g) sea salt

RUSSIAN DRESSING

1 small shallot, diced
1 garlic clove, minced
¼ tsp (1.25g) kosher salt
½ tsp (0.5g) freshly ground black pepper
1 cup (230g) mayonnaise
¼ cup (59g) ketchup
1 tbsp (12g) sugar
2 tbsp (32g) prepared horseradish
2 tsp (10ml) Worcestershire sauce
1 tbsp (15ml) hot sauce
1 tsp (3g) sweet paprika

ASSEMBLY

2 tbsp (28g) unsalted butter
4 slices rye bread or sourdough
1 lb (454g) corned beef, sliced to your preferred thickness
4 slices Swiss cheese

SPECIAL EQUIPMENT

Disposable kitchen gloves
Wooden pestle

Note

To make your own corned beef, try the Corned Beef and Cabbage recipe earlier in the book (page 61).

1. Cut the cabbage into quarters, place in a large bowl, and add water to cover. Add the vinegar, and let sit for 5 minutes. Rinse the cabbage under running water, place it cut-side down on a paper towel, and let sit for 10 minutes.
2. Slice the cabbage into ¼-inch (0.5cm) strips, cut the strips into 1-inch (2.5cm) pieces, and place in a large bowl. Add the garlic, chiles, and caraway seeds, and sprinkle evenly with salt.
3. Wearing disposable kitchen gloves, use both hands to combine all the ingredients, squeezing and mixing vigorously. Mix until the cabbage changes color, becomes pliable, and releases its juices, about 10 to 15 minutes.
4. Add the cabbage, a small portion at a time, to a 2-quart (2-liter) sterilized jar, pressing down with a wooden pestle to release the air from the cabbage. (If you don't have a pestle, you can push down the cabbage with a gloved fist.) Add the cabbage juice to the jar, close the lid, and let sit at room temperature for one week. You can use a silicone lid that will allow the gas to escape automatically as the cabbage ferments, or use a lid with a tube to vent, or just close the lid loosely.
5. To make the Russian dressing, whisk together all the dressing ingredients in a small bowl. Cover with plastic wrap, and set in the refrigerator.
6. Preheat the broiler to 500°F (260°C).
7. Butter one side of each of 2 slices of the rye bread and place them buttered-sides up on a baking sheet. Divide the corned beef into two ½-pound (225g) patties, top each with 2 slices of Swiss cheese, and place them on the baking sheet but not on top of the bread slices. Place under the broiler for 1 or 2 minutes to melt the cheese and toast the bread slices.
8. Place the beef and cheese on the toasted pieces of bread, top each with ⅓ cup (45g) of sauerkraut and 3 tablespoons (45ml) of dressing, and serve with extra sauerkraut and dressing on the side.

Butter Shrimp and Black Bun Sandwiches

PREP TIME: 20 minutes plus 2 hours to rise • **COOK TIME:** 35 minutes • **MAKES:** 2 sandwiches and 4 extra buns

This sandwich is filled with succulent Argentine shrimp and a rich butter sauce, which are tucked into a black bun made with squid ink. The unique colors and flavors delight both the eyes and the palate, and the combination of the soft bread, fresh shrimp, and savory butter sauce creates a perfect harmony. A squeeze of lemon adds a refreshing brightness that enhances the overall taste of this stunning sandwich.

BLACK DOUGH

⅓ cup (79ml) warm water
½ cup (118ml) warm milk
2¼ tsp (7g) active dry yeast
400g bread flour, plus more for dusting
2 tbsp (25g) sugar
1 tsp (5g) kosher salt
1 large egg
1 tbsp (24g) squid ink
7 tbsp (98g) unsalted butter, divided, at room temperature

FILLING

1 tbsp (15g) kosher salt, for washing
12 5/9 Argentine shrimp (about 28 oz/800g)

BUTTER SAUCE

½ cup (115g) unsalted butter
¼ cup (59ml) white wine
2 garlic cloves, crushed

CREAM SAUCE

¼ cup (58g) unsalted butter
3 garlic cloves, minced
1 shallot, minced
1 tsp (5g) kosher salt
¼ cup (59ml) heavy cream
¼ tsp (0.25g) freshly ground black pepper
1 tbsp (6g) chopped fresh parsley

ASSEMBLY

2 stems of fresh parsley, leaves only
Lemon wedges

1. To make the dough, mix the warm water, warm milk, and yeast in a small bowl using a wooden spoon. Cover with a towel, and let rest for 10 minutes.
2. Meanwhile, whisk together the flour, sugar, and salt in a large bowl. (You also can do this in the bowl of a stand mixer fitted with a dough hook.)
3. Beat together the egg and squid ink in a small bowl.
4. Add the yeast mixture and the egg mixture to the flour mixture and combine using a stand mixer or handheld electric mixer set to low. Add 5 tablespoons butter and mix on medium for about 10 minutes. The dough will look runny but will not stick to your hands. Remove the dough from the bowl, shape it into a ball, and return it to the bowl, seam side down. Cover with a tea towel and let rise in a warm place until doubled in size, about 1 hour.
5. Turn out the dough onto a floured work surface, press down with your hands to lightly deflate. Use a scraper to divide the dough into 6 equal portions and shape each portion into a ball. Cover with a towel and let rest for 15 minutes.
6. Line a baking sheet with parchment paper. Place one ball of dough on a work surface, and use your hands to flatten it to about ½-inch (1.25cm) thick. Place your hands on the ends of the dough and roll from the top to the bottom, pinching the ends of the dough together. Working from the center outward, roll the dough with both hands to stretch it out to 6 inches (15cm). Transfer to the prepared baking sheet and repeat with the remaining balls. Cover with a tea towel, and let rise for 45 minutes.
7. Preheat the oven to 400°F (200°C).
8. Cut a ⅛-inch (3mm) deep slit in the top of each dough ball. Divide the remaining 2 tablespoons (28g) of butter into six equal-size portions and insert a portion into each slit. Bake the buns for 15 minutes and then transfer to a wire rack to cool.
9. Meanwhile, to make the filling, pour 4 cups (945ml) water into a large bowl, add the salt, and stir to dissolve. Add the shrimp, and shake to rinse. Transfer the shrimp to a fine-mesh sieve, and gently rinse under running water. Remove the heads and set them aside on a large paper towel–lined plate. Peel the shrimp, make a cut ⅛ inch (3mm) deep from the back to the tail, remove and discard the guts, and set aside the cleaned shrimp with the heads. (If the guts have burst, rinse the shrimp under running water to remove the waste.)
10. To make the butter sauce, place the shrimp heads, butter, white wine, and garlic in a large skillet over low heat. Cover and simmer for 2 minutes, uncover, turn over, and re-cover. Cook for 3 more minutes. Strain the butter sauce through a fine-mesh sieve, and set aside. Discard the solids.
11. Wipe the skillet clean with a paper towel and return it to low heat. To make the cream sauce, add the butter to the skillet to melt, along with the garlic and shallot, and cook for 5 minutes. Increase the heat to medium and add the shrimp and salt.

Tilt the pan to one side, and cook, tossing the shrimp in the melted butter, for 3 to 5 minutes. When the shrimp have turned from transparent to white, transfer them to a bowl, cover with plastic wrap, and set aside.

12. Add the butter sauce and heavy cream to the skillet, stir, and simmer until the sauce has thickened, about 5 minutes. Remove from the heat. Add the pepper and parsley, mix well, and keep warm.

13. Cut a long slit in the middle of two buns, and add 6 shrimp, with their juices, to each. Garnish with parsley leaves. Just before serving, stir the cream sauce and drizzle generously over the shrimp. Finish with a squeeze of lemon and serve.

14. The remaining buns can be stored in a zipperlock bag at room temperature for up to 3 days or frozen for up to 3 months.

Open-Faced

Baked Eggplant Sandwiches

PREP TIME: 20 minutes • **COOK TIME:** 40 minutes • **SERVINGS:** 2

The joy of creating delicious food with healthy ingredients makes me love cooking even more, and this eggplant open-faced sandwich is a great example. You'll love the combination of golden, tender, baked eggplant with lightly melted mozzarella and roasted cherry tomatoes.

- 1 large (18 oz/500g) eggplant
- 2 tsp (6g) everything bagel seasoning
- 4 tbsp (59ml) extra-virgin olive oil, divided
- 5.5 oz (150g) cherry tomatoes, halved
- ½ tsp (2.5g) kosher salt
- ½ tsp (0.5g) freshly ground black pepper, plus more for topping
- ¼ tsp (0.25g) dried sage
- ¼ tsp (0.25g) dried thyme
- ¼ tsp (0.25g) dried rosemary
- 2 thick slices artisan bread
- ½ garlic clove, halved
- 2 tsp (10ml) maple syrup
- 8 oz (226g) fresh mozzarella, sliced
- 1 cup baby arugula
- 6 slices prosciutto

1. Preheat the oven to 400°F (200°C). Line a 9 × 9-inch (23 × 23cm) baking dish with parchment paper.
2. Cut the eggplant in half without removing the stem. Using a sharp knife, make a grid pattern on the inside of the eggplant without cutting through the skin. Season the eggplant with the everything bagel seasoning, drizzle with 2 tablespoons (30ml) of extra-virgin olive oil, and place skin-side down in the prepared baking dish.
3. Place the cherry tomatoes in a small baking dish. Add the salt, ¼ teaspoon (0.2g) of ground black pepper, 1 tablespoon (15ml) of olive oil, sage, thyme, and rosemary, and stir to coat the tomatoes in the oil and seasonings.
4. Place the baking dishes in the oven, and roast for 40 minutes, or until the eggplant is tender.
5. While the eggplant is roasting, heat a grill pan over high heat. Drizzle the remaining 1 tablespoon (15ml) olive oil over the bread, add the bread to the pan, and toast both sides.
6. Rub the cut garlic on the toasted bread and set aside.
7. Remove the eggplant from the oven Holding the stem, remove the eggplant flesh from the skin and mash the flesh with a spoon. Spread about half of the eggplant on each slice of bread and then drizzle each slice with ½ teaspoon (2.5ml) of maple syrup.
8. Crush the roasted tomatoes with a fork, and mix well. Set aside.
9. To assemble the sandwiches, place half of the fresh mozzarella slices on top of each eggplant-topped toast, drizzle each with ½ teaspoon (2.5ml) of maple syrup, and heat with a blowtorch until the cheese melts. (If you don't have a torch, add to the warm oven until the cheese melts.)
10. Top each open-faced sandwich with half of the baby arugula, 3 slices of prosciutto, half of the roasted tomatoes, and the remaining pepper, and serve.

Picnic Sandwiches

PREP TIME: 30 minutes plus 2 hours to rise • **COOK TIME:** 20 minutes • **MAKES:** 15 mini sandwiches

These sandwiches are the perfect meal for outdoor adventures. The fresh vegetables, savory ham, and creamy spread come together in a delightful bite that enhances the joy of dining in the open air. They're a simple yet flavorful way to elevate your picnic experience.

DOUGH

400g bread flour, plus more for dusting
1 tsp (5g) kosher salt
¼ medium red onion, finely diced
¼ medium yellow bell pepper, finely diced
¼ medium red bell pepper, finely diced
½ small carrot, finely diced
½ cup (118ml) warm water
2¼ tsp (7g) active yeast
2 tbsp (28g) sugar
2 large eggs
3 tbsp (42g) mayonnaise
2 tbsp (28g) unsalted butter
2 egg yolks, beaten

CREAM CHEESE SPREAD

1 cup (120g) cream cheese, at room temperature
2 tbsp (28g) unsalted butter, at room temperature
⅛ tsp (0.6g) kosher salt
2 tbsp (30ml) maple syrup

ASSEMBLY

9 slices ham
2 handfuls of spring mix
⅛ tsp (0.6g) kosher salt
⅛ tsp (0.25g) freshly ground black pepper
1 tbsp (15ml) extra-virgin olive oil
¼ cup (25g) shredded cheddar
15 sandwich picks

SPECIAL EQUIPMENT

Stand mixer or handheld electric mixer

1. To make the dough, mix the flour, salt, onion, bell peppers, and carrot in a large bowl using your hands. Set aside.
2. Combine the warm water, yeast, and sugar in a cup, cover with a tea towel, and let sit until foamy, about 10 minutes.
3. Meanwhile, whisk together the eggs and mayonnaise in a small bowl. Add to the flour mixture. Add the yeast mixture to the flour mixture, and mix with a wooden spoon.
4. Turn out the dough onto a work surface, add the butter, and knead until the dough is smooth and doesn't stick to your hands, 10 to 15 minutes. (If using a stand mixer, knead until the dough doesn't stick to the bowl, 8 to 10 minutes.) Return the dough to the bowl, cover with a tea towel, and let rise until doubled in size, about 1 hour.
5. Meanwhile, to make the cream cheese spread, add the cream cheese, butter, salt, and maple syrup in a small bowl, and mix well with a spoon. Cover with plastic wrap, and set in the refrigerator.
6. Turn out the dough onto a floured surface, and press down with your hands to release the gas. Cut the dough into 15 equal pieces and shape each into a ball. Cover with a tea towel and let rest for 15 minutes.
7. Line a 9 × 13-inch (23 × 33cm) baking dish with parchment paper.
8. Add the dough to the pan in five even rows of three balls. Cover the pan with a tea towel, and let the dough rise until it's ¼ inch (6mm) from the top of the pan, 40 to 50 minutes.
9. Preheat the oven to 360°F (185°C).
10. Brush the dough twice with the egg yolks.
11. Bake for 20 minutes, or until browned on top.
12. Remove from the oven and allow to cool in the pan slightly. Lift the parchment paper from the pan and transfer the bread to a wire rack to cool completely.
13. Cut the cooled bread in half horizontally and open the halves. Spread the cream cheese mixture on the bottom half. Fold the sliced ham over the cream cheese, top with a couple handfuls of spring mix, season with salt and pepper, drizzle with extra-virgin olive oil, and sprinkle the cheddar evenly over the top. Add the top half of the bread. Stick a sandwich pick in each mini sandwich and use a sharp knife to separate the bread into individual sandwiches. Serve or package several sandwiches in a storage container and take on a picnic.

CHAPTER 8

Scones & Biscuits

Country White Gravy and Biscuits

PREP TIME: 25 minutes • **COOK TIME:** 13 minutes • **MAKES:** 9 biscuits and 2½ cups (600ml) white gravy

Biscuits and gravy are a favorite breakfast combination, and the gravy used is usually either country gravy or white gravy. The biggest difference between country and white gravy is whether bacon grease or flour is added to the roux. The country white gravy in this recipe is the best of both, combining the lightness of flour with the savory flavor of bacon grease. When served with these freshly baked biscuits, the creamy gravy perfectly accompanies the warm, fluffy layers.

BISCUITS

¼ cup (58g) unsalted butter
240g all-purpose flour, plus more for dusting
2 tsp (9.6g) baking powder
¼ tsp (1.5g) baking soda
½ tsp (2.5g) salt
1 cup (240g) sour cream

COUNTRY WHITE GRAVY

¼ cup (58g) unsalted butter
4 slices (100g) maple-flavored bacon, diced
1 tbsp (14g) all-purpose flour
½ medium sweet onion, finely grated
½ medium russet potato, finely grated
2 cups (473ml) whole milk
½ tsp (2.5g) salt
¼ tsp (0.25g) freshly ground black pepper

SPECIAL EQUIPMENT

Cheese grater
3- or 4-inch (7.5 or 10cm) round cookie or biscuit cutter

1. To make the biscuits, place the butter in the freezer for 15 minutes.
2. Add the flour, baking powder, baking soda, and salt to a large bowl, and mix well.
3. Remove the butter from the freezer, and grate it with a cheese grater using the largest holes. Add the grated butter to the flour mixture, and gently toss to coat.
4. Add the sour cream and use a dough scraper to mix the dough.
5. Turn out the mixture onto a work surface, and use the dough scraper to press and fold until the dough comes together.
6. Use the dough scraper to cut the dough in half. Stack the two pieces of dough, and press them together. Repeat cutting in half, stacking, and pressing four or five times to create layers in the dough.
7. Preheat the oven to 450°F (230°C). Line a baking sheet with parchment paper.
8. Lightly dust a work surface with flour, place the dough on top, and roll out to ½-inch (1.25cm) thickness. Using a 3-inch (7.5cm) round biscuit cutter, cut the dough into 9 pieces, gathering and re-rolling the dough scraps to use all the dough. Place the biscuits on the prepared baking sheet.
9. Bake for 13 minutes, or until golden brown. Transfer to a rack to cool slightly.
10. While the biscuits are baking, make the gravy. Heat a medium skillet over medium heat. Add the butter and bacon, and stir-fry the bacon until the grease comes out, about 5 minutes.
11. Add flour, and cook, stirring constantly, until brown, about 3 minutes.
12. Add the onion, potato, and milk, and stir until thick.
13. Season with salt and pepper, and serve with the warm biscuits.

Sunflower Biscuits

PREP TIME: 20 minutes plus 20 minutes to freeze • **COOK TIME:** 35 minutes • **MAKES:** 8 scones

Sunflower Biscuits are a sensory delight, combining vibrant colors, enticing shapes, and a symphony of flavors and textures. The buttery biscuit, layered with savory ham and melted cheddar, offers a harmonious taste experience, and each petal-like slice offers a tender crumb and rich filling. The touch of maple syrup and poppy seeds add a subtle sweetness and a delightful crunch. Representing the sunflower's promise of abundance, these biscuits bring a sense of prosperity to your baking.

⅓ cup (76g) unsalted butter
300g all-purpose flour
1 tsp (5g) baking powder
⅓ tsp (2g) baking soda
½ tsp (2.5g) kosher salt
1 cup (237ml) heavy cream
6 slices deli ham
6 slices cheddar
1 large egg yolk, for egg wash
½ tsp (1.5g) poppy seeds, or everything bagel seasoning
1 tbsp (15ml) maple syrup

SPECIAL EQUIPMENT

Cheese grater
2-inch (5cm) round cookie cutter

1. Place the butter in the freezer for 20 minutes.
2. Preheat the oven to 365°F (185°C). Line a baking sheet with parchment paper.
3. Add the flour, baking powder, baking soda, and salt to a medium bowl, and mix well with a whisk or your hands.
4. Grate the cold butter into the flour mixture, and stir until the butter is evenly coated in the flour mixture.
5. Add the heavy cream, and mix well with a wooden spatula.
6. When the dough comes together, turn it out onto a work surface and form it into a mound. Divide the dough into three equal portions.
7. Place one piece of dough on your work surface, and cut it in half using a scraper. Stack the two pieces, and press down with your hands. Repeat the cutting, stacking, and pressing two more times to create layers. Roll out the layered dough to a ⅛-inch (3mm) thick circle. Set aside and repeat with the remaining two pieces of dough.
8. Place the ham slices on top of the first piece of dough. Top the ham with the second piece of dough. Place the cheddar slices on the second piece of dough, and top with the third piece of dough. Gently press and lightly roll the stack with a rolling pin to help the cheese and ham stick to the dough. Transfer the stack to the prepared baking sheet.
9. Using a 2-inch (5cm) round cutter, mark a circle in the center of the dough. Using the scraper, gently press down on the dough to mark eight equal portions. When you have the portions equally marked, use the scraper to cut the sections, leaving a 2-inch (5cm) circle in the center uncut. (This forms the sunflower petals and center portion.)
10. Again leaving the circle uncut in the center, cut each petal in half, twist each half of the petal outward two times, and then pinch the ends together to make the petal. (You'll create eight total petals.)
11. Brush the petals and center two times with the egg yolk, and sprinkle the center with the poppy seeds or everything bagel seasoning.
12. Bake for 15 minutes. Reduce the oven temperature to 330°F (165°C), and bake for 20 minutes.
13. Transfer to a large plate, drizzle with maple syrup, and serve. Store any leftovers in an airtight container for up to 3 days, or freeze and reheat in the microwave for 1 or 2 minutes.

Cinnamon Kouign-Amann Biscuits

PREP TIME: 10 minutes plus 2 hours to rest • **COOK TIME:** 20 minutes • **MAKES:** 8 biscuits

These special biscuits reinterpret a Kouign-Amann, a traditional French dessert, with a cinnamon twist. The exterior is crisp and the interior is tender, and there's a hint of saltiness that beautifully complements the sweetness. Enjoying it with ice cream enhances the sweetness even further. This easy-to-make recipe allows you to savor the flavors of a French bakery at home.

300g cake flour, plus more for dusting
1 tsp (5g) baking powder
½ tsp (3g) baking soda
1 tsp (5g) kosher salt
¾ cup (170g) cold unsalted butter
¾ cup (177ml) buttermilk
1 cup (200g) sugar
¼ cup (33g) ground cinnamon
2 tbsp (28g) unsalted butter, at room temperature

SPECIAL EQUIPMENT

Cheese grater
Mortar and pestle
Muffin tin

1. Sift together the flour, baking powder, baking soda, and ½ teaspoon (2.5g) of salt in a medium bowl.
2. Coat the cold butter in the flour mixture, and grate the butter through the coarse part of a cheese grater in two or three batches, stirring with the flour mixture after each grating to evenly coat.
3. Add the buttermilk in two or three batches, and mix with a wooden spoon after each addition until the dough comes together.
4. Turn out the lumpy dough onto a work surface, press and gather with a scraper, and shape into a 5 × 5-inch (12.5 × 12.5cm) square. Wrap in parchment paper, and place in the refrigerator for 30 minutes. (The dough won't be smooth and will be cracked in some spots, but that's okay.)
5. Meanwhile, grind the remaining ½ teaspoon (2.5g) of kosher salt with a mortar and pestle, and transfer to a small bowl. Add the sugar and cinnamon, and stir to combine. Set aside.
6. Turn out the dough on a floured work surface, and sprinkle generously on both sides with some of the sugar mixture. Using a scraper and a rolling pin, flatten the dough into a 6 × 12-inch (15 × 30.5cm) rectangle. Sprinkle both sides of the dough with more of the sugar mixture, and roll over the dough so the sugar is embedded in the dough. Cut the dough in half with a scraper, sprinkle more of the sugar mixture on top of one half, and cover with the other half. (Always sprinkle the dough with the sugar mixture just before layering.) Roll out to 5 × 10 inches (12.5 × 25.5cm). Sprinkle both sides with the sugar mixture again. Cut the dough in half, sprinkle the top of one half with the sugar mixture, and cover with the other half. Roll out and then wrap in parchment paper and place in the refrigerator for 1 hour.
7. Remove from the refrigerator and sprinkle both sides of the dough generously with the sugar mixture. Cut the dough in half, sprinkle the sugar mixture on half of the dough, and cover with the other half of the dough. Roll out to 6 × 12 inches (15 × 30.5cm), and trim the ends of the dough neatly with a scraper.
8. Dust both sides again with the sugar mixture, and cut into eight 3 × 3-inch (7.5 × 7.5cm) pieces. Refrigerate for 30 minutes.
9. Preheat the oven to 420°F (215°C). Grease a muffin tin with the soft butter and then dust each cup with some of the sugar mixture.
10. Remove the dough from the refrigerator, fold each corner of the squares to the center, and press each into a muffin divot.
11. Reduce the oven temperature to 375°F (190°C), and bake for 20 minutes.
12. Flip the muffin tin onto a wire rack to remove the biscuits, and allow the biscuits to cool before serving.

Strawberry and Chocolate Scones

PREP TIME: 30 minutes plus 4 hours to freeze • **COOK TIME:** 35 minutes • **MAKES:** 9 scones

You'll love the combination of fresh strawberries and rich chocolate in these delightful scones. Each bite offers a luscious blend of creamy chocolate and juicy strawberries, creating a treat that's both decadent and refreshing. Perfect for any occasion, these scones are sure to impress!

CHOCOLATE STRAWBERRY FILLING

1 cup (170g) dark chocolate chips

2 tbsp (30ml) heavy cream

3 fresh strawberries, finely diced

DOUGH

1 cup (227g) cold unsalted butter

456g cake flour, plus more for dusting

2 tbsp (28g) baking powder

2 tbsp (25g) sugar

1 tsp (5g) kosher salt

½ cup (89g) hot cocoa mix (with sugar)

1 cup (170g) chocolate chips (I prefer 50% dark chocolate)

1 cup (240g) sour cream

⅓ cup (79ml) heavy cream

SPECIAL EQUIPMENT

Mini muffin pan

Mini paper cupcake liners

Cheese grater

3-inch (7.5cm) round pastry cutter

1. Place the chocolate chips and cream in a small bowl in a double boiler, and set over medium-high heat. Cook, stirring, until the chocolate chips are melted, about 15 minutes. Add the strawberries, and mix well.
2. Line a mini muffin pan with mini paper cupcake liners and fill each liner with the chocolate strawberry filling. Place the muffin pan in the freezer until the chocolate has cooled and hardened, at least 3 or 4 hours. (These can be made a day ahead.)
3. Grate the cold butter through the large holes of a cheese grater into a small bowl. Freeze for 5 minutes.
4. Whisk together the flour, baking powder, sugar, and salt in a large bowl until well combined. Add the cold butter and use your hands to toss to coat. Stir in the hot cocoa mix and chocolate chips until the flour mixture is light brown in color. Add the sour cream and heavy cream, and mix with a wooden spoon until a shaggy dough forms.
5. Turn out the dough onto a work surface. Using a scraper and your hands, gather and press the dough into a flat mound. Cut the dough in half, stack the two pieces, and press to a thickness of 1 inch (2.5cm). Do this four or five times to create layers.
6. Using a scraper, press and flatten the dough to 1 inch (2.5cm), wrap well in parchment paper, and place in the freezer for 1 hour.
7. Remove the dough from the freezer and place on a floured work surface. Cut the dough in half, and roll out one half to a ½-inch (1.25cm) thickness using a rolling pin.
8. Line a baking sheet with parchment paper. Using a 3-inch (7.5cm) round pastry cutter, cut out the scones and place them on the prepared baking sheet. Gather the remaining dough, roll it out, and cut it again. You should have 9 pieces. Repeat with the other half of the dough for a total of 18 pieces. Cover with a tea towel and place in the refrigerator, removing two at a time to work with.
9. Preheat the oven to 425°F (220°C).
10. Place the two pieces of dough on your work surface and press down on the center of each using a spoon. (This will create room for the frozen chocolate strawberry filling.)
11. Remove one chocolate strawberry filling from the freezer, peel off the paper liner, place in the center of the dough, and cover with another piece of dough. Seal the two pieces of dough well to prevent the filling from leaking out. Return the filled scones to the baking sheet in the refrigerator to prevent the butter from melting, and repeat with the rest of the dough and chocolate strawberry filling.
12. Place the scones in the oven, reduce the temperature to 360°F (185°C), and bake for 20 minutes.
13. Transfer the scones to a wire rack to cool before serving.

Cheese and Leek Scones

PREP TIME: 20 minutes plus 30 minutes to rest • **COOK TIME:** 30 minutes • **MAKES:** 6 scones

Scones are a quick bread that are believed to have originated in the United Kingdom. They're a popular baked good for new home bakers because they're relatively easy and forgiving. I really love leeks, and these scones are packed with the umami of leeks and the creaminess of cheddar and mozzarella. Let the smell of baking scones fill your home, and invite your loved ones over for a cup of tea.

240g all-purpose flour
1 tsp (5g) baking powder
½ tsp (2.5g) kosher salt
¼ tsp (1.5g) baking soda
¼ cup (50g) sugar
½ cup (115g) cold unsalted butter
1 cup (110g) trimmed and chopped leeks
1 cup (118g) shredded cheddar
1 cup (118g) shredded mozzarella
½ cup (123g) sour cream
2 egg yolks

SPECIAL EQUIPMENT
Pastry blender

1. Add the flour, baking powder, salt, baking soda, and sugar to a large bowl, and mix well.
2. Add the butter to the flour mixture. Using a pastry blender, cut the unsalted butter into small pieces (about the size of a pea) as you work it into the flour mixture.
3. Add the leeks, cheddar, and mozzarella, and mix to coat evenly with the flour mixture.
4. Make a well in the center of the dry ingredients and add the sour cream. Scoop the flour mixture over the sour cream and work it into the flour mixture until well combined.
5. Turn out the dough onto a work surface. Using your hands, flatten the dough to a 1-inch (2.5cm) thickness and then cut in half. Stack the two pieces of dough and press them together. Repeat cutting in half, stacking, and pressing four or five times to create layers in the dough.
6. After you create the last layer, form the dough into a 6 × 8-inch (15 × 20cm) rectangle that's 1 inch (2.5cm) thick.
7. Wrap the dough in parchment paper or plastic wrap, and place in the freezer for 30 minutes.
8. Preheat the oven to 420°F (215°C). Line a baking sheet with parchment paper.
9. Remove the dough from the freezer, and cut the dough into 9 equal-size pieces. Place on the prepared baking sheet.
10. Whisk the egg yolks in a small bowl. Brush each scone twice with the egg.
11. Reduce the oven temperature to 360°F (180°C). Bake for 30 to 35 minutes, until golden brown on top.
12. Serve immediately. Store any leftovers in an airtight container at room temperature for up to 3 days, reheating in the microwave for about 15 to 20 seconds, or freeze and then thaw to room temperature.

Black Cheese Scones

PREP TIME: 25 minutes plus 30 minutes to rest • **COOK TIME:** 25 minutes • **MAKES:** 9 scones

These scones are a delightful twist on the classic, offering a striking visual appeal and a rich, cheesy flavor. The squid ink gives these scones their unique black color, while the blend of cheddar and cheese curds brings a smooth, creamy texture. Fresh parsley adds a burst of freshness, complementing the savory notes of the cheese. These scones are incredibly tender, and each bite will melt in your mouth. Enjoy them as a savory snack or a delicious addition to any meal.

½ cup (115g) cold unsalted butter
300g all-purpose flour, plus more for dusting
1 tsp (4.8g) baking powder
¼ tsp (1.25g) baking soda
2 tbsp (25g) sugar
¾ cup (170g) cold cheese curds, cut into ½-inch (1.25cm) cubes
¾ cup (170g) cold cheddar, cut into ½-inch (1.25cm) cubes
¼ cup (16g) finely chopped fresh flat-leaf parsley
¾ cup (177ml) heavy cream
2 tsp (16g) squid ink

SPECIAL EQUIPMENT

Cheese grater
3- or 4-inch (7.5 or 10cm) round cookie or biscuit cutter

Note

You can reheat the scones in the microwave for about 20 seconds to get that freshly baked flavor back.

1. Grate the cold butter through the thickest holes of a grater, and place it in the freezer while you prepare the flour mixture.
2. Using your hands or a whisk, mix the flour, baking powder, baking soda, and sugar in a medium bowl.
3. Add the butter to the flour mixture, and toss to coat evenly with the flour.
4. Add the cheese curds, cheddar, and parsley, and toss to coat.
5. In a small bowl, stir together the cream and squid ink. Pour into the flour mixture and lightly mix the ink so it spreads evenly.
6. Turn out the dough onto a floured work surface. Use a dough scraper to gather and press the dough together, and shape it into a square about 1 inch (2.5cm) thick. Cut the dough in half, stack the two pieces, and press until 1 inch (2.5cm) thick. Repeat four or five times to create layers.
7. Roll out the dough to 1 inch (2.5cm) thick, wrap in parchment paper, and place in the freezer for 30 minutes.
8. Preheat the oven to 400°F (200°C). Line a baking sheet with parchment paper.
9. Turn out the dough onto a floured work surface, and roll it to ½-inch (1.25cm) thickness. Cut the dough with a 3- or 4-inch (7.5 or 10cm) round cookie or biscuit cutter. Gather the remaining dough, roll out again to ½-inch (1.25cm) thickness, and cut again. You should have 9 scones. Place the scones on the prepared baking sheet.
10. Bake for 10 minutes. Reduce the heat to 330°F (165°C), and bake for 15 minutes.
11. Transfer the scones to a wire rack to cool before serving.

CHAPTER 9

Cakes

Black Forest Cake

(Forêt-Noire Gâteau)

PREP TIME: 50 minutes plus at least 6 hours to cool • **COOK TIME:** 30 minutes • **MAKES:** 1 (9-inch or 23cm) cake (12 servings)

This cake originates from the Schwarzwald (Black Forest) region of Germany, known for its abundance of cherries and production of Kirschwasser, a cherry brandy. The cake is believed to have been inspired by the region's traditional cherry, cream, and chocolate desserts, with the earliest known recipe appearing in the 1930s. Some historians trace its name to the Black Forest's dark, dense woodlands, while others suggest it comes from the traditional Bollenhut, a hat worn by women in the region that features red pom-poms resembling cherries. The cake is a beloved classic in Germany, Austria, and Switzerland as well as in France and North America. My decoration varies from the original, with cut cherries alternating in direction.

CHERRY COMPOTE

1 lb (454g) cherries

¾ cup (150g) brown sugar, firmly packed

3 tbsp (45ml) gold rum

3 tbsp (45ml) fresh lemon juice

1 cinnamon stick

CAKE

120g cake flour (sifted, then measured)

¼ cup (25g) cocoa powder

2 tbsp (15g) cornstarch

1 cup (237ml) boiling water

3 egg yolks

4 large eggs, at room temperature

¼ tsp (1.25g) kosher salt

½ cup (100g) granulated sugar

1 tbsp (15ml) corn syrup

3 tbsp (45ml) whole milk

2 tbsp (28g) unsalted butter, melted

WHIPPED CREAM

4¼ cups (1 liter) heavy cream

¾ cup (98g) confectioners' sugar

¼ tsp (1.25g) kosher salt

GARNISH

1 lb (454g) cherries

½ cup (42g) grated unsweet or dark chocolate

SPECIAL EQUIPMENT

Stand mixer or handheld electric mixer

9-inch (23cm) round cake pan

Thermometer

1. Make the cherry compote at least 6 hours before making the cake (see Notes). Using a small knife, insert the point into a cherry so the knife touches the pit, rotate the knife around the center of the cherry, and cut the cherry in half. Twist the halves back and forth to split them, remove the pit, and place the halves in a small saucepan. (You also can use a cherry pitter.)
2. Add the brown sugar, rum, lemon juice, and cinnamon stick to the saucepan. Set over medium heat and cook until the sugar dissolves, tossing the cherries gently with a wooden spoon, about 3 to 5 minutes. (Be careful not to overcook the cherries or they will become mushy.) Transfer the mixture to a bowl, let cool, cover tightly with plastic wrap, and set in the refrigerator for at least 6 hours or up to 1 day.
3. The next day, preheat the oven to 375°F (190°C). Line the bottom and sides of a 9-inch (23cm) round cake pan with parchment paper.
4. Sift the flour, cocoa powder, and cornstarch into a medium bowl, and set aside.
5. Pour the boiling water into a large bowl. Combine the egg yolks, eggs, salt, granulated sugar, and corn syrup in another large bowl, or in the bowl of a stand mixer. Set the bowl over the hot water, and continuously stir the egg mixture with a wooden spoon until it reaches 100°F (38°C). Remove the bowl from the hot water, and mix with a handheld electric mixer or the stand mixer on high until pale and stiff peaks form, 5 to 7 minutes. Reduce the speed to low, and mix for 1 minute more. (The dough should hold its shape briefly when lifted and dropped.)
6. Add the flour mixture in two or three batches, folding the dough from the outside in and shaking the spatula to distribute the flour mixture. Mix quickly and evenly to avoid air bubbles.
7. Combine the milk and butter in a small, heatproof bowl, and microwave at 122°F (50°C) for about 20 seconds. Add about ¼ cup (59ml) of the dough to the milk-butter mixture, stir to combine, and pour the combination into the dough. Fold the dough about 10 times to incorporate the butter mixture evenly.
8. Pour the batter into the prepared pan, and use a skewer to draw a swirl from the center outward, flattening the batter and smoothing out any air bubbles. Drop the cake pan vertically on a work surface to pop any large air bubbles.
9. Bake for 10 minutes. Reduce the temperature to 350°F (180°C), and bake for another 15 to 20 minutes. The cake is done when a skewer inserted in the center comes out clean. Remove from the oven, drop the cake pan once onto a heatproof surface to allow the steam to release, and then turn the pan upside down onto a wire rack to cool.
10. Remove the cherry compote from the refrigerator, strain the cherries from the remaining liquid, and set aside both.

11. Beat the heavy cream, confectioners' sugar, and salt in a large bowl or in the bowl of a stand mixer with the mixer on medium-high until stiff peaks form, about 5 minutes.
12. Remove the parchment paper from the cake. Place about 1 tablespoon (15ml) of the whipped cream in the center of a rotating cake stand, set the cake on top, and use a long, serrated knife to cut the cake into three even layers. Using a pastry brush, brush the entire surface of the first layer with cherry compote syrup. Cover with about 1 cup (237ml) of the whipped cream, and spread the whipped cream to a smooth layer using a long cake spatula. Top with a generous dollop of cherry compote, spread into an even layer, add another ½ cup (118ml) of whipped cream, and spread that into a smooth layer, too. Top with the second layer of cake, repeat the layers, and then cover with the third layer of cake and brush with the compote syrup.
13. Spread the top and sides of the cake with whipped cream so they're covered with an even ½-inch (1.25cm) layer of cream, starting with the top, then the sides, then the top again, dragging the cream from the outside to the center. (You may find it easier to use a wide spatula for this.)
14. Slide a thin, wide spatula under the base of the cake, and transfer it to a serving plate or cake stand.
15. Using a small knife, cut the garnish cherries in half as directed in step 1, and decorate the sides of the cake in your choice of pattern. Dust the top with grated chocolate, and garnish with a single cherry before cutting and serving.
16. Store any leftovers in the refrigerator for up to 3 days.

Notes

You can also make the cherry compote the day before you make the cake.

Step 3 is important. Be sure to preheat the oven and line the cake pan with parchment paper before moving on to the next step.

You can bring eggs cold from the refrigerator to room temperature quickly by soaking them in warm water for about 10 minutes.

Also, if you want to make the cake a day ahead, you can store it in a plastic bag until ready to use: When the internal temperature of the baked cake has cooled to 100°F (38°C), place it in a plastic bag, seal the bag, and store the cake at room temperature. The cake will still be moist the next day.

Whipped Ganache Cake

PREP TIME: 50 minutes and 3 hours to cool • **COOK TIME:** 45 minutes • **MAKES:** 1 (9-inch or 23 cm) cake

This cake is a true celebration of rich flavors. The soft, moist chocolate cake soaks up the deep, aromatic rum syrup, creating a wonderfully balanced taste. The whipped ganache cream wraps the cake in a velvety smoothness, adding a creamy and satisfying texture. The pistachios bring a delightful crunch and savory flavor that perfectly complement the chocolate, creating a beautiful harmony in every bite. A light dusting of cocoa powder finishes it off. The combination of chocolate and pistachio makes each bite indulgent and satisfying, and after a few hours in the refrigerator, the flavors truly come together for a memorable treat.

GANACHE CREAM

2 cups (340g) semisweet chocolate chips

2½ cups (591ml) heavy cream

½ tsp (2.5g) kosher salt

1 cup (237ml) cold heavy cream

CHOCOLATE CAKE

180g cake flour

½ cup (50g) unsweetened cocoa powder

1 tsp (2g) ground cinnamon

6 large eggs

⅓ cup (65g) sugar

½ cup (118ml) sweetened condensed milk

½ tsp (2.5g) kosher salt

½ tsp (2.5ml) vanilla extract

⅓ cup (76g) unsalted butter, melted

⅔ cup (158ml) whole milk

RUM SYRUP

3 tbsp (36g) sugar

¼ cup (59ml) warm water

½ tsp (1g) ground cinnamon

2 tbsp (30ml) spiced rum

DECORATION

1 milk chocolate bar

1 cup (150g) shelled pistachios, chopped

¼ cup (25g) unsweetened cocoa powder

SPECIAL EQUIPMENT

Thermometer

Stand mixer or handheld electric mixer

1. To make the ganache cream, place the chocolate chips in a heatproof bowl and melt in the microwave in 30-second intervals (this should take about three times) until the chocolate reaches 104°F (40°C), stirring the chocolate evenly for 1 minute between each interval to melt it.
2. Place the heavy cream in a heatproof bowl, and microwave it for 1 or 2 minutes until it reaches 104°F (40°C). Pour it into the melted chocolate, add the salt, and stir, starting in the middle, to combine.
3. Pour the ganache into a large bowl, and gradually whisk in the cold heavy cream until well combined. Cover the chocolate mixture tightly with plastic wrap, and set in the refrigerator for at least 3 hours.
4. Preheat the oven to 350°F (180°C). Line a 9-inch (23cm) round cake pan with parchment paper.
5. To make the cake, sift together the flour, cocoa powder, and cinnamon in a large bowl, and mix by hand until light brown.
6. Separate the eggs, and place the yolks in a medium bowl and the whites in a large bowl or in the bowl of a stand mixer.
7. Add the sugar to the egg whites and beat with the stand mixer or a handheld electric mixer on low, gradually increasing the speed to high to make a stiff meringue, about 3 to 5 minutes. Set aside.
8. Add the condensed milk, salt, vanilla extract, and melted butter to the egg yolks, and whisk well.
9. Microwave the whole milk in a heatproof bowl for about 1 minute or until it reaches 122°F (50°C). Add it to the egg yolk mixture and whisk well. (Be sure the temperature of the warmed milk does not exceed 140°F/60°C).
10. Add the sifted flour mixture to the egg yolk mixture in two batches, mixing well with a whisk after each addition. Add about 2 cups (80g) of the meringue in two batches, mixing thoroughly with the flour mixture after each addition. Pour all the flour mixture into the meringue bowl, and fold with a spatula to mix gently but thoroughly until just combined.
11. Pour the batter into the prepared cake pan. Holding the pan about 10 inches (25.5cm) high, drop the pan onto a work surface two or three times to release any air pockets.
12. Bake for 15 minutes. Reduce the oven temperature to 340°F (170°C), and bake for another 20 minutes. The cake is done when a toothpick inserted in the center comes out clean. Drop the cake pan onto a work surface one more time to let the steam escape. Set a wire rack on top of the cake pan, hold the rack and the pan together, and invert. Remove the cake pan, and let the cake cool on the rack until its internal temperature is about 100°F (38°C). (If you're not assembling the cake until later, you can store it in a plastic bag when its temperature reaches 100°F/38°C. Be sure to press out all the air from the bag.)
13. Heat the broiler to 500°F (260°C).

14. To make the rum syrup, whisk together the sugar, warm water, and cinnamon in a small bowl until the sugar dissolves. Add the rum, whisk well, and set aside.

15. Remove the ganache from the refrigerator. Whip until soft peaks form, and set aside.

16. Remove the parchment paper from the cake. Place about 1 tablespoon (12.5g) of the ganache cream in the center of a rotating cake stand, set the cake on top, and use a long, serrated knife to cut the cake into three even layers. (For a very delicate texture of the finished cake, you can remove the top and bottom crusts from the cake before slicing into layers.) Using a pastry brush, brush the entire surface of the first layer with the rum syrup. Cover with about 1½ cups (300g) of the ganache cream, and spread it to a smooth layer using a long cake spatula. (The flattened cream should be about ½ inch/1.25cm high.) Top with the second layer of cake, and cover with ganache cream, working in small batches so the top and sides of the cake are covered with a consistent ½ inch (1.25cm) of cream. (You may find it easier to use a straight, wide dough scraper.) Coat the sides of the cake with the ganache cream.

17. Place the top layer of the cake on a baking sheet, drizzle lightly with more rum syrup, and top with the chocolate bar. Broil for about 30 seconds to 1 minute to slightly melt the chocolate bar. Remove the cake from the oven and use a wide spatula to transfer the cake to the top of the two frosted layers.

18. Using your hands, coat the sides of the cake evenly with the pistachios. Dust the top evenly with cocoa powder, and serve. Store any leftovers in an airtight container in the refrigerator for up to 3 days.

Strawberry Jelly Cake

PREP TIME: 20 minutes plus 5 hours to cool • **COOK TIME:** 2 minutes • **MAKES:** 1 Jelly Cake

Making this cake felt like creating a little work of art. The combination of fresh strawberries and creamy sweet jelly turned out to be even more delicious than I imagined. The soft texture of the jelly and the refreshing sweetness of the strawberries create a delightful experience with every bite. The process of making it is so much fun, especially as you layer the ingredients and watch the cake come together. A helpful tip is to gently warm the mold, just enough so the jelly doesn't melt too much. This way, the sweet and creamy jelly cake will come out beautifully, with a perfect finish.

1½ lb (681g) fresh strawberries

1 tbsp (15ml) white vinegar

3 (1 oz/22.5g) pouches unflavored powdered gelatin

2½ cups (591ml) whole milk

1½ cups (355ml) sweetened condensed milk

SPECIAL EQUIPMENT

6-inch (15cm) pan or gelatin mold

1. Place the strawberries in a large bowl. Cover with water, add the vinegar, and let sit for 3 minutes. Drain the berries in a colander and rinse them once under running water. Drain again.
2. Place a 6-inch (15cm) pan or gelatin mold on a work surface. Cut 3 or 4 of the strawberries into slices ⅛ inch (3mm) thick, near the stem end to get the largest circle possible, until you have 10 to 12 slices. Place the strawberry slices in a circle around the inside edge the pan, so the slices bend along the edge of the pan. (Try to arrange the slices in a pretty design because these will be the decoration on the top edge of the cake when it's removed from the pan.)
3. Cut a third of the remaining strawberries into ¾-inch (2cm) cubes. Cut another third of the strawberries into ½-inch (1.25cm) cubes. Cut the remaining strawberries into ¼-inch (0.5cm) cubes. Fill the center of the bottom of the pan with half of the ¼-inch strawberries, then add all the ¾-inch strawberries, flattening them, followed by all the ½-inch strawberries, then the remaining half of the ¼-inch strawberries, flattening them, too.
4. Add the gelatin to a large bowl and pour in ½ cup (118ml) of the whole milk. Mix well, and let sit for about 5 minutes.
5. Warm the remaining whole milk in a heatproof bowl in the microwave for 2 minutes. Pour the warm milk over the gelatin mixture, and mix well. Add the condensed milk, and stir until combined.
6. Using a ladle, pour the milk mixture over the strawberries in the pan in small portions. Cover with plastic wrap, and refrigerate for at least 4 hours.
7. Fill a bowl with hot water. Remove the pan from the refrigerator, dip the pan into the hot water for about 10 seconds to loosen the jelly cake from the pan, and then remove the pan from the hot water. Turn the pan from side to side to see if the jelly cake slides around. If it doesn't, put it back in the water for 5 or 10 seconds more.
8. Place a plate or cake stand over the pan, hold the pan and plate together, and invert both to allow the jelly cake to come out of the pan. If it doesn't come out, dip the pot in the hot water for another 5 seconds or so and try again.
9. Soak up any melted gelatin with paper towels, clean the plate, and return the jelly cake to the refrigerator to chill for at least 1 hour.
10. To cut the jelly cake, dip a sharp knife in hot water for about 2 minutes, wipe it dry with a towel, and cut the cake cleanly. Serve cool.

Mini Pistachio Baklava Cakes

with Lemon Diplomat Cream

PREP TIME: 50 minutes plus 2 hours 30 minutes to cool • **COOK TIME:** 30 minutes • **MAKES:** 6 cakes

Some desserts take you by surprise with their delightful contrast of textures and flavors. This is one of them. Delicate, buttery phyllo pastry is layered to crispy perfection and infused with the nutty richness of pistachios and a hint of bright lemon zest. Between those golden, flaky layers is a smooth and airy lemon diplomat cream that melts on your tongue, adding just the right touch of citrusy freshness. It's like a classic baklava meets a refined French pastry—unexpected yet perfectly harmonious. Serve it in a clear glass to showcase the beautiful layers, and just before taking a bite, squeeze a little fresh lemon juice on top. The balance of crisp and creamy with sweet and tangy makes every spoonful worth savoring.

DIPLOMAT CREAM

- 1 vanilla bean, or 1 tsp (5ml) vanilla extract
- 2 cups (473ml) whole milk
- 6 egg yolks
- ½ cup (100g) sugar
- ¼ tsp (1.25g) kosher salt
- 5 tbsp (50g) cornstarch
- 3 tbsp (43g) unsalted butter, cubed, at room temperature
- 1 cup (237ml) heavy cream
- 2 tsp (10ml) lemon juice
- 6 lemon wedges

PISTACHIO BAKLAVA

- 1 cup (150g) coarsely chopped pistachios
- ½ tsp (2.5g) kosher salt
- ½ cup (50g) confectioners' sugar
- 1 tbsp (6g) lemon zest
- 1¼ cups (283g) melted unsalted butter or ghee
- 1 lb (454g) frozen phyllo pastry (19 sheets), thawed

SPECIAL EQUIPMENT

- 4-inch (10cm) round cookie or biscuit cutter

Note

When brushing the phyllo pastry with the melted butter, dip the brush only slightly into the butter to use just the ghee that's floating at the top. (The butter solids will fall to the bottom.)

1. Cut the vanilla bean in half, split open the skin, and use the back of a knife to scrape out the vanilla beans. Add the beans and skins to a heatproof medium bowl. Pour in the milk, microwave on high for 2 or 3 minutes, and stir. Pour the milk through a sieve into another medium bowl. Discard the solids.
2. Whisk together the egg yolks, sugar, salt, and cornstarch in a medium saucepan until well combined, about 3 minutes. Gradually add the milk mixture to the egg mixture, whisking constantly to combine. Set the saucepan over medium-low heat, and cook, whisking constantly, until the mixture is thick, about 7 to 8 minutes.
3. Remove from the heat and add the butter, stirring until completely mixed.
4. Transfer the mixture to a large bowl, and allow it to cool slightly. Cover tightly with plastic wrap to prevent air pockets, and set in the refrigerator for about 2 hours.
5. Pour the heavy cream into a large, deep bowl, and beat with an electric mixer fitted with a whisk attachment on low, gradually increasing the speed to high, until stiff peaks form, about 3 minutes.
6. Remove the milk mixture from the refrigerator, beat with an electric mixer fitted with a whisk attachment on low, gradually increasing the speed to high, until soft peaks form, and add the whipped cream. Add the lemon juice and fold in. Cover the cream tightly with plastic wrap, and return to the refrigerator until ready to use.
7. To make the pistachio baklava, use a wooden spoon to combine the pistachios, salt, confectioners' sugar, and lemon zest in a small bowl. Add 3 tablespoons (45ml) of the melted butter, and mix well. Set aside.
8. Preheat the oven to 370°F (187°C).
9. Line a work surface with a piece of parchment paper that's about the size of a baking sheet. Unroll 1 sheet of the pastry, brush it with the melted butter, and spread it thinly. Sprinkle about 2 tablespoons (13g) of the pistachio mixture over the pastry. Cover with another sheet of pastry, and press down lightly. Repeat for a total of 19 buttered layers. (Be sure to butter the edges, too, so they don't dry out and crumble.)
10. Using a 4-inch (10cm) round cookie or biscuit cutter, cut out 12 circles from the dough. Set a baking sheet horizontally at the edge of your work surface, and carefully slide the parchment paper containing the baklava onto the baking sheet.
11. Bake for about 20 minutes, or until evenly golden brown. (If there is a lot of color variation between the edges and the center of the baklava, cover the partially browned areas with foil and bake for 2 or 3 minutes more.) Transfer the baklava to a rack and allow to cool completely, about 30 minutes.
12. In each of six glass dishes that are 4 inches (10cm) wide, add a layer of the baklava on the bottom, top with about ⅓ cup (85g) of the cream mixture, followed by another layer of the baklava, and finally another ⅓ cup (85g) of the cream mixture. Garnish with lemon slices and some pistachios, and serve, squeezing the lemon wedges over the top just before eating.

Carrot Loaf Cake

PREP TIME: 50 minutes • **COOK TIME:** 45 minutes • **MAKES:** 1 (9 × 5-inch [23 × 13cm]) loaf cake (12 servings)

This delightful twist on classic carrot cake brings a touch of whimsy with hidden cream cheese "carrots" nestled inside. The cake is moist and rich, with a medley of warm spices, toasted nuts, and bursts of dried fruit. Each slice reveals a soft, spiced crumb with a garden-inspired surprise: carrot-shaped cream cheese frosting in the cake's center. A dusting of cocoa powder mimics soil, while fresh herbs add the finishing touch of green carrot tops. Perfect for special occasions or an everyday treat, this cake is as fun to make as it is to eat.

CARROT CAKE

¼ cup (40g) raisins
⅓ cup (40g) dried cranberries
¼ cup (59ml) boiling water
1 tbsp (15ml) gold rum
1 cup (100g) walnut halves
⅓ cup (40g) pumpkin seeds
⅔ cup (110g) pineapple chunks
2 cups (220g) grated carrot
400g all-purpose flour
1 tsp (2.6g) ground cinnamon
1½ tsp (7.5g) baking powder
4 large eggs
½ tsp (2.5g) kosher salt
¾ cup (150g) granulated sugar
⅔ cup (158ml) vegetable oil, plus more for greasing
Fresh herbs, for garnish

CREAM CHEESE FROSTING

1 cup (225g) cream cheese, at room temperature
½ cup (113g) unsalted butter, at room temperature
½ cup (118ml) heavy cream
⅓ cup (55g) confectioners' sugar
1 tsp (5ml) pure vanilla extract
¼ tsp (1.25g) kosher salt
2 or 3 drops of red and yellow food coloring
1 tbsp (7g) black or regular cocoa powder, plus more for garnish

SPECIAL EQUIPMENT

Handheld electric mixer
Five small stainless-steel horn molds, brushed with oil
Pie weights
Two pastry bags, one with a basket weave tip attached

1. Preheat the oven to 350°F (175°C). Line a 9 × 5-inch (23 × 13cm) loaf pan with parchment paper.
2. Combine the raisins and cranberries in a small heatproof bowl. Pour the boiling water into the bowl, stir, and let sit for 1 to 2 minutes. Strain the fruit and return it to the bowl. Add the rum, and set aside.
3. Spread the walnuts and pumpkin seeds on a baking sheet, and toast in the oven for 5 to 10 minutes, until golden brown. Remove from the oven and allow to cool slightly.
4. Transfer the toasted nuts and seeds to a cutting board, and chop. Add the raisins, cranberries, and pineapple chunks to the cutting board and chop everything evenly.
5. Transfer the fruit, nuts, and seeds to a large bowl. Add the carrot. Sift in the flour, cinnamon, and baking powder, and toss with a wooden spoon to coat the chopped ingredients in the flour mixture.
6. Beat the eggs and salt in a medium bowl using a handheld electric mixer. With the mixer on medium-high, slowly add the granulated sugar, and beat until the sugar is dissolved and the mixture is foamy, about 7 minutes. Continue mixing and slowly pour in the oil, mixing until combined.
7. Add half of the flour mixture, mix until combined, and then add the remaining flour mixture and mix until just combined (be careful not to overmix). Pour the batter into the prepared loaf pan, and smooth the top.
8. Press the oiled horn molds deep into the batter until the tips touch the bottom of the pan. Place some pie weights in the horn molds to prevent them from rising as the cake bakes.
9. Bake for about 40 to 50 minutes.
10. Meanwhile, to make the cream cheese frosting, mix together the cream cheese and butter in a large bowl, scraping down the sides of the bowl as needed, until no lumps remain.
11. Using a handheld electric mixer, beat the heavy cream, confectioners' sugar, vanilla, and salt in another large bowl until stiff peaks form.
12. Add the cream mixture to the cream cheese mixture in two batches, mixing well after each addition.
13. Transfer half of the frosting to the empty bowl, add 2 or 3 drops of red and yellow food coloring, and mix well until the frosting is orange. Add the cocoa powder to the other half of the frosting to tint it brown. Attach a basket weave tip to a pastry bag, and transfer the brown frosting to the pastry bag. Place the orange frosting in a pastry bag without a tip. Place both bags in the refrigerator.
14. Test the cake for doneness by inserting a skewer into the center of the cake. When it comes out clean, remove from the oven and transfer the cake to a wire rack to cool completely.

15. Once cool, place the cake on a platter, remove the horn molds, and dust the entire top with cocoa powder to represent soil. Fill the empty spaces left by the horn molds with the orange frosting, and decorate the ends with herbs to represent the carrot leaves. Pipe the brown frosting on the outside of the cake to represent the garden bed. Cut into slices to show the "carrots" inside, and serve. Store any leftovers in an airtight container in the refrigerator for up to 3 days.

Note

To make mini cakes, instead of a loaf pan use muffin tins lined with tulip liners. Add the horn molds filled with pie weights, and bake for about 25 minutes. Decorate as directed.

Chocolate Loaf Cake

PREP TIME: 30 minutes • **COOK TIME:** 55 minutes • **MAKES:** 1 loaf cake

This indulgent loaf cake is a decadent treat that's perfect for chocolate lovers. With a combination of rich cocoa and a hint of spice, it's a delightful dessert or snack any time of day. Serve it warm with melted chocolate for a gooey experience, or let it cool for a firmer texture. Fresh berries and a pistachio cream add a burst of flavor and color.

PISTACHIO CREAM

2 tbsp (20g) pistachios, shelled
2 tbsp (20g) semisweet chocolate chips
1¼ cups (296ml) cold heavy cream
¼ cup (25g) confectioners' sugar
⅛ tsp (0.6g) kosher salt

TOPPING

⅔ cup (85g) fresh blueberries
⅔ cup (85g) fresh raspberries
3 or 4 sprigs of mint
1 tbsp (15ml) white vinegar

CHOCOLATE LOAF CAKE

1 tbsp (14g) plus ¾ cup (170g) unsalted butter, at room temperature
120g cake flour
¾ cup (60g) cocoa powder
1 tsp (2g) freshly grated nutmeg
½ tsp (1.3g) ground cinnamon
½ tsp (2.4g) baking powder
¼ tsp (1.25g) kosher salt
1 cup (200g) granulated sugar
3 large eggs
½ cup (120g) sour cream
Your favorite chocolate bar (7 oz/200g)

SPECIAL EQUIPMENT

Mortar and pestle or food processor
Handheld electric mixer

Note

The chocolate topping will be soft on the day the cake is baked but will harden over time, adding a nice, crunchy texture to the cake.

1. Crush the pistachios and chocolate chips in a mortar and pestle or a food processor.
2. Combine the heavy cream, confectioners' sugar, and salt in a medium bowl, and whisk until firm. Add the chopped pistachios and chocolate chips, and mix well with a spatula. Cover with plastic wrap and set in the refrigerator.
3. Combine the blueberries, raspberries, and mint in a small bowl. Add enough water to cover, along with the vinegar, and let sit for 3 minutes. Transfer the berries and mint to a colander, and rinse under running water. Transfer to paper towels, and set aside.
4. Preheat the oven to 350°F (180°C). Grease a 6-cup (1.5-liter; 10¼ × 6 × 3-inch/ 26 × 15 × 7.5cm) loaf pan evenly with 1 tablespoon (14g) of butter.
5. Sift together the flour, cocoa powder, nutmeg, cinnamon, and baking powder in a medium bowl. Add the salt, and whisk to combine. Set aside.
6. Using a handheld electric mixer, whisk the remaining ¾ cup (170g) softened butter in another medium bowl until smooth. Add the granulated sugar in two batches, beating after each addition until the butter and sugar are evenly distributed and the color has lightened slightly, about 5 minutes.
7. Add the eggs, one at a time, and beat until the butter and eggs are light and fluffy, about 5 or 6 minutes. Add the sour cream, and mix with a spatula.
8. Add the flour mixture in two or three batches, mixing after each batch. (Be careful not to overmix.)
9. Pour the batter into the prepared loaf pan, and smooth the top with a spatula. Set the pan on a baking sheet, and bake for 50 minutes, or until a toothpick inserted in the center of the loaf comes out clean.
10. Turn off the oven. Remove the pan from the oven, remove the loaf from the pan, and transfer the loaf to a wire rack. Place the chocolate bar to the top of the cake and return the loaf to the oven until the chocolate bar is melted and bends at the ends, about 3 to 5 minutes. Remove the loaf from the oven and allow to cool completely.
11. Slice the loaf. Spread with the pistachio cream; garnish with the blueberries, raspberries, and mint; and serve. Store any leftover cake in an airtight container at room temperature for up to 3 days. Store any leftover pistachio cream, berries, and mint in airtight containers in the refrigerator for up to 3 days.

CHAPTER 10

Desserts

Peach Cookies

PREP TIME: 25 minutes plus 30 minutes to rest • **COOK TIME:** 12 minutes • **MAKES:** 15 medium or 20 small cookies

Peach cookies are a beloved Italian treat, often made for special celebrations and family gatherings. They may look like real peaches, but inside, they're soft, buttery, and filled with rich chocolate. The bright citrus zest, smooth chocolate, and a hint of anise create a flavor combination that's both comforting and delightfully unexpected. Rolling them in tinted syrup and sugar gives them a peachy glow, making them as beautiful as they are delicious. With just one bite, you'll feel like you've stepped into a cozy Italian bakery, where every sweet is made with love. Serve them with coffee or dessert wine, and watch them disappear in no time!

DOUGH

360g all-purpose flour, plus more for dusting
1 tbsp (14g) baking powder
¼ tsp (1.25g) kosher salt
2 large eggs
¾ cup (150g) sugar
⅔ cup (151g) unsalted butter, melted
½ cup (118ml) whole milk
Zest of 1 lemon

CHOCOLATE FILLING

½ cup (48g) almond flour
1 tbsp (6g) unsweetened cocoa powder
½ tsp (1g) ground nutmeg
¼ tsp (1.25g) kosher salt
1 cup (170g) semisweet chocolate chips
⅓ cup (79ml) heavy cream
2 tbsp (30ml) corn syrup

DECORATION

2 tbsp (30ml) fresh lemon juice
2 tbsp (30ml) anise liquor
¼ tsp (1.25ml) red food coloring
1 tsp (5ml) yellow food coloring
1 cup (200g) sugar, for coating
Grissini, broken into 1-inch (2.5cm) pieces
Fresh mint leaves

SPECIAL EQUIPMENT

Melon baller
Thermometer

Note

These beautiful cookies are perfect for gift-giving. Package them in a see-through box, and watch your recipient's face light up when they see them!

1. To make the dough, sift together the flour and baking powder in a small bowl. Add the salt, and mix evenly by hand.
2. Beat the eggs in a large bowl. Add the sugar and mix well. Add the melted butter, milk, and lemon zest. Add the flour mixture and mix evenly with a wooden spatula.
3. Turn out the dough onto a generously floured work surface, fold in the dough with a scraper, press down with your hands, and knead for about 5 minutes. When the dough no longer sticks to your hands, return it to the bowl and set it in the refrigerator for 30 minutes.
4. Preheat the oven to 350°F (180°C). Line a baking sheet with parchment paper.
5. Remove the dough from the refrigerator. Pinch off portions of the dough, form into balls about 1 to 1½ inches (2.5 to 3.75cm) in diameter, and place them on the prepared baking sheet. Forming 1-inch (2.5cm) balls will yield about 40 balls, or enough for 20 small cookies; forming 1½-inch (3.75cm) balls will yield about 30 balls, or enough for 15 medium cookies.
6. Bake for 12 minutes, or until they are golden brown on the bottom but not on top. Remove from the oven, and allow to cool completely.
7. Using a melon baller, scoop out the centers of the flat sides of the cookies and add to a medium bowl. Roll and crush the scooped-out cookie centers with your hands to make a fine crumble. Add the almond flour, cocoa powder, nutmeg, and salt to the cookie crumbs, and mix well by hand.
8. Place the chocolate chips in a heatproof bowl, and microwave in 30-second intervals to melt, stirring the chocolate chips from the bottom each time and using the residual heat from the bowl to melt the chocolate. It should take about two or three 30-second intervals to melt them all.
9. Microwave the heavy cream in another heatproof bowl for 30 to 40 seconds to warm it to about 100°F (38°C). Pour the cream into the melted chocolate, add the corn syrup, and mix well. Add the chocolate mixture to the cookie crumbs, and mix well.
10. Fill the hollows of two cookies with chocolate filling, flatten out the filling, and "glue" the bottoms together to form a single cookie. Repeat with the remaining cookies.
11. To make the decoration, add ½ cup (118ml) of water, 1 tablespoon (15ml) of fresh lemon juice, and 1 tablespoon (15ml) of anise liquor to each of two small bowls. To one bowl, add the red food coloring. To the other bowl, add the yellow food coloring. Stir both well to combine.
12. Pour the sugar into a medium bowl.
13. Roll the cookies in the red dye first, about 60 to 70 percent covered, and then

roll the rest of the cookie in the yellow dye to create the varied coloration of real peaches.

14. Immediately place the cookie in the bowl of sugar, and roll to lightly coat. Garnish with a piece of broken grissini for a stem and some mint leaves. Repeat with the remaining cookies, and serve. Store any leftover cookies in a loosely covered (not airtight) or paper container at room temperature for up to 3 days. (Storing them in an airtight container may cause the sugar to dissolve.)

Koesisters

(Spiced Doughnuts)

PREP TIME: 20 minutes plus 1 hour to rise • **COOK TIME:** 40 minutes • **MAKES:** 32 doughnuts

A classic Cape Malay treat from South Africa, these spiced doughnuts are a delight, bursting with warm, fragrant spices like cinnamon, ginger, cardamom, and anise. The dough is enriched with a touch of orange zest and a hint of sweetness, and after frying, it's soaked in a spiced syrup and coated in shredded coconut, making each bite a journey of taste and texture. Koesisters are wonderful for breakfast with coffee.

DOUGH

½ tbsp (4g) ground cinnamon
1 tsp (1g) ground ginger
1 tsp (1g) ground anise
½ tsp (0.5g) ground cardamom
½ tsp (3g) orange zest
1 cup (237ml) whole milk
⅓ cup (65g) sugar, divided
2¼ tsp (7g) active dry yeast
1 small yellow potato, peeled
1 large egg, room temperature
1 tbsp (14g) unsalted butter, room temperature
¼ tsp (1.25g) kosher salt
300g all-purpose flour, plus more for dusting
½ tsp (2.4g) baking powder
¼ cup (59ml) vegetable oil
Canola oil, for frying

SYRUP

1 cup (100g) sugar
2 cinnamon sticks
Peel of ½ orange
6 cardamom pods, or ½ tsp (1g) ground cardamom
½ cup (50g) shredded coconut

SPECIAL EQUIPMENT

Handheld electric mixer
Deep-fry thermometer

1. Make the dough: Stir together the cinnamon, ginger, anise, cardamom, and orange zest in a small bowl. Set aside.
2. Warm the milk in the microwave for 15 seconds and then add 1 tablespoon (7.5g) of sugar and the yeast and stir well with a wooden spoon. Cover with a tea towel, and let sit until bubbles appear, about 10 minutes.
3. Meanwhile, fill a small saucepan with enough water to cover the potato. Add the potato, and bring to a boil over high heat. Boil until fork-tender, 15 to 20 minutes.
4. Drain, transfer to a medium bowl, and mash with a fork. Add the remaining sugar, and the egg, butter, and salt, and blend with a handheld electric mixer set to high until smooth, about 3 minutes.
5. Sift the flour and baking powder into the potato mixture, add the yeast mixture, and mix well with a wooden spatula. Cover with a tea towel, and let rise until doubled in size, about 1 hour.
6. Lightly coat a large plate or baking pan with vegetable oil, and set aside.
7. Turn out the dough onto a lightly floured work surface. The dough will be very sticky. Use a scraper to cut the dough into strips 2 inches (5cm) long and then cut the strips into 1½-inch (3.75cm) pieces. Use your hands to shape the pieces into balls about the size of a small egg, and place on the prepared plate or baking pan. Keep the balls covered while you shape the rest of the dough.
8. Heat a large, deep skillet over medium-high heat. Add 3 inches (7.5cm) of canola oil, and heat to 345°F (175°C).
9. Meanwhile, to prepare the syrup, add the sugar, 1 cup (237ml) of water, the cinnamon sticks, orange peel, and cardamom pods to a medium saucepan, and set over medium heat. Cook, stirring, until thickened, 10 to 15 minutes. Turn off the heat, but leave the pot on the stove to keep it warm. (When hot donuts meet warm syrup, the donuts absorb the syrup well.)
10. When the oil is hot, grease your hands again, pick up a ball of dough, stretch it two or three times into an oval, and carefully place it in the oil. Working in batches, fry about 10 balls at a time. When the dough is puffed and plump and the side that has been in contact with the oil is golden, turn it over. Fry until the doughnuts are golden brown, about 3 to 5 minutes. Transfer the doughnuts to a paper towel-lined plate, and repeat with the remaining balls.
11. Roll the fried dough in the warm sugar syrup, taking care to ensure each is evenly coated on all sides. Place the coconut in a shallow bowl. Roll the syrup-soaked doughnuts in shredded coconut to coat, and serve, either warm or cooled, with extra shredded coconut sprinkled on top. Store any leftovers in an airtight container at room temperature for up to 3 days or in the freezer for 1 month. Defrost at room temperature, and reheat in the microwave for 10 to 15 seconds.

Pineapple Cupcakes
with Sweet Coconut Cream

PREP TIME: 25 minutes plus 1 day to dry • **COOK TIME:** 3 hours 25 minutes • **MAKES:** 12 medium or 20 small cupcakes

There's something magical about the way a pineapple transforms into a delicate, sun-kissed flower when dried—its golden flesh bursting with tropical sweetness. As I sliced the pineapple for this recipe as thinly as possible and arranged the pieces to dry, I couldn't help but marvel at how nature had already designed them to bloom. The core, once the heart of the fruit, remained at the center, just like a real flower. These pineapple cupcakes capture that same beauty—light, airy cake infused with bright pineapple and a touch of lemon all crowned with a cloud of coconut cream. The dried pineapple flowers rest on top like nature's own delicate decoration. Each cupcake is a small, edible celebration of transformation, where simple ingredients come together to create something extraordinary.

PINEAPPLE DRIED FLOWER AND PUREE

1 golden pineapple

¼ cup (50g) sugar

SWEET COCONUT CREAM

2 cups (200g) shredded sweetened coconut

3 cups (710ml) cold heavy cream

⅓ cup (65g) sugar

¼ tsp (1.25g) kosher salt

PINEAPPLE CUPCAKES

6 large eggs

¼ cup (50g) sugar

⅓ cup (76g) unsalted butter, melted

½ tsp (2.5g) kosher salt

1 tsp (4.8g) baking powder

⅓ cup (79ml) sweetened condensed milk

2 tbsp (30ml) lemon juice

About 2 cups (473ml) pineapple puree, divided

½ tsp (2.5ml) vanilla extract

150g cake flour, sifted

Note

If you're not decorating and serving the cupcakes right away, place them in a ziplock bag or airtight container to retain moisture. The cupcakes should be topped with the cream just before serving. The cupcakes will keep for up to 3 days at room temperature in an airtight container,. The cream will keep for about 3 days in the refrigerator.

1. Peel the pineapple with a knife, and cut it in half at the widest middle part to get the largest circle for the pineapple flowers. Slice the pineapple as thinly as possible into 12 slices. Place the slices on a wire rack, set the rack on a baking sheet, and place in the oven. Heat the oven to 175°F (80°C), and dry the pineapple for 1 hour and 30 minutes. Open the oven to release the moisture. Dry for about 1 hour and 30 minutes more or until the pineapple dries and shrinks to the thickness of thick paper and the center of the pineapple looks like the stamens of a flower. Remove the pineapple from the oven and dry at room temperature for an additional 1 to 2 days to make dried pineapple flowers. (You can also use a food dehydrator for this.)
2. Place the remaining pineapple in a blender with the sugar, and blend until pureed. Transfer to an airtight container and store in the refrigerator until ready to use.
3. To make the sweet coconut cream, add the shredded coconut to a food processor and pulse until like coarse sand.
4. Combine the cold heavy cream, sugar, salt, and 1 cup of the coconut flour in a large bowl, and whip with a handheld electric mixer until stiff, about 5 minutes. Transfer to an airtight container, and set in the refrigerator to cool.
5. To make the pineapple cupcakes, preheat the oven to 350°F (180°C). Line a 12-cup muffin tin with tulip-shaped sheets of parchment paper.
6. Place a medium bowl and the clean, dry bowl of a stand mixer on a work surface. Crack the eggs, placing the yolks in the medium bowl and the whites in the stand mixer bowl. Add the sugar to the whites, and beat with the mixer on high until stiff peaks form, about 3 or 4 minutes.
7. Add the melted butter, salt, baking powder, condensed milk, lemon juice, ½ cup pineapple puree, and vanilla to the egg yolks, and whisk until well combined. Add the remaining processed coconut in two or three batches and mix until well combined.
8. Add about 2 cups (80g) of the meringue to the flour mixture in two batches and mix well. Add all of the flour mixture to the meringue and fold to combine the meringue and flour mixture. Evenly divide the batter among the 12 muffin cups using an ice-cream scoop.
9. Bake for 15 minutes. Reduce the oven temperature to 340°F (170°C), and bake for another 10 minutes. Check for doneness by poking a cupcake with a toothpick about 5 minutes before they're due to come out of the oven. The cupcakes are done when the toothpick comes out clean. Remove from the oven, transfer to a wire rack, and cool to an internal temperature of 100°F (38°C).
10. Using a large ice-cream scoop, add a generous scoop of the coconut cream to each cupcake.
11. Transfer the pineapple puree to a piping bag, and pipe about 2 tablespoons (30ml) into the center of the coconut cream on each cupcake. Sprinkle the remaining coconut flour on top, garnish each with a dried pineapple flower, and serve.

Red Pear Chocolate Turnovers

PREP TIME: 40 minutes plus 1 hour 50 minutes to rest • **COOK TIME:** 40 minutes • **MAKES:** 13 or 14 turnovers

These turnovers are a delightful fusion of buttery, flaky pastry and a rich, fruity filling. The sweet red pears, caramelized with brown sugar and cocoa, create a uscious contrast to the crisp pastry. A splash of rum adds a touch of warmth and sophistication. Imagine savoring these turnovers on a cozy afternoon. A fruity aroma would fill the air and each bite would bring pure joy.

PASTRY

1 cup (227g) cold unsalted butter

200g cake flour

40g bread flour, plus more for dusting

2 tbsp (25g) granulated sugar

1 tsp (5g) kosher salt

6 tbsp (90ml) ice water

2 large egg yolks

RED PEAR CHOCOLATE FILLING

2 pears, peeled, cored, and chopped

2 tbsp (28g) unsalted butter

2 tbsp (26g) brown sugar

2 tbsp (12g) unsweet cocoa powder

1 tsp (5ml) rum

SPECIAL EQUIPMENT

Cheese grater

Round cutter

Note

If you are a chocolate person, you can drizzle melted chocolate over the cooled turnovers before serving.

1. Grate the butter into a small bowl, cover, and place in the freezer for 15 minutes.
2. Combine cake flour, bread flour, granulated sugar, salt, and grated butter in a medium bowl. Stir until the butter is evenly coated with the flour.
3. Using a measuring spoon, gradually add the ice water, 2 tablespoons (30ml) at a time, to the flour mixture, mixing well after every addition until a shaggy dough forms. Form the dough into a ball, wrap it in parchment paper, and place it in the refrigerator for 30 minutes.
4. Turn out the dough onto a floured work surface. Using a rolling pin, roll out the dough into an 8 × 12-inch (20 × 30.5cm) rectangle, dusting as you go so the dough does not stick to the rolling pin.
5. Brush off any excess flour. Fold the left third of the dough to the center and then fold the right third to the center, over the left side. Roll out the dough again to 8 × 12 inches (20 × 30.5cm), dusting with extra flour, as needed. Brush off any excess flour once again, and fold both sides toward the center again. Wrap in parchment paper, and set in the refrigerator for 30 minutes.
6. Roll out the dough to 8 × 12 inches (20 × 30.5cm) a third time. Fold both sides toward the center again. Wrap and refrigerate again for 30 minutes.
7. Roll out the dough to ½-inch (1.25cm) thick and then cut in half. Return one half to the refrigerator, and roll out the other half to about ⅛-inch (3mm) thick. Using a 4- or 5-inch (10 or 12.5cm) round cutter, cut out 6 circles of dough, place them on a parchment-lined baking sheet, and refrigerate for 20 minutes. Repeat with the remaining dough half. Collect the leftover dough scraps, roll out, and cut out 1 or 2 more pieces. Store in the refrigerator until ready to use.
8. Heat the pears, butter, brown sugar, cocoa powder, and rum in a medium saucepan over low heat. Cook until the moisture has evaporated, about 10 minutes. Remove from the heat.
9. Preheat the oven to 400°F (200°C). Line a baking sheet with parchment paper.
10. Place one piece of dough on the work surface. Using a rolling pin, gently roll from the center of the dough to the edges three or four times. Place 1 tablespoon (14g) of the pear filling in the center of the dough and then brush the edges with water. Fold the dough in half over the filling and seal the edges, using the water to adhere the dough rather than pinching or pressing it together. (If you pinch or press the edge, the butter layer will disappear.) Transfer to the prepared baking sheet, and repeat with the remaining dough pieces.
11. In a small bowl, beat the egg yolks until frothy. Brush the turnovers twice with the egg yolk. Use a fork to score a leaf design on top of the each turnover and then use a skewer, toothpick, or knife point to pierce a few vents holes on the folded edge of each turnover.
12. Bake for 15 minutes. Reduce the oven temperature to 375°F (190°C), and bake for 15 more minutes.
13. Serve warm.

Apple Tarte Tatin

PREP TIME: 20 minutes plus 3 hours 30 minutes to rest • **COOK TIME:** 2 hours • **SERVINGS:** 6

In this French-style Apple Tarte Tatin, tender, caramelized apples are balanced with a flaky, buttery crust. Each bite is a rich and comforting experience, with a hint of rum and cinnamon that adds depth to the sweet and tart flavors. Served with a scoop of vanilla ice cream, it's a taste of indulgence that brings back memories of cozy autumn days.

DOUGH

240g all-purpose flour, plus more for dusting

1 tbsp (7.5g) granulated sugar

1 tsp (5g) kosher salt

1 cup (227g) unsalted butter, cut into ½-inch (1.25cm) cubes and frozen for 15 minutes

½ cup (118ml) ice water

APPLE FILLING

¾ cup (170g) unsalted butter, at room temperature

½ cup (100g) dark brown sugar, firmly packed

½ tsp (2.5g) kosher salt

7 large red apples (about 3lb/1.35kg)

2 tbsp (30ml) gold rum

1 tbsp (15ml) lemon juice

1 tbsp (8g) ground cinnamon

SPECIAL EQUIPMENT

9½-inch (24cm) pie pan

Melon baller

1. Make the dough: Add the flour, granulated sugar, salt, and cold butter to a medium bowl, and roughly mix.
2. Pour the ice water evenly over the dough, allowing it to come together, and shape it into a flat square. (Work as quickly as possible to avoid melting the cold butter. Don't worry if you still see the chunks of butter in the dough.) Wrap the dough in parchment paper, and refrigerate for 1 hour.
3. Turn out the dough onto a floured work surface. Roll the dough into a 8 × 12-inch (20 × 30.5cm) rectangle. If the dough sticks to the work surface, dust with flour.
4. Fold one-third of each side of the dough toward the center, placing one on top of the other to make three layers (fold 1). Cover with parchment paper, and refrigerate for 1 hour.
5. Repeat Steps 3 and 4 two more times, refrigerating for 30 minutes each time (folds 2 and 3).
6. Once again, fold the dough on top of itself (fold 4), and then roll out the dough until it is ⅛-inch thick (3mm) and will fit in a 10-inch (25.5cm) square pan or a 9½-inch (24cm) pie pan.
7. Invert the pie pan over the dough, and cut the dough ¼-inch (6mm) wider than the pan. Wrap the dough in parchment paper, and refrigerate for at least 30 minutes.
8. Preheat the oven to 360°F (185°C).
9. Make the apple filling: Grease the bottom of the pie pan with the butter. Evenly sprinkle the brown sugar and salt over the butter.
10. Peel the apples, cut them in half, use a melon baller to scoop out the seeds, and remove the stems.
11. Place the halved apples upright in the pan, leaning them against the sides of the pan and working inward to fill the pan, taking care to press the apples down lightly into the butter.
12. Drizzle the rum and lemon juice over the apples, and sprinkle evenly with the ground cinnamon.
13. Bake for 1½ hours.
14. Remove the pan from the oven, and cover with the refrigerated pastry dough, using a spatula to tuck the edge of the dough into the pan around the apples. Poke the dough 4 or 5 times with a knife or fork. Bake for 30 minutes, or until golden brown.
15. Remove the pan from the oven. Invert a plate face down on top of the pan, and flip over the plate and the pan. Remove the pan.
16. Cut the tarte tatin into 6 slices, and serve.

Beignets

PREP TIME: 20 minutes plus 1 hour to rest • **COOK TIME:** 10 minutes • **MAKES:** 16 beignets

Beignets are a delightful treat that will transport you straight to New Orleans. Made with warm buttermilk and whole milk, these airy, French-style fried doughnuts have a light and fluffy texture and a subtle sweetness. A dusting of confectioners' sugar adds a classic finishing touch, and a drizzle of honey enhances their irresistible flavor. Beignets are perfect for breakfast or a sweet snack.

¾ cup (177ml) warm buttermilk
⅓ cup (79ml) warm whole milk
2¼ tsp (7g) active dry yeast
1 tbsp (12.5g) granulated sugar
300g bread flour, plus more for dusting
¼ tsp (1.5g) baking soda
¼ tsp (1.25g) kosher salt
2 qt (2 liters) canola oil, for frying
½ cup (58g) confectioners' sugar
¼ cup (59ml) honey

SPECIAL EQUIPMENT

Pastry cutter
Deep-fry thermometer

1. Combine the buttermilk, whole milk, yeast, and granulated sugar in a small bowl. Cover with a tea towel and let sit for 10 minutes or until foamy.
2. Whisk together the flour, baking soda, and salt in a large bowl.
3. Add the yeast mixture to the flour mixture, and mix, using a wooden spoon, for 5 minutes. Cover the bowl with a tea towel, and let the dough rise in a warm place until doubled in size, about 1 hour.
4. Line a baking sheet with parchment paper, and sprinkle the parchment paper with flour.
5. Turn out the dough onto a floured work surface. Press the dough and stretch it slightly with your hands to form a 9 × 9-inch (23 × 23cm) square about ½-inch (1.25cm) thick.
6. Using a pastry cutter or knife, cut the square into 4 strips lengthwise and 4 strips widthwise to create 16 equal-size pieces. Transfer the pieces to the prepared baking sheet.
7. Pour 2 inches (5cm) of oil into a large, heavy-bottomed skillet set over medium-high heat. Attach a deep-fry thermometer to the side of the skillet and bring the oil to 350°F (180°C).
8. Just before placing the dough into the oil, gently stretch each dough piece with both hands to form a rectangle. Place 5 or 6 pieces of dough in the skillet, and fry until golden brown on both sides, about 3 to 5 minutes. Transfer to a cooling rack, and repeat with the remaining pieces of dough. If the temperature starts to drop below 340°F (170°C), reduce the number of dough pieces you cook at a time.
9. Let cool slightly, about 5 minutes, then dust with confectioners' sugar and/or drizzle with honey, and serve.

Orange Custard Cream Éclairs

PREP TIME: 30 minutes • **COOK TIME:** 40 minutes • **MAKES:** 12 éclairs

There's something magical about the combination of citrus and chocolate, and these éclairs, filled with a luscious orange custard cream, capture that magic perfectly. While I was thinking about pairing chocolate and orange, I imagined how special it would be to fill an éclair with a tangy orange cream. The moment I added orange zest to the custard, the kitchen filled with a sweet, citrusy aroma. It reminded me of orange cream popsicles from my childhood, reimagined in a more elegant and indulgent way. The smooth chocolate ganache on top adds the perfect finishing touch, creating a beautiful balance with the tart, creamy filling. Freshly made, these éclairs offer the perfect combination of crispy pastry and silky cream—be sure to enjoy them while they're at their best.

ORANGE CUSTARD CREAM

1 large orange

3 egg yolks

¼ tsp (1.25g) kosher salt

¼ cup (50g) sugar

1 tbsp (8g) cornstarch

1 tsp Grand Marnier (optional)

¼ cup (58g) unsalted butter, cubed

CHOUX PASTRY

⅓ cup (79ml) whole milk

⅓ cup (76g) unsalted butter, cubed

1 tbsp (12g) sugar

¼ tsp (1.25g) kosher salt

120g cake flour or all-purpose flour, sifted

3 large eggs

GANACHE

1 cup (170g) 50% cacao chocolate chips

¼ cup (59ml) heavy cream

SPECIAL EQUIPMENT

Pastry bag fitted with a ½-inch (1.25cm) cream tip

Thermometer

1. To make the orange custard cream, use a microplane to zest the orange part of the orange peel. Set aside in a small bowl.
2. Remove all the peel from the orange. Cut the orange into quarters, add to a blender, and puree it. Pour the juice through a fine-mesh sieve, and press down with a spatula on the pulp to extract as much juice as possible. (You also can use a juicer for this.)
3. Whisk together the egg yolks and salt in a small saucepan. Whisk in the sugar in two batches and then whisk in the cornstarch.
4. Add the orange zest, orange juice, and Grand Marnier (if using), and stir to combine. Set the pan over low heat, and simmer for about 10 minutes.
5. Remove the pan from the heat, add the butter, and stir until completely mixed. Transfer to a bowl, and allow to cool to room temperature. Cover tightly with plastic wrap, and set in the refrigerator until ready to use.
6. Preheat the oven to 400°F (200°C).
7. To make the choux pastry, place ⅓ cup (79ml) of water, the milk, butter, sugar, and salt in a medium saucepan. Set over low heat to melt the butter, and remove from the heat when the edges of the butter are just sizzling. Sift in the flour, and stir with a wooden spatula to combine into a lump of dough.
8. Return the pan to low heat and stir, pressing and rolling the dough until it lightly coats the bottom of the pan, about 2 minutes.
9. Gather the dough into a ball, transfer it to a large bowl, and spread it out to cool slightly. Add the eggs one at a time, mixing vigorously with a wooden spatula after each addition. Be sure each egg is completely incorporated before adding the next.
10. Transfer the dough to a pastry bag fitted with a ½-inch (1.25cm) cream tip. Squeeze a little of the dough into the corners of a baking sheet, and line the baking sheet with parchment paper, sticking it to the dough so it won't move when you pipe the éclairs. Squeeze the rest of the dough into twelve 4-inch (10cm) lengths.
11. Bake for 10 minutes. Reduce the oven temperature to 375°F (190°C), and bake for 15 minutes. Transfer to a wire rack to cool.
12. Make three small holes in the bottom of each éclair using a skewer, and fill each éclair with the orange custard cream.
13. Place the chocolate chips in a heatproof bowl at least 4 inches (10cm) in diameter, and melt in the microwave in 30-second intervals until the chocolate reaches 105°F (40°C), about three times, stirring the chocolate evenly between each interval to melt it.
14. Place the heavy cream in a heatproof bowl, and microwave for about 20 seconds. Pour it into the melted chocolate, and stir to combine.
15. Dip the tops of the éclairs in the chocolate ganache, and place on a serving plate. The éclairs can be served immediately, but the ganache will take 2 or 3 hours to set. Store the éclairs in an airtight container in the refrigerator for up to 3 days.

Cinnamon Twist Doughnuts

PREP TIME: 20 minutes plus 12 hours to ferment and 1 hour 30 minutes to rise • **COOK TIME:** 8 minutes • **MAKES:** 16 dougnuts

These doughnuts were a favorite treat when I ran my shop, where I wanted to share the taste of Korean-style doughnuts with my Canadian neighbors. Some customers would stop by daily, while others came weekly to pick up a batch to share with their visiting grandchildren or family. It was so heartwarming and rewarding to see a taste from my childhood become something beloved in a different culture. These doughnuts are especially delightful when dipped into a cup of rich, velvety hot chocolate. The key to their fluffy texture is giving the dough plenty of time to ferment. Serve them warm, and you'll be greeted with the sweet aroma of cinnamon and the feeling of pure happiness with every bite.

POOLISH

½ cup (118ml) warm water
1 tsp (2.8g) active dry yeast
100g bread flour

DOUGH

¼ cup (59ml) warm whole milk
2 tbsp (25g) sugar
1 tsp (2.8g) active dry yeast
300g bread flour, plus more for dusting
1 tsp (5g) kosher salt
3 large eggs, beaten
¼ cup (58g) unsalted butter, at room temperature

FOR FRYING

2 qt (2 liters) canola oil

CINNAMON SUGAR

1 cup (200g) sugar
2 tbsp (16g) ground cinnamon

SPECIAL EQUIPMENT

Stand mixer fitted with a dough hook

Note

If you want to make mini doughnuts, you can use a 1- or 2-inch (2.5 or 5cm) round doughnut cutter to cut them out. Once the doughnuts are puffed, press them under the oil to cook. You'll be rewarded with super soft and fluffy donuts!

1. Prepare the poolish the day before. Pour the warm water into a 1-quart (1-liter) jar, add the yeast, and let it dissolve. Add the flour, mix well, and close the lid. Mark the amount of poolish on the jar, and place the jar in the refrigerator for 12 hours. The next day, remove the jar from the refrigerator and let it sit at room temperature until the dough has tripled in size, about 1 hour 30 minutes.
2. To make the dough, combine the milk, sugar, and yeast in a small bowl. Cover with a tea towel, and let sit for 10 minutes.
3. Add the flour and salt to the bowl of a stand mixer fitted with a dough hook, and mix well by hand. Add the poolish and the eggs and mix by hand using the dough hook portion of a stand mixer until no visible streaks of flour remain. Add the butter, fit the dough hook into the mixer, and mix on medium for 10 minutes. The dough should come out clean when you lift it with the dough hook.
4. Using floured hands, fold and pinch the dough into a round shape. Return it to the bowl, cover with plastic wrap, and let rise until tripled in size, between 1 hour and 30 minutes to 2 hours.
5. To make the cinnamon sugar, add the sugar and cinnamon to a large bowl and mix well with a fork or whisk. Set aside.
6. Turn out the dough onto a floured work surface, and roll out with a rolling pin to 16 inches × 10 inches (40 × 25.5cm). Mark every 1 inch (2.5cm) along the long side to divide it into 16 pieces, and cut the dough into pieces 1 inch (2.5cm) wide by 10 inches (25.5cm) long.
7. Lay out a strip of dough horizontally in front of you. Place a hand on each end of the strip of dough, and twist the dough two or three times, one hand twisting upward while the other twists downward. Then lift and attach the ends of the dough together at the same time, which will twist the dough together. Place the doughnut on a floured baking sheet, and cover with a tea towel. Repeat with the remaining 15 strips.
8. Add the oil to a large, wide saucepan or wok, and heat over medium heat to 330°F (165°F).
9. Add 8 doughnuts to the pan and cook for 2 minutes. Flip and cook the other side until golden brown, 1 to 2 minutes more. Transfer the doughnuts to a wire rack, allow to cool slightly, and roll them in the cinnamon sugar. Repeat with the remaining 8 doughnuts. Serve warm.

Cookie Choux
with Cinnamon Chocolate Ganache Drip

PREP TIME: 30 minutes plus 30 minutes to freeze • **COOK TIME:** 45 minutes • **MAKES:** 12 choux buns

There's something so comforting about the combination of crisp cookie and airy choux. The first time I made these, I couldn't wait for them to cool—I broke one open right away, letting the steam escape, and took a bite. It was warm, crisp, and so delicate it almost melted on my tongue. But then I added a scoop of ice cream and a drizzle of rich ganache, and it became something even more special—a perfect harmony of textures and flavors. Whether you enjoy them fresh with ice cream and berries, save them for later, or fill them with a luscious lemon diplomat cream, they are a delightful reminder that sometimes the simplest things bring the most happiness.

COCOA COOKIES

¼ cup (58g) unsalted butter, at room temperature and very soft
¼ cup (50g) golden sugar
30g cake flour
6g almond flour
½ tbsp (3.5g) unsweetened cocoa powder
½ tsp (1g) ground nutmeg or ground cinnamon (optional)

CHOUX

½ cup (118ml) whole milk
½ cup (115g) unsalted butter
1 tbsp (12g) granulated sugar
½ tsp (2.5g) kosher salt
120g cake flour
1 tsp (5ml) vanilla extract
4 large eggs, beaten

GANACHE DRIP

½ cup (87.5g) semisweet chocolate chips
½ cup (118ml) heavy cream
½ tsp (1g) ground cinnamon

FOR SERVING

Vanilla ice cream
Fresh berries of choice (optional)

SPECIAL EQUIPMENT

2-inch (5cm) round cookie or biscuit cutter
Pastry bag with a ½-inch (1.25cm) tip
Thermometer
Ice-cream scoop

1. To make the cocoa cookies, beat the butter with a spatula in a medium bowl until soft. Add the golden sugar, and mix well. Sift in the cake flour, almond flour, cocoa powder, and nutmeg (if using), and mix until just combined. Turn out the dough onto a sheet of parchment paper, cover with another sheet of parchment paper, and roll out with a rolling pin to a circle or square ⅛ inch (3mm) thick. Place the cookie dough on a plate or tray, and set in the freezer for 30 minutes.
2. Preheat the oven to 400°F (200°C).
3. To make the choux, place a medium skillet over medium-high heat. Add ½ cup (118ml) of water, and the milk, butter, granulated sugar, and salt, and bring to a boil. Cook for 2 or 3 minutes. Turn off the heat, add the flour, and mix evenly with a spatula. Turn the heat to high, and cook, pressing and rolling the dough, for 2 minutes. A film of flour dough will form on the bottom of the pan.
4. Transfer the choux dough to a medium bowl and spread it out with a wooden spatula to allow it to cool slightly. Add the vanilla and stir in the eggs in about three batches, making sure the eggs are completely incorporated into the dough. When you lift the dough with a wooden spatula, it should form a V shape and drop very slowly. Transfer the dough to a pastry bag with a ½-inch (1.25cm) tip.
5. Line a baking sheet with a silicone pad, and squeeze out choux circles 2 inches (5cm) round and 1 inch (2.5cm) high. Leave about 2 inches (5cm) of space between each mound.
6. Remove the cookie dough from the freezer, cut out cookies with a 2-inch (5cm) round cookie or biscuit cutter, and place one cookie on top of each choux circle.
7. Bake for 25 minutes. Then reduce the oven temperature to 375°F (190°C), and bake for 15 minutes, or until the bottoms of the choux are golden brown. (Do not open the oven door while the cookies are baking.) Transfer to a wire rack to cool completely.
8. To make the ganache drip, combine the chocolate chips and heavy cream in a small heatproof bowl, and swirl the bowl to completely coat the chocolate chips in the heavy cream. Microwave for 30 seconds, then let stand for 2 minutes. Add the cinnamon to the center of the bowl, and stir to completely combine. Allow to cool to 85°F (30°C), stirring occasionally.
9. Slice the cooled choux horizontally through the middle. Scoop out balls of vanilla ice cream using an ice-cream scoop, place a scoop in each cut choux, and cover with the top. Garnish with berries (if using) and serve with shot glasses of ganache for drizzling.

Note

You can freeze any leftover uncut choux and fill them with lemon diplomat cream (see Mini Pistachio Baklava Cakes with Lemon Diplomat Cream, page 186) instead of ice cream when they've thawed. Simply skewer holes in the bottom of the uncut choux, and pipe in some diplomat cream to fill.

Panna Cotta

with Fruity Gin Jellies

PREP TIME: 30 minutes plus 6 hours to cool • **COOK TIME:** 10 minutes • **SERVINGS:** 6 to 8

Panna means "cream" in Italian, and cotta means "cooked." This sweet "cooked cream" pudding is made by boiling heavy cream and sugar, flavoring it with vanilla, adding gelatin, and then cooling it to solidify. It's topped with fruity gin jellies, which are made by pouring gelatin into molds and adding fruit. This recipe is as beautiful as it is delicious, especially when paired with more fruit, or caramel, or even coffee.

FRUITY GIN JELLIES

¾ cup (100g) fresh raspberries
½ cup (100g) fresh blueberries
⅔ cup (100g) fresh blackberries
1 tbsp (15ml) white vinegar
2 (0.25 oz/7g) envelopes unflavored gelatin
½ cup (118ml) boiling water
¼ cup (50g) sugar
1 (7 fl oz/200ml) bottle grapefruit flavored tonic water
⅓ cup (79ml) gin

PANNA COTTA

2 cups (473ml) heavy cream
2 (0.25 oz/7g) envelopes unflavored gelatin
½ cup (100g) sugar
1 vanilla bean
2 cups (473ml) whole milk

SPECIAL EQUIPMENT

Mini-ball ice cube mold (see Notes)
Muffin pan

Notes

I used a silicone mold to make the fruity gin jellies. It held about 50 mini-balls.

Do not boil the heavy cream. Carefully warm it over a low heat and remove the pan from the heat before the mixture begins to boil.

1. Prepare the fruity gin jellies: Place the raspberries, blueberries, and blackberries in a large bowl, and add water to cover. Add the vinegar, and let sit for 3 minutes.
2. Drain and rinse the berries under running water. Place them on a tea towel to absorb any remaining moisture and then set aside.
3. Pour ½ cup (118ml) of water into a medium bowl. Stir in the gelatin powder and then let stand for about 5 minutes to allow the gelatin to absorb the water.
4. Add the boiling water and sugar, and whisk well to dissolve. Allow to cool to room temperature.
5. Add the tonic water and gin to the gelatin mixture, and stir. Use a spoon to remove and discard any foam from the top of the mixture.
6. Fill a silicone mini-ball ice cube mold about half full with the gelatin liquid and then add a single raspberry, blueberry, or blackberry to each mold. Add more gelatin liquid to cover, close the top of the mold, and place it in the freezer.
7. Meanwhile, to make the panna cotta, pour the heavy cream into a medium saucepan over low heat, and sprinkle in the gelatin powder. When the gelatin begins to absorb the cream, add the sugar, stir well, and cook for 5 minutes.
8. Halve the vanilla bean lengthwise, scrape out the seeds with the back of a knife, and add both to the cream mixture. Cook over low heat, stirring constantly. When the cream begins to bubble (see Note 2), immediately strain it into a large bowl. (This will separate out the vanilla bean pod and produce a softer-texture panna cotta.) Set aside to cool for 10 minutes.
9. Add the whole milk, and mix well.
10. Place a damp towel over a muffin pan, and add 6 to 8 small serving bowls or glasses to the muffin cups, tilted at a 45-degree angle. Pour the cream mixture into the glasses until they are about one-third full and refrigerate for 6 hours.
11. Remove the panna cotta from the refrigerator, top each with several fruity gin jellies and some of the remaining fresh berries, and serve.

Lime Pavlovas

PREP TIME: 40 minutes • **COOK TIME:** 1 hour 5 minutes • **MAKES:** 2 pavlovas

When I make this dessert, whipping the meringue to perfection and filling it with the creamy lime curd, I find joy in watching everything come together. The process of combining all the different elements feels like a reminder to find little moments of happiness in everyday life. Adding the cream and lightly sprinkling the thyme into the dessert makes this treat feel extra special, and the fresh tanginess of the strawberries brings the flavors into perfect harmony. These pavlovas are an ideal dessert for a small celebration or a quiet moment of joy. Each bite feels like a little piece of sunshine on your tongue.

MERINGUE

3 large egg whites (120g), at room temperature

¼ tsp (1.25ml) fresh lime juice

¾ cup (150g) granulated sugar

⅓ vanilla bean or ½ tsp (2.5ml) vanilla extract

2 tsp (5g) cornstarch

LIME CURD

3 large egg yolks (100g)

¼ cup (50g) granulated sugar

Zest of 2 limes

¼ cup (59ml) fresh lime juice

¼ cup (58g) unsalted butter, cubed

FILLING AND TOPPING

1 cup (237ml) heavy cream

3 tbsp (23g) confectioners' sugar

⅛ tsp (0.6g) kosher salt

8 strawberries, diced, plus a few more to garnish

½ lime, sliced

1 sprig of fresh thyme

SPECIAL EQUIPMENT

Stand mixer or electric hand mixer

1. Preheat the oven to 210°F (100°C). Line a baking sheet with parchment paper.
2. To make the meringue, add the egg whites and lime juice to a large bowl or the bowl of a stand mixer and beat on medium for about 2 minutes.
3. Add the granulated sugar in three batches, mixing on medium after each addition until combined.
4. Add the vanilla bean and cornstarch, increase the mixer speed to high, and continue to whip until all the sugar crystals are dissolved (touch the meringue with your fingers to check) and the meringue is whipped to stiff peaks, about 5 minutes.
5. Fill a pastry bag with the meringue, and cut off about 1½ inches (3.75cm) of the end. Holding the bag vertically over the prepared baking sheet, squeeze out two circles of meringue, each about 5 inches (12.5cm) wide and 2½ inches (6.25cm) high.
6. Using a small spatula, start at the bottom of each meringue and drag upward, gently and slightly pulling the meringue upward to create a pattern. At the top, start at the center and work outward, pressing and dragging to create a small round indentation in the meringue to hold the filling.
7. Bake for 1 hour. Turn off the oven and let the pavlovas dry inside the oven with the door closed for about 15 minutes.
8. Meanwhile, to make the lime curd, whisk the egg yolks and granulated sugar in a small saucepan for about 5 minutes.
9. Set the saucepan over low heat. Add the lime zest and lime juice, and cook, whisking constantly, until the mixture is thick and shiny, 3 or 4 minutes.
10. Remove from the heat, and add the butter in two or three batches, stirring to incorporate all the butter after each addition. Set aside to cool.
11. To make the filling and topping, whip the heavy cream, confectioners' sugar, and salt in a medium bowl until soft peaks form, about 10 minutes.
12. Place the pavlovas on a serving plate, crack the center with a spoon to create a space. Divide the whipped cream into two portions and fill each pavlova with the whipped cream. Top with the lime curd and some diced strawberries. Garnish with more strawberries, lime slices, and some thyme leaves, and serve.

Rochers Coco

PREP TIME: 20 minutes plus 24 hours to rest • **COOK TIME:** 30 minutes • **MAKES:** 20 cookies

When I first encountered coconut in Southeast Asia, I remember drinking the sweet water inside the hard, round, brown fruit with amazement. Then, I scraped the inner wall of the fruit with a spoon and enjoyed the sweet, jelly-like texture of the coconut meat. This coconut cookie, sometimes called a coconut macaroon, is a wonderful dessert that goes well with chocolate fondue or seasonal fruits.

4 cups (340g) unsweetened shredded coconut
3 large eggs, or 4 egg whites
½ tsp (2.5g) kosher salt
1 cup (200g) sugar
1 cup (237ml) warm whole milk
1.75 oz (50g) unsweetened chocolate or dark chocolate
1 tbsp (12.5g) pearl sugar (optional)
2 tbsp (15g) unsweetened cocoa powder

SPECIAL EQUIPMENT

Spice grinder or coffee grinder
Ice-cream scoop

1. To make the coconut flour, grind half of the shredded coconut in a spice or coffee grinder until fine and sand-like, about 5 minutes. Set aside.
2. In a small bowl, whisk together the eggs and salt.
3. Combine the sugar and warm milk in a medium bowl, and stir until the sugar is dissolved, about 5 minutes.
4. Add the remaining shredded coconut, the coconut flour, and the egg mixture, and mix well.
5. Cover with parchment paper, and gently press down to release the air between the dough and the parchment paper. Place in the refrigerator for 24 hours.
6. Preheat the oven to 360°F (185°C). Line a baking sheet with parchment paper.
7. Remove the coconut dough from the refrigerator. Use an ice-cream scoop to portion out the dough. You should have about 20 mounds of dough (One portion is about 3 tablespoons/35g.) Place one portion in your left hand, and squeeze the dough into a conical shape between the fingers (not the thumb) and pad of your right hand. Place the cone on the prepared baking sheet, and repeat with the remaining dough.
8. Bake for 30 minutes, or until golden brown.
9. Meanwhile, to melt the chocolate, fill a medium bowl with boiling water, set a smaller bowl in the hot water. (Don't let any of the hot water get into the small bowl.) Add the chocolate to the small bowl, and allow it to melt until it reaches 100°F (38°C).
10. Remove the cookies from the oven, and transfer them to a wire rack to cool.
11. Drizzle with the melted chocolate, sprinkle with pearl sugar (if using), and dust with cocoa powder. Cool to room temperature before serving. Store any leftovers in an airtight container at room temperature for up to 5 days, or freeze and then thaw to room temperature.

White Chocolate–Coated

Candied Lemon Peels

PREP TIME: 50 minutes plus 25 hours 30 minutes to rest • **COOK TIME:** 2 hours 50 minutes • **MAKES:** 1½ pounds (680g)

These candied lemon peels covered in white chocolate are a perfect treat if you love a mix of sweet and tangy flavors. This recipe does take a little time, but it's totally worth it! You can enjoy these peels on their own, or chop them up and add them to cakes, cookies, or even stir them into your favorite tea. Don't forget to save the leftover syrup—it's perfect for baking or adding to drinks. If you're in the mood for something different, use orange peels instead of lemon for a tasty twist.

9 large lemons (I recommend using organic lemons)
2 tbsp (28g) baking soda
4 or 5 cups (800g to 1kg) sugar
¼ cup (59ml) lemon juice
1 cup (175g) white chocolate chips

Note

These coated lemon peels are great for cutting into small pieces and using as an ingredient in a variety of baked goods. You can also bottle the leftover lemon-flavored syrup and use in baked goods. Or mix it with hot lemon tea or sparkling water for a lemony drink.

1. Place the lemons in a large bowl, add enough water to cover halfway, and sprinkle the baking soda over the lemons.
2. Scrub each lemon with the baking soda, distributing it evenly over the entire peel. Return the lemon to the bowl, wipe all over with water, and then rinse thoroughly under running water.
3. Cut off the top and bottom of each lemon, and make four light slits around the lemon through the rind only, cutting from top to bottom. Slide a spoon between the skin and the flesh of the lemon, peel off the rind, and cut the peels into long slices ¼ inch thick.
4. Place all the lemon peels in a large, wide saucepan. Add enough water to cover the peels, and set over medium heat. Bring to a boil and simmer for 10 minutes. Transfer the lemon peels to a colander, and rinse under running water. Return the peels to the saucepan, and add fresh water. Bring to a boil, and simmer for another 10 minutes. Transfer the peels to a strainer, and rinse again under running water.
5. Pour 1½ quarts (1.5 liters) of water into the saucepan, add the lemon peels and the sugar, and set over medium heat. Bring to a boil, and simmer for 30 minutes. Turn off the heat, cover, and let stand for 24 hours.
6. The next day, add the lemon juice to the saucepan, set over medium heat, and cook until the white pith becomes translucent, about 1 hour to 1 hour 30 minutes.
7. Set a wire rack on a baking sheet. Transfer the lemon peels, one at a time, to the wire rack. Add the peels to the oven, heat the oven to 170°F (75°C), and dry for 1 hour. Turn off the oven, and let the peels stand in the closed oven for 1 more hour.
8. Add some water to a small saucepan, set over medium heat, and bring to a boil. Place a medium bowl over the pan to make a double boiler. Add the white chocolate to the bowl, and stir to melt, about 10 minutes. Pour the chocolate into a small, narrow cup, and dip each lemon peel into the chocolate, leaving about 1 inch (2.5cm) of the peel uncoated.
9. Place the coated peels in an even layer on a parchment paper–lined baking sheet, and set in the refrigerator for about 30 minutes to allow the chocolate to set.
10. Serve with flavored tea.

Variation: For Chocolate-Coated Candied Orange Peels, substitute orange peels for the lemons and coat them in melted semisweet chocolate.

Chocolate Baklava

with Hazelnuts

PREP TIME: 1 hour 45 minutes plus 2 or 3 hours to soak • **COOK TIME:** 1 hour 15 minutes • **MAKES:** 40 baklava

The first time I made baklava from scratch, I remember feeling both excitement and a little bit of fear—all of those delicate layers of phyllo seemed so intimidating! But once I got into the rhythm of rolling, stacking, and brushing, I found it to be almost meditative. This chocolate version takes the traditional nutty, syrup-soaked treat to a whole new level, with rich, cocoa-infused pastry and the deep, toasty flavor of hazelnuts. The real magic happens when the crisp, golden layers soak up the warm cinnamon syrup, turning each bite into a perfect balance of crunch and melt-in-your-mouth decadence. It's a labor of love, but trust me, it's worth every moment.

PHYLLO PASTRY

400g bread flour, plus more for dusting

⅓ cup (35g) cocoa powder

2 tsp (10g) baking powder

1 large egg

½ cup (118ml) 2% milk

½ cup (118ml) corn oil, plus 3 or 4 tbsp (45 to 60ml) more for drizzling

¼ tsp (1.25g) kosher salt

1 cup (120g) wheat starch, for dusting

HAZELNUT FILLING

2 cups (300g) chopped hazelnuts

¼ cup (25g) unsweetened cocoa powder

1 tsp (2g) grated nutmeg

GHEE

½ lb (227g) unsalted butter

CINNAMON SYRUP

1½ cup (300g) sugar

1 tsp (2g) ground cinnamon

SPECIAL EQUIPMENT

12-inch (30.5cm) pan

1. Whisk together the flour, cocoa powder, and baking powder in a medium bowl until the cocoa powder is evenly distributed.
2. Whisk together ½ cup (118ml) of water with the egg, milk, oil, and salt in a large bowl. Add the flour mixture, and mix with a wooden spoon until a dough comes together. Turn out the dough onto a floured work surface and knead for 10 minutes. Form the dough into a ball, cover with a tea towel, and let rest for 10 minutes.
3. Meanwhile, to make the hazelnut filling, combine the hazelnuts, cocoa powder, and nutmeg in a medium bowl. Set aside.
4. Sift the wheat starch into a bowl, and set it aside.
5. Divide the dough into quarters with a scraper. Remove one quarter, and cover the rest with the tea towel. Weigh the dough on a scale and then divide it equally into 10 portions. Shape each portion into a round, dust the rounds generously with the wheat starch, and press the rounds into disks.
6. Sprinkle your work surface with wheat starch. Use a rolling pin to roll out the dough, one disk at a time, into a 5- to 6-inch (12.5 or 15cm) circle, and stack the 10 circles of dough on top of one another. Press the palm of your hand down on the overlapping sheets of dough to hold them together and then evenly roll them out again in all directions to form a 12-inch (30.5cm) circle. You can use wheat starch as you roll to keep the dough from sticking to the work surface and tearing. The process in steps 5 and 6 will take about 20 to 30 minutes per quarter.
7. Bend the ends of the dough up so you can better see the edges of each sheet of dough. Gently peel off the first sheet with your hands, being careful not to tear it. Place the first sheet on a piece of parchment paper, and cover it with a tea towel. Repeat peeling off the sheets. You may be able to take off all 10 sheets, but if you can't, just take off as many as you can.
8. Trim the dough to fit the size of a 12-inch (30.5cm) pan. Grease the pan, and stack the 10 sheets of dough inside, drizzling a few drops of oil between each layer. When the sheets from the first quarter of dough are all in the pan, sprinkle about one-third of the hazelnut filling evenly over the top. Repeat steps 5 through 8 with the second and the third quarters of the dough.
9. Finally, for the last batch of dough, repeat steps 5 through 7, and lightly stack the sheets in the pan. Place the last sheet on top, smooth the dough, and tuck in the edges around the outside of the pan. Cut a long strip across the center of the pan 1½ inches (3.75cm) wide. Rotate the pan 90 degrees, and cut the same width again. Keep going until you've cut about 40 squares.
10. Preheat the oven to 375°F (190°C).
11. Place the butter in a small saucepan, set over medium heat, and cook for 10 to 15 minutes, skimming off the foam as it boils. Slowly pour the melted butter through a fine-mesh sieve into a bowl to strain out the solids from the clear ghee. Pour all the ghee into the pan over the pastry sheets, tilting the pan to distribute it evenly.
12. Bake for 35 minutes.

13. Meanwhile, to make the cinnamon syrup, combine 1½ cups (355ml) of water, the sugar, and the cinnamon in a small saucepan. Set over medium heat, bring to a boil, and cook for 20 minutes. Reduce the heat to medium-low, and simmer until the syrup drips from a spoon slowly, about 10 minutes.

14. Remove the baklava from the oven when both the top and the bottom are golden brown. Immediately pour the cinnamon syrup over the top, drizzling it evenly over the cooked baklava. (The hot pan and the hot syrup will make a sizzling sound.) Let the baklava stand for 2 or 3 hours to soak up the syrup before serving.

Lemony Nougat

PREP TIME: 40 minutes plus 4 hours to cool and harden • **COOK TIME:** 1 hour • **MAKES:** 15 pieces

Every time I make this nougat, I'm amazed by how the ingredients come together in such a magical way. The scent of honey and lemon rising from the saucepan fills the kitchen with a sweet, zesty fragrance, and when I slowly pour the hot syrup into the whipped egg whites, watching it transform is such a wonderful moment. At first, I worried the nougat was too soft, but as it cooled, that softness turned into the perfect smooth, chewy texture, filled with the bright, refreshing taste of lemon and the rich flavor of nuts. Each time I share this treat, it brings warmth and joy to everyone around.

- 1 cup (150g) hazelnuts
- 1 cup (150g) almonds
- 1½ cup (225g) pistachios
- 4 (8 × 11-inch/20 × 28cm) sheets of edible wafer paper (optional)
- Zest of 3 lemons
- 3 large egg whites
- ½ cup (170g) honey
- ¼ cup (59ml) lemon juice
- 1½ cups (300g) sugar
- ¼ cup (85g) glucose syrup
- ½ cup (65g) Candied Lemon Peels (see page 218), diced
- ½ cup (70g) dried cranberries

SPECIAL EQUIPMENT

- 8 × 11-inch (20 × 28cm) baking pan
- Disposable kitchen gloves
- 15 candy wrappers
- Thermometer
- Handheld electric mixer or stand mixer

1. Preheat the oven to 150°F (65°C).
2. Spread the hazelnuts, almonds, and pistachios on a baking sheet, and toast for 20 to 25 minutes or until light golden brown. Remove from the oven, and let the nuts cool for 30 minutes. Rub the nuts with your hands to remove some of the skins and then set aside.
3. Line an 8 × 11-inch (20 × 28cm) baking pan with wafer paper (if using) or parchment paper brushed with a thin layer of oil, cut to fit and fold over the sides of the pan.
4. Add the lemon zest and egg whites to a large, clean, dry bowl, or the bowl of a stand mixer. Set aside.
5. Combine the honey and lemon juice in a small saucepan. Set over medium-low heat, and bring to 250°F (120°C).
6. Add the sugar to another small saucepan. Set the sugar over medium-high heat, and bring to a boil. Add the glucose, and bring to 250°F (120°C).
7. When the honey reaches 210°F (100°C), begin beating the egg whites with an electric mixer until stiff peaks form, slowly increasing the speed of the mixer from low to high.
8. When the honey reaches 250°F (120°C), set the mixer to high and slowly pour the honey mixture into the egg white mixture. Beat for 3 minutes.
9. When the sugar reaches 250°F (120°C), reduce the speed to medium-high, and slowly pour into the bowl. Continue beating for 3 more minutes.
10. Transfer the mixture to a large saucepan. Set over very low heat and simmer, stirring slowly and continuously flipping and mixing with a wooden spatula, for 30 to 40 minutes. Scoop out 1 teaspoon of the nougat and put it in cold water to be sure it doesn't dissolve completely. If it dissolves completely, simmer for another 5 to 10 minutes and test again. (If you skip this step, you may end up with a very soft nougat.)
11. Pour the toasted nuts and the candied lemon peels and cranberries into the nougat, mix well with a spatula, and transfer to the prepared pan. Don a pair of disposable kitchen gloves and lightly oil your gloved hands. Press the nougat hard to release the air and flatten the top. Cover with another layer of wafer or parchment paper, and leave at room temperature for at least 4 hours.
12. Transfer the nougat from the pan to a cutting board and use a serrated knife to cut it into 15 equal pieces (three rows of five pieces).
13. Wrap each piece of nougat in a clear candy wrapper or a piece of parchment paper and place in a container. Store at room temperature for up to 3 months or in the freezer for 6 months. If frozen, let stand at room temperature for 1 hour before eating.

Gin-Filled Pavé Chocolates

PREP TIME: 20 minutes plus 5 hours 35 minutes to rest • **COOK TIME:** 20 minutes • **MAKES:** 15 chocolates

These gin-filled pavé chocolates are the perfect blend of elegance and indulgence. Each little bite is packed with flavors like raspberry, pistachio, or candied lemon peel, all enhanced with your favorite gin. The smooth, rich chocolate shell melts away, revealing a deliciously boozy center that just bursts with flavor. When you take a bite, the chocolate melts in your mouth and the bold flavors unfold. Whether you're serving these chocolates at a party or sharing them with friends, they're sure to leave a lasting impression. Pair them with a glass of gin for the ultimate treat!

PAVÉ CHOCOLATES

8 oz (225g) chopped semisweet baking chocolate

4 oz (112g) chopped unsweetened baking chocolate

⅔ cup (158ml) heavy cream

1½ tbsp (22.5g) corn syrup

⅓ cup (76g) unsalted butter, at room temperature

RASPBERRY PUREE

2 cups (340g) fresh raspberries

1 tbsp (15ml) white vinegar, for washing

½ cup (100g) dark brown sugar, firmly packed

2 tsp (10ml) fresh lemon juice

RASPBERRY GIN FILLING

½ cup (120g) raspberry puree

2 tbsp (30ml) gin

PISTACHIO GIN FILLING

½ cup (50g) finely chopped pistachios

1 tbsp (12.5g) dark brown sugar

2 tbsp (30ml) gin

CANDIED LEMON PEEL GIN FILLING

½ cup (120g) lemon jam

2 tbsp (30ml) gin

¼ cup (20g) finely chopped Candied Lemon Peels (see page 218)

CHOCOLATE COATING POWDERS

¼ cup (30g) freeze-dried raspberry powder

¼ cup (30g) pistachio powder

¼ cup (25g) cocoa powder

SPECIAL EQUIPMENT

Round silicone molds

Melon baller

Culinary heat gun

1. Pour boiling water into a large, shallow bowl. Add the semisweet and unsweetened chocolates to a medium bowl, and set the medium bowl into the large bowl, being careful not to let any water into the chocolate. Let the chocolate sit for about 5 minutes to melt.
2. Meanwhile, set a small saucepan over low heat, add the heavy cream, and bring to a boil so the cream is bubbling around the edges, about 105°F (40°C). Remove from the heat.
3. Stir the chocolate with a silicone spatula to melt. When it reaches 105°F (40°C), add the corn syrup and the warm cream, and stir well to combine. Add the butter, and stir again. Stop stirring when the temperature reaches between 97°F (36°C) and 99°F (37°C). Again, be careful not to let any water into the chocolate.
4. Pour the chocolate into a piping bag and fill 1½-inch (3.8 cm) round silicone molds with the chocolate. You'll need to fill 30 molds in total, so you end up with 15 balls of filled chocolates. Set aside at room temperature for 4 hours and then transfer to the refrigerator for 1 hour.
5. Meanwhile, to make the raspberry puree, place the raspberries in a bowl and cover with water. Add the vinegar, and allow to soak for about 3 minutes. Drain the berries using a fine-mesh sieve, rinse once under running water, and place in a medium saucepan. Add the sugar and lemon juice, set over medium heat, and simmer for 15 to 20 minutes or until it thickens. Remove from the heat and cool completely.
6. To make the gin fillings, mix all the ingredients for each type of filling in a separate small bowl and set aside.
7. Remove the chocolate from the refrigerator and allow to rest at room temperature for about 15 minutes.
8. Dip a melon baller in a bowl of hot water and then wipe dry with a paper towel. Using the warmed melon baller, carve out a hole in the center of each chocolate to hold the filling. As you work, dip the melon baller in and out of the hot water to keep it warm, blotting it with a paper towel to prevent water from getting into the chocolate. Repeat with all 30 chocolates.
9. Fill 10 hollowed-out chocolates with the raspberry filling, 10 with the pistachio filling, and 10 with the candied lemon peel filling, smoothing the tops so they don't dome. Remove 5 chocolates of each type of filling from the molds (15 pieces total).
10. Using a culinary heat gun, lightly melt the top of the chocolates that remain in the molds and then attach a piece of the removed chocolates with the same kind of filling to form a ball. Refrigerate the balls for 20 minutes.

11. Place each of the chocolate coating powders in a separate small bowl. Remove the chocolates from the molds, divide them by filling, and roll them in the appropriate powder to match the filling – raspberry for the raspberry-filled balls, pistachio for the pistachio-filled balls, and cocoa for the candied lemon peel-filled balls. If the powder doesn't stick, use a heat gun to slightly melt the chocolate to help it stick better.

CHAPTER 11

Frozen Desserts

Pomegranate Sorbet

PREP TIME: 15 minutes plus 5 hours • **COOK TIME:** 5 minutes • **CHURN TIME:** 30 minutes • **MAKES:** 9 cups (1.8kg)

I love the freshness of sorbet; it's simple but delicious. Pair it with pomegranates, which are good for the blood vessels, and you get a sweet, refreshing pomegranate sorbet. Note that you will need an ice-cream maker for this recipe.

3 large pomegranates, halved (see Note)
1 cup (200g) sugar
2 (½ inch × 3 inch/1.25cm × 7.5cm) slices fresh lemon peel
1 cinnamon stick
1 whole star anise
2 whole cloves
½ tsp (2.5g) kosher salt

SPECIAL EQUIPMENT
Blender
Ice-cream maker

Note

The pomegranate peels can be used as sorbet bowls. After removing the seeds, use a spoon to scoop out the inside of the pomegranate. Set the hollowed-out pomegranate peel cups on a baking sheet, and place them in the freezer for at least 2 hours. Serve a scoop or two of the sorbet in each frozen cup.

1. If your ice cream bowl must be frozen before churning, place it in the freezer the night before.
2. Hold a pomegranate half over a large bowl. Using a spoon, strike the pomegranate peel all over to dislodge the seeds into the bowl. Repeat with the remaining pomegranates.
3. Using a blender, blend the seeds until they are like juice, about 5 minutes. Filter the juice through a fine-mesh strainer and set aside. You should have 3 cups (710ml) of juice. Discard the solids. (You can also use a juicer for this step.)
4. Combine 3 cups (710ml) of water, the sugar, lemon peel, cinnamon stick, star anise, cloves, and salt in a medium saucepan over medium heat. Bring to a boil, and cook until the sugar dissolves, about 5 minutes.
5. Transfer the mixture to a clean medium bowl and allow to cool to room temperature.
6. Remove the lemon peel and spices, and add the pomegranate juice. Mix well with a wooden spoon. Cover and refrigerate for at least 3 hours or up to 12 hours.
7. Pour the chilled pomegranate juice mixture into the prepared ice-cream maker bowl, and churn until smooth and thick, about 30 minutes.
8. Transfer the sorbet to a freezer-proof airtight container, and freeze for at least 2 hours.
9. Remove from the freezer about 15 minutes before serving. Store any leftovers in the airtight container in the freezer for up to 3 months.

Orange Thyme Sorbet
with Blood Orange Compote

PREP TIME: 15 minutes plus 6 hours • **COOK TIME:** 25 minutes • **CHURN TIME:** 30 minutes • **MAKES:** 9 cups (1.8kg)

Oranges are popular citrus fruits all throughout the year, and this orange and thyme sorbet will be a hit during warm summer months. In this recipe, the orange sorbet is marbled with a compote made from blood oranges. It's colorful, cool, and refreshing. Note you will need an ice-cream maker for this recipe.

BLOOD ORANGE COMPOTE

6 blood oranges
1 cup (200g) sugar
1 tbsp (15ml) lemon juice
¼ tsp (1.25g) kosher salt

ORANGE SORBET

6 oranges
2 tbsp (34g) baking soda
½ cup (100g) sugar
½ tsp (2.5g) kosher salt
10 sprigs fresh thyme

SPECIAL EQUIPMENT

Blender
Ice-cream maker

Note

Use the halved orange peels as ice cream cups. After juicing, use a spoon to scoop out any remaining pulp. Set the hollowed-out orange peel cups on a baking sheet, and freeze for at least 2 hours. Serve a scoop or two of the sorbet in each frozen cup.

1. The day before, place the bowl of the ice-cream maker in the freezer.
2. To make the blood orange compote, cut off the tops and bottoms of the blood oranges to expose some of the flesh. Using a sharp knife, peel the blood orange from top to bottom, cutting down to the inner skin to expose the pulp. Make a V-shaped cut to separate the pulp from the segment walls. Cut the pulp into small pieces.
3. Combine the pulp, sugar, lemon juice, and salt in a medium saucepan over medium heat, and cook, stirring often, until thick, about 20 to 30 minutes.
4. Remove the pan from the heat. Use a blender to blend the mixture until mostly smooth. Cool to room temperature and then transfer to the refrigerator.
5. To make the sorbet, place the oranges in a large, shallow bowl, and add enough water to cover the oranges halfway. Submerge the orange halves in the water and sprinkle the baking soda evenly over the top. Scrub the oranges thoroughly, one at a time, until the water and baking soda are dissolved. (If the scrub feels too dry, add a little more water with your hands.) Rinse the oranges with clean water and then dry with a towel.
6. Zest 2 oranges. You should have 4 tablespoons (24g) of orange zest. Set aside. Juice the oranges until you have 3 cups (710ml) of juice. Set aside.
7. Place a medium saucepan over medium heat, and add 3 cups (710ml) of water, the sugar, and 2 tablespoons (12g) orange zest. Bring to a boil and cook until the sugar dissolves, about 5 minutes.
8. Pour the sugar mixture into a large heatproof bowl, add the salt, orange juice, and 1 sprig of thyme. Gently stir to combine. Allow to cool to room temperature. Refrigerate at least 3 hours or overnight.
9. Add the remaining 2 tablespoons (12g) of orange zest to the orange-sugar mixture, and stir until combined.
10. Pour the mixture into the frozen ice-cream maker bowl, and churn until smooth and thick, about 30 to 40 minutes.
11. Transfer the sorbet to a freezer-proof airtight container. Add the blood orange compote sparingly and stir with a fork until evenly distributed. Cover and freeze for at least 3 hours.
12. Remove from the freezer about 15 minutes before serving. Store any leftovers in the airtight container in the freezer for up to 3 months.

Lemon Basil Sorbet

PREP TIME: 15 minutes plus at least 5 hours to cool and freeze • **COOK TIME:** 10 minutes • **CHURN TIME:** 30 minutes • **MAKES:** 9 cups (1.8kg)

This lemon basil sorbet tastes fresh and tart and sweet—it's the taste of summer. If you can get your hands on Italian lemons, use them; standard grocery store lemons will produce an amazing flavor, too. Note you will need an ice-cream maker for this recipe.

12 lemons
1 tbsp (17g) baking soda
2 tsp (10ml) white vinegar
1 cup (25g) fresh basil leaves
2 cups (400g) sugar
½ tsp (2.5g) kosher salt

SPECIAL EQUIPMENT

Handheld electric mixer
Ice-cream maker

Notes

This sorbet is eye-catching when served in a lemon cup. Cut off the top of a lemon, and use a spoon to scoop out any remaining pulp. Set the hollowed-out lemon peel cups and lids on a baking sheet, and place in the freezer for at least 2 hours. Serve a scoop or two of the sorbet in each frozen cup.

Because you're using 12 lemons in this recipe, you'll have a lot of lemon peels left over, even after zesting a few. If you don't use them for lemon cups, you can use them to make lemon salt or lemon pepper. Zest leftover lemon peels, spread the zest in an even layer on a baking sheet lined with parchment paper, and let it dry at room temperature for a few days. For each lemon, you'll get about 1 tablespoon (6g) of fresh lemon zest, which will reduce down to about 1 teaspoon (1-1.5g) when dried. For lemon salt, combine 4 parts salt with 1 part dried lemon zest. For lemon pepper, combine 1 part pepper with 1 part dried lemon zest. Store in small jars for up to 3 months.

1. The day before, place the bowl of the ice-cream maker in the freezer.
2. Place the whole lemons in a large, shallow bowl, and add enough water to cover the lemons halfway. Submerge the lemons in the water and sprinkle the baking soda evenly over the top. Scrub the lemons thoroughly, one at a time, until the water and baking soda are dissolved. (If the scrub feels too dry, add a little more water with your hands.) Rinse the lemons with clean water and then dry with a towel.
3. Prepare the lemon zest and juice. For the zest, use a zester to grate only the yellow part of 2 lemons. You need 2 tablespoons (12g) of zest. Set aside. Juice the lemons. You should have 3 cups (710ml) of juice.
4. Add the basil and vinegar to a small bowl. Fill the bowl with water until the basil is covered. Let sit for 3 minutes. Rinse with clean water. Spread the basil out on a tea towel, and set aside.
5. Heat a medium saucepan over medium-low heat, and add 3 cups (710ml) of water, the sugar, and 1 tablespoon (6g) of the lemon zest. Cook, stirring constantly, until the sugar is completely dissolved, about 10 minutes.
6. Pour the sugar mixture into a clean medium bowl, add the basil and the salt, and whisk until the salt is dissolved, about 2 minutes. Add the lemon juice, and stir to combine. Let cool to room temperature. Cover and refrigerate for at least 3 hours or overnight.
7. Strain the chilled lemon-basil mixture through a fine-mesh strainer, and discard the zest and basil. Add the remaining lemon zest to the juice, and mix well.
8. Pour the mixture into the frozen ice-cream maker bowl, and churn until smooth and thick, about 30 to 40 minutes.
9. Transfer the sorbet to a freezer-proof airtight container, and place in the freezer for about 2 hours.
10. Remove from the freezer about 15 minutes before serving. Store any leftovers in the airtight container in the freezer for up to 3 months.

Lime Cheesecake Gelato

PREP TIME: 30 minutes plus 15 hours • **COOK TIME:** 30 minutes • **CHURN TIME:** 20 minutes • **MAKES:** 8 cups (1.6kg)

Elevate your gelato experience with this Lime Cheesecake Gelato. Tangy lime compote meets rich, creamy, cheesecake goodness. This homemade gelato bursts with fresh, vibrant flavors and a velvety texture. Each bite is a perfect blend of zesty lime and smooth cheesecake, topped with a delightful crunch of Lotus cookies. Note that you will need an ice-cream maker for this recipe.

LIME COMPOTE

4 limes

½ cup (100g) sugar

1 tbsp (15ml) honey

LIME GELATO

2 cups (473ml) whole milk

1 cup (237ml) heavy cream

1 cup (200g) sugar

2 tbsp (20g) cornstarch

1 tbsp (15ml) pure vanilla extract

¼ tsp (1.25g) kosher salt

2 cups (454g) cream cheese

1 tbsp (15ml) liquid pectin

Juice of 4 limes (about ⅔ cup/150ml)

10 Lotus cookies, crushed, plus whole Lotus cookies, for serving

Lime slices, for serving

SPECIAL EQUIPMENT

Ice-cream maker

1. If your ice cream bowl must be frozen before churning, place it in the freezer the night before.
2. To make the lime compote, place a lime on a cutting board, and cut off the top and bottom, exposing a bit of the pulp. Set the lime cut side down, and slice off the skin from top to bottom. Cut the lime in half from top to bottom, and then cut into each segment, toward the center, to remove the pulp from the skin. Transfer the pulp to a small saucepan, and repeat with the remaining limes.
3. Add the sugar and honey to the saucepan, set over medium heat, and simmer for 10 minutes. Remove from the heat, cool to room temperature, and refrigerate.
4. Meanwhile, to make the lime gelato, whisk together the milk, heavy cream, sugar, cornstarch, vanilla extract, and salt in a medium saucepan. Set over medium heat, and cook, whisking constantly, until the mixture thickens, about 20 minutes.
5. Add the cream cheese to a large bowl, and whip with a whisk until soft. Slowly pour in the thickened cream mixture, and stir to combine. Add the pectin and lime juice, and whisk to combine. Cover with a tea towel, cool to room temperature, and then transfer to the refrigerator to chill at least 12 hours.
6. Pour the lime-cream mixture into the frozen ice-cream maker bowl, and churn until smooth and thick, 20 to 30 minutes.
7. Transfer the mixture to a freezer-proof airtight container. Add the crushed Lotus cookies, and mix with a spoon. Add 1 cup of lime compote, and stir to distribute. Cover and freeze for at least 3 hours.
8. Remove from the freezer about 10 minutes before serving. Serve each bowl, garnished with a lime slice and a whole Lotus cookie. Store any leftovers in the airtight container in the freezer for up to 3 months.

Brown Butter Ice Cream
with Pumpkin Spice Puree

PREP TIME: 15 minutes plus 14 hours • **COOK TIME:** 1 hour 20 minutes • **MAKES:** 8 cups (1.6kg)

The combination of creamy pumpkin puree and brown butter in this ice cream is truly delightful, and with its rich and sweet flavors, this is a special fall dessert that allows you to enjoy the taste of pumpkin in a unique way. Plus, this ice cream is easy to make, without the need for an ice-cream machine. (But feel free to use a machine if you have one.)

PUMPKIN SPICE MIX

¼ cup (33g) ground cinnamon
1 tbsp (6g) ground ginger
1 tsp (2g) ground nutmeg
½ tsp (1g) ground cloves
½ tsp (1g) ground allspice

PUMPKIN SPICE PUREE

4 lb (1.8kg) pie pumpkin (also known as a sugar pumpkin), halved
2 cups (400g) dark brown sugar, firmly packed
2 tbsp (16.5g) ground cinnamon
1 tbsp (15ml) pure vanilla extract
1 tsp (5g) kosher salt

BROWN BUTTER ICE-CREAM BASE

2 cups (473ml) whole milk
1 (14 oz/300g) can condensed milk
1 tsp (5g) kosher salt
6 egg yolks
2 tsp (10ml) pure vanilla extract
½ cup (115g) unsalted butter
3 cups (710ml) cold heavy cream

SPECIAL EQUIPMENT

Handheld electric mixer or stand mixer

Notes

For an eye-catching presentation, remove the seeds from several mini pumpkins and freeze the shells to use as serving bowls for the ice cream.

Store any leftover pumpkin puree in an airtight container in the refrigerator for up to 7 days, and enjoy with store-bought vanilla ice cream or in a pumpkin spice latte.

1. Preheat the oven to 400°F (200°C).
2. To make the pumpkin spice mix, stir together the cinnamon, ginger, nutmeg, cloves, and allspice in a small bowl until evenly combined. Set aside.
3. To make the pumpkin spice puree, remove the seeds from the pumpkin and discard. Place the pumpkin skin-side up on a baking sheet, and roast for 1 hour or until tender.
4. Scoop out the cooked pumpkin flesh using an ice-cream scoop, and place in a large bowl. Add 3 tablespoons (22.5g) of the prepared pumpkin spice mix, the brown sugar, cinnamon, vanilla, and salt. Using a potato masher or a handheld electric mixer, mash until well combined. Cover with plastic wrap or parchment paper, and allow to cool to room temperature. Transfer to the refrigerator, and cool to about 40°F (5°C), about 4 hours. (You can speed up this process by chilling the bowl in an ice water bath.)
5. Meanwhile, prepare the brown butter ice-cream base. Add the whole milk, condensed milk, and salt to a medium saucepan set over low heat. Bring to a simmer, and cook, stirring constantly with a whisk to prevent the condensed milk from sticking to the pan or burning, for 10 minutes. Remove from the heat and allow to cool slightly.
6. Whisk the egg yolks and vanilla in a medium bowl until light and fluffy, about 5 minutes. Slowly pour in the condensed milk mixture, and stir until combined. Cover with parchment paper or plastic wrap, and allow to cool to room temperature. Transfer to the refrigerator, and cool to about 40°F (5°C), about 4 hours (or use an ice water bath).
7. After the pumpkin puree and condensed milk mixture have cooled (or the next day), place the butter in a small skillet set over low heat, and cook until the butter is bubbling and brown, about 10 minutes. (Do not burn the butter.) Add the remaining prepared pumpkin spice mix to the browned butter, stir to combine, transfer it to a bowl, and allow to cool to room temperature. Set aside.
8. Place the heavy cream in a large bowl, and whisk with a handheld electric mixer or stand mixer on high until stiff peaks form, about 10 minutes. With the mixer on, slowly add the condensed milk mixture and whisk until just combined. Add the brown butter mixture, and whip on medium until combined.
9. Transfer the cream mixture to a large freezer-proof container, and freeze for 4 to 6 hours. The mixture will be about half frozen. Remove it from the freezer and blend on high until smooth.
10. Using an ice-cream scoop, add the pumpkin puree to the ice cream, and stir with a fork to distribute. Smooth the top of the ice cream with a spatula, cover with parchment paper, and return to the freezer until the ice cream is firm, about 5 hours.
11. Allow the ice cream to sit at room temperature for 5 to 10 minutes before serving.

CHAPTER 12

Liquors

Apple Liquor

PREP TIME: 20 minutes plus at least 3 months to infuse • **COOK TIME:** 15 minutes • **MAKES:** 6 (12 oz/375ml) bottles

This liquor is infused with the sweet and tangy aroma of apples, evoking crisp, sun-kissed autumn days. Each sip carries the essence of ripe apples, subtly enhanced by the warmth of grain alcohol, creating a delightful harmony of flavors. The infusion process draws out the natural sweetness of the apples, and the simple syrup brings a smoothness. Best served chilled, it's a refreshing burst of apple goodness.

8 small apples, any variety
1 tbsp (15ml) white vinegar
2 tbsp (34g) baking soda
1 (24 oz/750ml) bottle 95 percent grain alcohol (I like Everclear Grain 95)
2½ cups (500g) sugar

Note

This is a sweet liquor with a high alcohol content. Enjoy it in small amounts as a dessert wine, over ice, or with sparkling water.

1. Place the apples in a wide, shallow bowl. Cover with water, add the vinegar, and let sit for 5 minutes. Discard the water, spread out the apples in a single layer, and sprinkle them all over with the baking soda. Rub the apples gently and then rinse clean under running water. Set on a kitchen towel to dry.
2. Cut each apple into 6 to 8 slices, remove the core and seeds, and place the apples in a 2-quart (2-liter) jar. Pour the alcohol over the apples, and use glass weights or a heavy, small bowl to keep the apples submerged in the alcohol. Cover and store in a cool, dark place for between 3 and 6 months.
3. To make the simple syrup, combine 6 cups (1.4 liters) water and the sugar in a large saucepan over high heat. Bring to a boil, and simmer for 15 minutes. Remove from the heat and cool to room temperature. Chill completely in the refrigerator for 2 hours. (You can save time by placing the covered saucepan in a large bowl of ice cubes.)
4. Place a colander in a large bowl, strain the apple mixture, and discard the apples. Add the simple syrup to the liquid and mix well.
5. Pour the liquid into bottles using a funnel, and store in the fridge for up to 3 months.
6. Remove from the fridge and place in an ice bucket just before serving.
7. To serve, pour sparkling water into a glass filled with ice, add about 2 shots of the apple liquor, and stir. You can also serve it straight or on the rocks. (It's also a great dessert wine.)

Pomegranate Liquor
(Original and Cream Versions)

PREP TIME: 20 minutes plus 2 hours to cool and 3 weeks to infuse • **COOK TIME:** 10 minutes • **MAKES:** 6 (12 oz/375ml) bottles

The vibrant, ruby-red seeds of the pomegranate hold numerous health benefits, antioxidants, and a burst of refreshing flavor. When infused with the warmth of cinnamon, star anise, and clove, pomegranate juice transforms into a luscious liqueur that's both invigorating and comforting. The delicate citrus notes from the lemon peels perfectly complement the richness of the pomegranate, making every sip a celebration of nature's finest gifts. This pomegranate liquor isn't just a treat for the senses—it's a liquid indulgence that brings vitality and charm to any occasion.

3 pomegranates
1 cinnamon stick
1 whole star anise
4 whole cloves
4 (½-inch × 3-inch/1.25cm × 7.5cm) slices of lemon peels
1 (24 oz/750ml) bottle 95-percent grain alcohol (I like Everclear Grain 95)
2½ cups (500g) sugar

Note

You can store these liquors for up to 6 months. Be sure to store them in bottles no smaller than 12 ounces (375ml) if freezing. If you use smaller bottles, the liquor could freeze and burst the bottles. To serve, bring the liquors to room temperature for a few minutes, shake to thaw, and enjoy.

1. Cut a thin slice off the top of the pomegranates, exposing some of the seeds, and cut the peel from the top down along the five corners of the pomegranate. Open the pomegranate using your hands, remove only the seeds, and place them in a 2-quart (2-liter) jar.
2. Add the cinnamon stick, star anise, cloves, and lemon peels to the jar. Pour in the alcohol. Cover and store in a cool, dark place for 3 weeks.
3. To make the simple syrup, combine 6 cups (1.4 liters) of water and the sugar in a large saucepan over medium heat. Bring to a boil, and simmer for about 10 minutes. Remove from the heat and cool to room temperature. Chill completely in the refrigerator for about 2 hours. (You can save time by placing the covered saucepan in a large bowl of ice cubes.)
4. Place a strainer over a large pitcher. Strain the pomegranate mixture into the pitcher. Discard the solids.
5. Pour the infused pomegranate liquor into the simple syrup, and mix well with a spoon.
6. Pour the pomegranate liquor into bottles using a funnel, and store it in the freezer for up to 6 months. (Because of the high alcohol content, it will not freeze.)
7. Just before serving, remove the bottle from the freezer. To serve, fill a glass with ice, add 2 shots of pomegranate liquor, and serve. Or fill the ice-filled glass two-thirds full with sparkling water and then add the pomegranate liquor.

Variations: To make a cream version of the pomegranate liquor, combine 3 cups (710ml) of 2% milk and 1¼ cups (250g) sugar in a medium saucepan over medium heat. Bring to a boil and simmer for about 10 minutes. Remove from the heat and cool to room temperature. Chill completely in the refrigerator for about 2 hours. Pour the infused pomegranate liquor into the milk syrup, and mix well with a spoon. Bottle and store as indicated for the non-cream version.

Limecello

(Original and Cream Versions)

PREP TIME: 25 minutes plus 2 hours to cool and 3 weeks to infuse • **COOK TIME:** 10 minutes • **MAKES:** 6 (12 oz/375ml) bottles

When I first tasted limoncello a few years ago, I was struck by the realization of how many incredible flavors I had yet to discover. Limoncello has a fresh, fruity aroma and a smooth yet vibrant taste. The pure joy of sipping something so refreshingly simple made it an unforgettable experience, and I instantly fell in love with fruit liqueurs. Since then, I've experimented with different versions (various fruits and even a cream version, which I've included here), and limecello has become my absolute favorite. The fresh lime peel infuses the alcohol beautifully, creating a bold and aromatic liqueur. Pouring it over ice with sparkling water creates a light and even more refreshing drink. Best of all, it's easy to make and perfect for gifting! Be sure to try both the original and the cream versions—and the limoncello and mandarincello variations, too.

10 large limes
1 tbsp (15ml) white vinegar
2 tbsp (34g) baking soda
1 (24 oz/750ml) bottle 95 percent grain alcohol (I like Everclear Grain 95)
1¼ cups (250g) sugar

MILK SYRUP

3 cups (710ml) 2% milk
1¼ cups (250g) sugar

Note

Pour the limecellos into tall limoncello bottles, wrap with a limoncello glass, and give as a gift!

You can store these liquors for up to 6 months. Be sure to store them in bottles no smaller than 12 ounces (375ml) if freezing. If you use smaller bottles, the liquor could freeze and burst the bottles. To serve, bring the liquors to room temperature for a few minutes, shake to thaw, and enjoy.

1. Place the limes in a wide, shallow bowl. Cover with water, add the vinegar, and let sit for 5 minutes. Discard the water, spread out the limes in a single layer, and sprinkle them all over with the baking soda. Rub the limes with the baking soda, wipe them off one by one, then rinse each under running water. Set aside on a kitchen towel to dry.
2. Using a potato peeler, remove the green part of the lime peels, leaving as little of the white part (pith) on the peels as possible. (Only the green part of the lime peel is needed. The pith is bitter.)
3. Place the peels in a 1-quart (1-liter) jar. Pour the alcohol over the peels. Cover and store in a cool, dark place for 3 weeks.
4. To make the simple syrup, combine 3 cups (710ml) of water and the sugar in a medium saucepan over medium heat. Bring to a boil, and simmer for about 10 minutes. Remove from the heat and cool to room temperature. Chill completely in the refrigerator for about 2 hours. (You can save time by placing the covered saucepan in a large bowl of ice cubes.)
5. To make the milk syrup, combine the milk and sugar in a medium saucepan over medium heat. Bring to a boil, and simmer for about 10 minutes. Remove from the heat and cool to room temperature. Chill completely in the refrigerator for about 2 hours.
6. Pour half of the infused lime alcohol into the simple syrup and half into the milk syrup. Use a spoon to mix the simple syrup mixture until combined and then the milk syrup mixture until combined.
7. Pour each version of limecello into separate bottles using a funnel, and store them in the freezer for up to 6 months. (Because of the high alcohol content, they will not freeze.)
8. Just before serving, remove the bottles from the freezer and place them an ice bucket. To serve, fill a glass with ice, fill the glass about two-thirds full with sparkling water, add about 2 shots of either limecello, and stir. Of course, you can also enjoy it straight or on the rocks.

Variations: This recipe is easy to customize with different citrus fruits. In place of the limes, use 8 large lemons to make limoncello or 20 mandarin oranges to make mandarincello. When choosing your mandarins, be sure they are hard-skinned.

Pineapplecello

(Original and Piña Colada Cocktail Versions)

PREP TIME: 10 minutes plus 2 hours to cool and 3 weeks to infuse • **COOK TIME:** 20 minutes • **MAKES:** 6 (12 oz/375ml) bottles

Pineapplecello is a tropical twist on the classic citrus-infused limoncello, bringing a rich, sun-kissed sweetness to every sip. The natural juiciness of pineapple combined with the smoothness of coconut milk creates a liqueur that feels like a tropical getaway in a glass. I love how the bright, tangy pineapple infusion contrasts with the creamy coconut syrup, making it perfect for both refreshing summer drinks and cozy winter nights. Whether enjoyed straight from the freezer or mixed with sparkling water, its vibrant flavor is always a delight. And if you're in the mood for something even more indulgent, the coconut milk version is like a silky, boozy piña colada—no blender required!

1 (2 lb or 907g) pineapple

1 (24 oz/750ml) bottle 95 percent grain alcohol (I like Everclear Grain 95)

1¼ cups (250g) sugar

COCONUT MILK SIMPLE SYRUP

1 cup (237ml) 2% milk

1 (14 oz/400ml) can coconut milk

1 (10 oz/300ml) can sweet condensed milk

Note

You can store these liquors for up to 6 months. Be sure to store them in bottles no smaller than 12 ounces (375ml) if freezing. If you use smaller bottles, the liquor could freeze and burst the bottles. To serve, bring the liquors to room temperature for a few minutes, shake to thaw, and enjoy.

1. Set the pineapple on a cutting board, and use a knife to cut off the top and bottom and then the skin. Place the peeled pineapple in a 2-quart (2-liter) glass container. Pour the alcohol over the pineapple. Cover and store in a cool, dark place for 3 weeks.
2. To make the simple syrup, combine 3 cups (710ml) of water and the sugar in a medium saucepan over medium heat. Bring to a boil, and simmer for about 10 minutes. Remove from the heat and cool to room temperature. Chill completely in the refrigerator for about 2 hours. (You can save time by placing the covered saucepan in a large bowl of ice cubes.)
3. To make the coconut milk simple syrup, combine the milk, coconut milk, and condensed milk in a medium saucepan over medium-low heat and bring to a boil whisking constantly. Simmer for 10 minutes while continuing to whisk. Remove from the heat and cool to room temperature. Chill completely in the refrigerator for about 2 hours.
4. Add 1½ cups (355ml) of the infused pineapple liqueur to both the simple syrup and the coconut milk syrup. Use a spoon to mix the simple syrup mixture until combined and then the coconut milk mixture.
5. Pour each version of the pineapplecello into separate bottles using a funnel, and store them in the freezer for up to 6 months.
6. Just before serving, remove the bottles from the freezer and place them in an ice bucket. To serve, fill a glass with ice, fill the glass about two-thirds full with sparkling water, add about 2 shots of of your choice of pineapplecello, and stir.

Strawberry Whiskey

PREP TIME: 10 minutes plus 5 to 10 days to age • **COOK T ME:** none • **MAKES:** 1½ cups (350ml)

This infused whiskey combines the sweetness of strawberries with the warmth of bourbon. The fresh strawberries blend beautifully with the whiskey's rich notes and the subtle sweetness of maple syrup or brown sugar. The result is perfect for sharing with someone you love—or wish to grow closer to.

15–20 strawberries
1 tbsp (15ml) white vinegar
2 tbsp (30ml) maple syrup, or brown sugar
1⅓ cups (317ml) bourbon

Note

The strawberries will taste bitter. I would not suggest eating them.

1. Place the strawberries in a large bowl, and fill with water until the berries are fully submerged. Add the vinegar, and let sit for 5 minutes. Drain and rinse the berries two or three times under running water.
2. Transfer the strawberries to a quart-size mason jar. Place a glass weight or small bowl on top of the strawberries so they are submerged under the whiskey.
3. Add the maple syrup or brown sugar to the jar, and fill with the whiskey.
4. Add the lid, and store in the refrigerator for at least 5 days and up to 10 days. (I recommend the full 10 days.)
5. Remove and discard the strawberries (see Note).
6. Serve neat or over ice. Store in the jar in the refrigerator for up to 6 months.

Index

A

aligot, Hamburger Steaks with, 73
allspice, 61, 237
almonds, Lemony Nougat, 223
anchovies, 47, 140
Apple and Cream Cheese Filled Buns, 144
Apple Liquor, 241
apples
- Apple and Cream Cheese Filled Buns, 144
- Apple Liquor, 241
- Apple Tarte Tatin, 202
- Boneless Beef Short Ribs, 66–67
- Lollipop Drumsticks, 90

Apple Tarte Tatin, 202
artisan bread, 153, 161
arugula
- Baked Eggplant Sandwiches, 161
- Black Ciabatta Egg Sandwich, 154
- Herbed Flatbread, 110–11

asparagus, Beef Tenderloins, 58–59
avocado, Grilled Shrimp, 39

B

bacon, 62, 167
Baked Beet Salad, 18
Baked Eggplant Rollatini, 25
Baked Eggplant Sandwiches, 161
Balsamic Glaze-Marinated Roasted Chicken Legs, 85
Balsamic Marinated Tomatoes, 17
barbecue sauce, Pork Shoulder Roast, 74
basil leaves, 13, 17, 22, 143, 233
basil olive oil burrata salad, Herbed Flatbread, 110–11
bay leaves, 40, 93
Beef, Pork & Lamb
- Beef Bourguignon, 62
- Beef Tenderloins, 58–59
- Boneless Beef Short Ribs, 66–67
- Bone Marrow Meatballs, 64–65
- Corned Beef and Cabbage, 61
- Crispy Porchetta, 70
- Hamburger Steaks, 73
- Lamb Chop Birria Tacos, 80–81
- Pork Shoulder Roast, 74
- Prime Rib Roast, 54–55
- Rack of Lamb Crown Roast, 76–77
- Rack of Lamb Cutlets, 79
- Spicy Pork Ribs, 69
- Steak with Pine Nut Sauce, 57

beef bones, Bone Marrow Meatballs, 64–65
Beef Bourguignon, 62
beef brisket, Corned Beef and Cabbage, 61
beef broth
- Beef Bourguignon, 62
- Beef Tenderloins, 58–59
- Bone Marrow Meatballs, 64–65
- Hamburger Steaks, 73
- Prime Rib Roast, 54–55

beef shank, Beef Bourguignon, 62
Beef Tenderloins, 58–59
beet hummus, Herbed Flatbread, 110–11
Beetroot-Cured Salmon, 48
beets
- Baked Beet Salad, 18
- Beetroot-Cured Salmon, 48
- Chicken Breast Rolls, 86–87

Beet Tortilla Mushroom Tacos, 34–35
Beignets, 205
bell peppers, 34–35, 162
blackberries, Panna Cotta, 213
Black Cheese Scones, 176
Black Ciabatta Egg Sandwich, 154
Black Forest Cake, 180–81
Black Red Onion Pies, 26–27
Black Squid Ink Pasta, 44
blood orange compote, Orange Thyme Sorbet, 230
blueberries, 191, 213
Boneless Beef Short Ribs, 66–67
Bone Marrow Meatballs, 64–65
bourbon, Strawberry Whiskey, 248
Braided Cinnamon Loaf, 107
breadcrumbs
- Beet Tortilla Mushroom Tacos, 34–35
- Bone Marrow Meatballs, 64–65
- Eggplant Parmesan, 30
- Hamburger Steaks, 73
- Rack of Lamb Cutlets, 79

Breads
- Braided Cinnamon Loaf, 107
- Cheesy Caramelized Onion Bread, 155
- Chocolate Babkas, 123
- Chocolate Bread, 120
- Herbed Flatbread, 110–11
- Hotel Bread, 103
- Monkey Bread, 116
- Pide Bread, 104–5
- Pumpernickel Bread, 108
- Raspberry Babka, 119
- Sandwich Bread, 100

Brioche, 132
Brown Butter Ice Cream, 237
brown sugar, 116, 135, 201
Brussels sprouts, Rack of Lamb Sandwiches, 153
Buns
- Anchovy Grilled Naan, 140
- Apple and Cream Cheese Filled Buns, 144
- Brioche, 132
- Butter Crumble Buns, 136
- Butter Eye Buns, 128
- Cardamom Butter Buns, 139
- Crunchy Cinnamon Balloon Buns, 127
- Meringue Cinnamon Rolls, 135
- Olive Fougasse, 143
- Pretzels, 131

Butter Crumble Buns, 136
Butter Eye Buns, 128
butter sauce, 54, 86, 140, 158
Butter Shrimp and Black Bun Sandwiches, 158

C

cabbage, 61, 74, 157
Cakes
- Black Forest Cake, 180–81
- Carrot Loaf Cake, 188–89
- Chocolate Loaf Cake, 191
- Mini Pistachio Baklava Cakes, 186
- Strawberry Jelly Cake, 185
- Whipped Ganache Cake, 182–83

Candied Lemon Peels, 218
- Gin-Filled Pavé Chocolates, 224–25
- Lemony Nougat, 223
- Roasted Turkey, 96–97

candied orange peel, Chocolate Babkas, 123
Caprese Salad Rolls, 13
caramelized onions, Cheesy Caramelized Onion Bread, 155
caraway seeds, Reuben Sandwiches, 157
cardamom, 128, 139, 197
Cardamom Butter Buns, 139
Carrot Loaf Cake, 188–89
carrots
- Beef Bourguignon, 62
- Bone Marrow Meatballs, 64–65
- Carrot Loaf Cake, 188–89
- Corned Beef and Cabbage, 61
- Lollipop Drumsticks, 90
- Picnic Sandwiches, 162
- Pork Shoulder Roast, 74
- Rack of Lamb Crown Roast, 76–77
- Turkey Breast, 94

celery stalks, 64–65, 96–97
cheese. *See* various recipes
Cheese and Leek Scones, 175
Cheese Crisps, Whole-Wheat Shiitake Mushroom Pasta with, 29

cheese potato balls, Prime Rib Roast, 54–55
Cheesy Caramelized Onion Bread, 155
cherries, Black Forest Cake, 180–81
cherry compote. *See* Black Forest Cake
chestnut mushrooms. *See* Eggplant Parmesan
chicken
- Balsamic Glaze–Marinated Roasted Chicken Legs, 85
- Chicken Breast Rolls, 86–87
- Chicken Soup, 93
- Creamy Chicken, 89
- Lollipop Drumsticks, 90

chicken. *See* Poultry
chicken breasts, 86–87, 89
chicken drumsticks, Lollipop Drumsticks, 90
chicken legs, Balsamic Glaze-Marinated Roasted Chicken Legs, 85
Chicken Soup, 93
chickpeas, Herbed Flatbread, 110–11
chiles, 80–81, 93
chocolate
- Black Forest Cake, 180–81
- Gin-Filled Pavé Chocolates, 224–25
- Rochers Coco, 217
- Whipped Ganache Cake, 182–83

Chocolate Babkas, 123
Chocolate Baklava, 220–21
Chocolate Bread, 120
chocolate chips
- Candied Lemon Peels, 218
- Chocolate Babkas, 123
- Chocolate Bread, 120
- Chocolate Loaf Cake, 191
- Cinnamon Kouign-Amann Biscuits, 171
- Cookie Choux, 210–11
- Orange Custard Cream Éclairs, 206
- Whipped Ganache Cake, 182–83

Chocolate Loaf Cake, 191
choux pastry, Orange Custard Cream Éclairs, 206
cilantro, Beet Tortilla Mushroom Tacos, 34–35
cinnamon
- Apple Tarte Tatin, 202
- Black Forest Cake, 180–81
- Braided Cinnamon Loaf, 107
- Brown Butter Ice Cream, 237
- Carrot Loaf Cake, 188–89
- Chocolate Baklava, 220–21
- Chocolate Bread, 120
- Chocolate Loaf Cake, 191
- Cinnamon Kouign-Amann Biscuits, 171
- Cinnamon Twist Doughnuts, 209
- Cookie Choux, 210–11
- Corned Beef and Cabbage, 61
- Crunchy Cinnamon Balloon Buns, 127
- Hotel Bread, 103
- Koesisters, 197
- Lollipop Drumsticks, 90
- Meringue Cinnamon Rolls, 135
- Monkey Bread, 116
- Pomegranate Liquor, 242
- Pomegranate Sorbet, 229
- Raspberry Babka, 119
- Roasted Turkey, 96–97
- Whipped Ganache Cake, 182–83

cinnamon chocolate ganache drip, Cookie Choux, 210–11
Cinnamon Kouign-Amann Biscuits, 171
Cinnamon Twist Doughnuts, 209
cocoa powder
- Beef Bourguignon, 62
- Black Forest Cake, 180–81
- Chocolate Baklava, 220–21
- Chocolate Loaf Cake, 191
- Gin-Filled Pavé Chocolates, 224–25
- Pumpernickel Bread, 108
- Red Pear Chocolate Turnovers, 201
- Rochers Coco, 217

coconut
- Koesisters, 197
- Pineapplecello, 246
- Pineapple Cupcakes, 198
- Rochers Coco, 217

Cookie Choux, 210–11
coriander seeds
- Beetroot-Cured Salmon, 48
- Corned Beef and Cabbage, 61

corned beef, Reuben Sandwiches, 157
Corned Beef and Cabbage, 61
corn tortillas, Lamb Chop Birria Tacos, 80–81
Country White Gravy and Biscuits, 167
cranberries
- Carrot Loaf Cake, 188–89
- Lemony Nougat, 223
- Roasted Turkey, 96–97

cream cheese
- Apple and Cream Cheese Filled Buns, 144
- Beetroot-Cured Salmon, 48
- Braided Cinnamon Loaf, 107
- Carrot Loaf Cake, 188–89
- Lime Cheesecake Gelato, 234
- Picnic Sandwiches, 162

Creamy Chicken, 89
Creamy King Oyster Mushroom Steaks, 21
Creamy Mussels, 40
Crispy Porchetta, 70, 150
Crunchy Cinnamon Balloon Buns, 127
cucumbers
- Beetroot-Cured Salmon, 48
- Fish and Chips, 47
- Grilled Shrimp, 39
- Rack of Lamb Crown Roast, 76–77

curing brine, Corned Beef and Cabbage, 61

D

Deep-Fried Lobster, 51
Desserts
- Apple Tarte Tatin, 202
- Beignets, 205
- Candied Lemon Peels, 218
- Chocolate Baklava, 220–21
- Cinnamon Twist Doughnuts, 209
- Cookie Choux, 210–11
- Gin-Filled Pavé Chocolates, 224–25
- Koesisters, 197
- Lemony Nougat, 223
- Lime Pavlovas, 214
- Orange Custard Cream Éclairs, 206
- Panna Cotta, 213
- Peach Cookies, 194–95
- Pineapple Cupcakes, 198
- Red Pear Chocolate Turnovers, 201
- Rochers Coco, 217

Diane sauce, Beef Tenderloins with, 58–59
Dijon blue cheese dipping sauce, Mushroom Wings, 33
dill seeds, Beetroot-Cured Salmon, 48
dough. *See* Breads; Buns; Desserts; Scones & Biscuits
Dutch-processed cocoa, 120, 123

E

eggplant
- Baked Eggplant Rollatini, 25
- Baked Eggplant Sandwiches, 161
- Eggplant Parmesan, 30
- French Tian, 22

Eggplant Parmesan, 30
eggs. *See* various recipes

F

fennel seeds, Crispy Porchetta, 70
Fish and Chips, 47
food coloring, Peach Cookies, 194–95
French Tian, 22
Frozen Desserts
- Brown Butter Ice Cream, 237
- Lemon Basil Sorbet, 233
- Lime Cheesecake Gelato, 234
- Orange Thyme Sorbet, 230
- Pomegranate Sorbet, 229

fruity gin jellies, Panna Cotta, 213

G

garlic cloves. *See various recipes*
garlic hot honey sauce, Mushroom Wings with, 33
gelatin, Panna Cotta, 213
Gin-Filled Pavé Chocolates, 224–25
ginger, 197, 237
grapefruit, Turkey Breast, 94
gravy, Roasted Turkey, 96–97
Grilled Shrimp, 39
ground beef, 64–65, 73
ground black pepper. *See* various entries

H

haddoc fillets, Fish and Chips, 47
ham, 162, 168
Hamburger Steaks, 73
hazelnuts, 220–21, 223
heavy cream
- Black Ciabatta Egg Sandwich, 154
- Bone Marrow Meatballs, 64–65
- Brioche, 132
- Creamy Chicken, 89
- Creamy King Oyster Mushroom Steaks, 21
- Creamy Mussels, 40
- Gin-Filled Pavé Chocolates, 224–25
- Lime Cheesecake Gelato, 234

Herbed Flatbread, 110–11
herbed olive oil. *See* French Tian
homemade taco seasoning, Beet Tortilla Mushroom Tacos, 34–35
honey
- Balsamic Marinated Tomatoes, 17
- Beignets, 205
- Lime Cheesecake Gelato, 234
- Mushroom Wings, 33
- Pide Bread, 104–5

horseradish
- Beetroot-Cured Salmon, 48
- Corned Beef and Cabbage, 61
- Reuben Sandwiches, 157

Hotel Bread, 103
hot sauce, Reuben Sandwiches, 157

IJ

instant coffee, Pumpernickel Bread, 108

jalapeños, 34–35, 90
juice. *See* lemons; limes; oranges

K

ketchup
- Grilled Shrimp, 39
- Hamburger Steaks, 73
- Lollipop Drumsticks, 90
- Reuben Sandwiches, 157
- Spicy Pork Ribs, 69

Koesisters, 197

L

Lamb Chop Birria Tacos, 80–81
leek
- Cheese and Leek Scones, 175
- Pork Shoulder Roast, 74

Lemon Basil Sorbet, 233
lemon cream sauce, Deep-Fried Lobster, 51
lemons
- Anchovy Grilled Naan, 140
- Apple Tarte Tatin, 202
- Baked Beet Salad, 18
- Balsamic Marinated Tomatoes, 17
- Beetroot-Cured Salmon, 48
- Beet Tortilla Mushroom Tacos, 34–35
- Black Forest Cake, 180–81
- Brioche, 132
- Butter Shrimp and Black Bun Sandwiches, 158
- Candied Lemon Peels, 218
- Chicken Breast Rolls, 86–87
- Corned Beef and Cabbage, 61
- Creamy King Oyster Mushroom Steaks, 21
- Crispy Porchetta, 70
- Deep-Fried Lobster, 51
- Fish and Chips, 47
- Gin-Filled Pavé Chocolates, 224–25
- Grilled Shrimp, 39
- Herbed Flatbread, 110–11
- Lemon Basil Sorbet, 233
- Lemony Nougat, 223
- Lollipop Drumsticks, 90
- Meringue Cinnamon Rolls, 135
- Mini Pistachio Baklava Cakes, 186
- Mushroom Wings, 33
- Olive Fougasse, 143
- Orange Thyme Sorbet, 230
- Peach Cookies, 194–95
- Pineapple Cupcakes, 198
- Pomegranate Liquor, 242
- Pomegranate Sorbet, 229
- Porchetta Sandwiches, 150
- Preserved Lemon, 14
- Prime Rib Roast, 54–55
- Rack of Lamb Crown Roast, 76–77
- Rack of Lamb Cutlets, 79
- Raspberry Babka, 119

lemon whipped cream, Brioche, 132
Lemony Nougat, 223
lettuce
- Boneless Beef Short Ribs, 66–67
- Deep-Fried Lobster, 51
- Grilled Shrimp, 39
- Herbed Flatbread, 110–11
- Rack of Lamb Crown Roast, 76–77

lettuce veggie cube bowl, Grilled Shrimp, 39
Limecello, 245
Lime Cheesecake Gelato, 234
Lime Pavlovas, 214
limes
- Lamb Chop Birria Tacos, 80–81
- Limecello, 245
- Lime Cheesecake Gelato, 234

liquid pectin, Lime Cheesecake Gelato, 234
Liquors
- Apple Liquor, 241
- Limecello, 245
- Pineapplecello, 246
- Pomegranate Liquor, 242
- Strawberry Whiskey, 248

lobster, Deep-Fried Lobster, 51
Lollipop Drumsticks, 90
Lotus cookies, Lime Cheesecake Gelato, 234
Louie dipping sauce, Grilled Shrimp, 39

M

mango salsa, Beet Tortilla Mushroom Tacos, 34–35
maple syrup
- Baked Eggplant Sandwiches, 161
- Boneless Beef Short Ribs, 66–67
- Deep-Fried Lobster, 51
- Fish and Chips, 47
- Herbed Flatbread, 110–11
- Hotel Bread, 103
- Lollipop Drumsticks, 90
- Olive Fougasse, 143
- Picnic Sandwiches, 162
- Pork Shoulder Roast, 74
- Prime Rib Roast, 54–55
- Rack of Lamb Crown Roast, 76–77
- Rack of Lamb Sandwiches, 153
- Strawberry Whiskey, 248
- Sunflower Biscuits, 168
- Tamago Sandwiches, 149

mayonnaise
- Black Ciabatta Egg Sandwich, 154
- Deep-Fried Lobster, 51
- Fish and Chips, 47
- Grilled Shrimp, 39
- Lollipop Drumsticks, 90
- Mushroom Wings, 33
- Picnic Sandwiches, 162
- Rack of Lamb Sandwiches, 153
- Reuben Sandwiches, 157
- Tamago Sandwiches, 149

melting cheese, Spicy Pork Ribs with, 69
Meringue Cinnamon Rolls, 135
Mini Pistachio Baklava Cakes, 186

molasses, Pumpernickel Bread, 108
Monkey Bread, 116
mozzarella balls, Herbed Flatbread, 110–11
mushroom balls, Beet Tortilla Mushroom Tacos, 34–35
mushroom gravy, Hamburger Steaks, 73
mushrooms
Beef Bourguignon, 62
Beet Tortilla Mushroom Tacos, 34–35
Chicken Breast Rolls, 86–87
Creamy King Oyster Mushroom Steaks, 21
Eggplant Parmesan, 30
Hamburger Steaks, 73
Mushroom Wings, 33
Steak with Pine Nut Sauce, 57
Whole-Wheat Shiitake Mushroom Pasta, 29
Mushroom Wings, 33
mussels, Creamy Mussels, 40
mustard
Beef Tenderloins, 58–59
Herbed Flatbread, 110–11
Lollipop Drumsticks, 90
Mushroom Wings, 33
Porchetta Sandwiches, 150
Rack of Lamb Crown Roast, 76–77
Rack of Lamb Sandwiches, 153

N

95-percent grain alcohol. *See* Liquors
nonpareil capers, 140, 143, 150
nutmeg
Brown Butter Ice Cream, 237
Chocolate Babkas, 123
Chocolate Baklava, 220–21
Chocolate Loaf Cake, 191
Cookie Choux, 210–11
Hamburger Steaks, 73
Peach Cookies, 194–95
Raspberry Babka, 119

O

octopus legs, Phyllo-Wrapped Seafood Papillote, 43
Old Bay Seasoning, Phyllo-Wrapped Seafood Papillote, 43
Olive Fougasse, 143
olives, 143, 85
onions
Beef Bourguignon, 62
Beef Tenderloins, 58–59
Beet Tortilla Mushroom Tacos, 34–35
Black Red Onion Pies, 26–27
Bone Marrow Meatballs, 64–65
Cheesy Caramelized Onion Bread, 155
Chicken Soup, 93
Corned Beef and Cabbage, 61
Country White Gravy and Biscuits, 167
Grilled Shrimp, 39
Hamburger Steaks, 73
Lamb Chop Birria Tacos, 80–81
Lollipop Drumsticks, 90
Phyllo-Wrapped Seafood Papillote, 43
Picnic Sandwiches, 162
Porchetta Sandwiches, 150
Pork Shoulder Roast, 74
Rack of Lamb Crown Roast, 76–77
Roasted Turkey, 96–97
Whole-Wheat Shiitake Mushroom Pasta, 29
Orange Custard Cream Éclairs, 206
oranges
Herbed Flatbread, 110–11
Koesisters, 197
Orange Custard Cream Éclairs, 206
Orange Thyme Sorbet, 230
Preserved Lemon, 14
Roasted Turkey, 96–97
Turkey Breast, 94
orange sauce, Turkey Breast with, 94
oregano
Black Red Onion Pies, 26–27
Creamy Mussels, 40
Eggplant Parmesan, 30
Pork Shoulder Roast, 74
Rack of Lamb Sandwiches, 153
Steak with Pine Nut Sauce, 57
Turkey Breast, 94
oyster mushrooms. *See* Creamy King Oyster Mushroom Steaks

P–Q

Panna Cotta, 213
parsley
Anchovy Grilled Naan, 140
Black Cheese Scones, 176
Butter Shrimp and Black Bun Sandwiches, 158
Cheesy Caramelized Onion Bread, 155
Chicken Breast Rolls, 86–87
Creamy King Oyster Mushroom Steaks, 21
Creamy Mussels, 40
Eggplant Parmesan, 30
Fish and Chips, 47
French Tian, 22
Hamburger Steaks, 73
Herbed Flatbread, 110–11
Porchetta Sandwiches, 150
Pork Shoulder Roast, 74
Steak with Pine Nut Sauce, 57
pasta
Black Squid Ink Pasta, 44
Creamy Chicken, 89
Whole-Wheat Shiitake Mushroom Pasta, 29
Peach Cookies, 194–95
peanut butter, Butter Crumble Buns, 136
pearl sugar, Chocolate Bread with, 120
pears, Red Pear Chocolate Turnovers, 201
peas, 47, 58–59
phyllo pastry. *See* Mini Pistachio Baklava Cakes; Phyllo-Wrapped Seafood Papillote

Phyllo-Wrapped Seafood Papillote, 43
Picnic Sandwiches, 162
Pide Bread, 104–5
pineapple
Boneless Beef Short Ribs, 66–67
Carrot Loaf Cake, 188–89
Pineapplecello, 246
Pineapple Cupcakes, 198
Pineapplecello, 246
pine nut cream sauce, Steak with Pine Nut Sauce, 57
pine nuts, Boneless Beef Short Ribs, 66–67
pistachios
Chocolate Loaf Cake, 191
Gin-Filled Pavé Chocolates, 224–25
Lemony Nougat, 223
Mini Pistachio Baklava Cakes, 186
Pide Bread, 104–5
Rack of Lamb Sandwiches, 153
Whipped Ganache Cake, 182–83
plain yogurt, Anchovy Grilled Naan, 140
Pomegranate Liquor, 242
pomegranate seeds, Rack of Lamb Crown Roast, 76–77
Pomegranate Sorbet, 229
poppy seeds, Sunflower Biscuits, 168
Porchetta Sandwiches, 150
pork belly, Crispy Porchetta, 70
Pork Shoulder Roast, 74
potatoes
Balsamic Glaze-Marinated Roasted Chicken Legs, 85
Bone Marrow Meatballs, 64–65
Chicken Breast Rolls, 86–87
Corned Beef and Cabbage, 61
Country White Gravy and Biscuits, 167
Creamy King Oyster Mushroom Steaks, 21
Deep-Fried Lobster, 51
Fish and Chips, 47
Hamburger Steaks, 73
Koesisters, 197
Phyllo-Wrapped Seafood Papillote, 43
Pork Shoulder Roast, 74
Prime Rib Roast, 54–55
Poultry. *See* chicken; turkey
Preserved Lemon, 14, 62
Pretzels, 131
Prime Rib Roast, 54–55
Pumpernickel Bread, 108
pumpkin seeds, 108, 188–89
pumpkin spice puree, Brown Butter Ice Cream, 237

R

Rack of Lamb Crown Roast, 76–77
Rack of Lamb Cutlets, 79
Rack of Lamb Sandwiches, 153
radicchio, Rack of Lamb Cutlets, 79
raisins, Carrot Loaf Cake, 188–89
raspberries
Chocolate Loaf Cake, 191
Gin-Filled Pavé Chocolates, 224–25
Panna Cotta, 213
Rack of Lamb Cutlets, 79
Raspberry Babka, 119
Raspberry Babka, 119
Red Pear Chocolate Turnovers, 201
red pepper. *See* various recipes
Reuben Sandwiches, 157
Roasted Turkey, 96–97
Rochers Coco, 217
rosemary
Baked Eggplant Sandwiches, 161
Beef Bourguignon, 62
Beef Tenderloins, 58–59
Creamy King Oyster Mushroom Steaks, 21
Crispy Porchetta, 70
Herbed Flatbread, 110–11
Olive Fougasse, 143
Phyllo-Wrapped Seafood Papillote, 43
Rack of Lamb Crown Roast, 76–77
Roasted Turkey, 96–97
Turkey Breast, 94
Russian dressing, Reuben Sandwiches, 157

S

sage
Baked Eggplant Sandwiches, 161
Beef Bourguignon, 62
Beef Tenderloins, 58–59
Chicken Breast Rolls, 86–87
Creamy King Oyster Mushroom Steaks, 21
Creamy Mussels, 40
Crispy Porchetta, 70
Eggplant Parmesan, 30
Herbed Flatbread, 110–11
Olive Fougasse, 143
Roasted Turkey, 96–97
Steak with Pine Nut Sauce, 57
Sandwich Bread, 100
Sandwiches
Baked Eggplant Sandwiches, 161
Black Ciabatta Egg Sandwich, 154
Butter Shrimp and Black Bun Sandwiches, 158
Picnic Sandwiches, 162
Porchetta Sandwiches, 150
Rack of Lamb Sandwiches, 153
Reuben Sandwiches, 157
Tamago Sandwiches, 149
sautéed green beans with lemon butter sauce, Prime Rib Roast, 54–55
savory butter sauce, Anchovy Grilled Naan, 140
scallops, Phyllo-Wrapped Seafood Papillote, 43
Scones & Biscuits
Black Cheese Scones, 176
Cheese and Leek Scones, 175
Cinnamon Kouign-Amann Biscuits, 171
Country White Gravy and Biscuits, 167
Sunflower Biscuits, 168
Seafood
Beetroot-Cured Salmon, 48
Black Squid Ink Pasta, 44
Creamy Mussels, 40
Deep-Fried Lobster, 51
Fish and Chips, 47
Grilled Shrimp, 39
Phyllo-Wrapped Seafood Papillote, 43
semolina, Black Squid Ink Pasta, 44
sesame seeds
Chicken Soup, 93
Crunchy Cinnamon Balloon Buns, 127
Pide Bread, 104–5
shallots
Balsamic Marinated Tomatoes, 17
Beef Bourguignon, 62
Beef Tenderloins, 58–59
Beet Tortilla Mushroom Tacos, 34–35
Butter Shrimp and Black Bun Sandwiches, 158
Creamy Mussels, 40
Eggplant Parmesan, 30
Fish and Chips, 47
Reuben Sandwiches, 157
Roasted Turkey, 96–97
shrimp
Butter Shrimp and Black Bun Sandwiches, 158
Grilled Shrimp, 39
Phyllo-Wrapped Seafood Papillote, 43
smoked paprika
Beet Tortilla Mushroom Tacos, 34
Lollipop Drumsticks, 90
Mushroom Wings, 33
Pretzels, 131
sorbets
Lemon Basil Sorbet, 233
Orange Thyme Sorbet, 230
Pomegranate Sorbet, 229
sour cream. *See various recipes*
sour cream sauce, Beet Tortilla Mushroom Tacos, 34–35
soy sauce. *See* various recipes
spaghetti. *See* pasta
spicy garlicky sauerkraut, Reuben Sandwiches, 157
spicy green onion soy sauce, Chicken Soup, 93
Spicy Pork Ribs, 69

spicy sticky sauce, Spicy Pork Ribs, 69
spinach, Creamy Chicken, 89
squash, French Tian, 22
squid ink
Black Cheese Scones, 176
Black Ciabatta Egg Sandwich, 154
Black Red Onion Pies, 26–27
Black Squid Ink Pasta, 44
Butter Shrimp and Black Bun Sandwiches, 158
star anise
Pomegranate Liquor, 242
Pomegranate Sorbet, 229
Roasted Turkey, 96–97
Steak with Pine Nut Sauce, 57
sticky sauce, Meringue Cinnamon Rolls, 135
strawberries
Butter Crumble Buns, 136
Cinnamon Kouign-Amann Biscuits, 171
Lime Pavlovas, 214
Strawberry Jelly Cake, 185
Strawberry Whiskey, 248
Strawberry Jelly Cake, 185
strawberry whipped cream, Butter Crumble Buns, 136
Strawberry Whiskey, 248
stuffing, Roasted Turkey, 96–97
Sunflower Biscuits, 168
sunflower seeds, Pumpernickel Bread, 108
sweet chili oil sauce, Lollipop Drumsticks, 90
sweet coconut cream, Pineapple Cupcakes, 198
Sweet Garlic Butter Leaves Bread, 112–13
sweet soy sauce marinade, Boneless Beef Short Ribs, 66–67
Swiss meringue, Meringue Cinnamon Rolls, 135

T

tacos. *See* Beet Tortilla Mushroom Tacos
Tamago Sandwiches, 149
thyme
Baked Beet Salad, 18
Beef Bourguignon, 62
Beef Tenderloins, 58–59
Black Red Onion Pies, 26–27
Creamy King Oyster Mushroom Steaks, 21
Creamy Mussels, 40
Eggplant Parmesan, 30
French Tian, 22
Lime Pavlovas, 214
Olive Fougasse, 143
Orange Thyme Sorbet, 230
Phyllo-Wrapped Seafood Papillote, 43
Pork Shoulder Roast, 74
Rack of Lamb Crown Roast, 76–77
Rack of Lamb Sandwiches, 153
Roasted Turkey, 96–97
Steak with Pine Nut Sauce, 57
Turkey Breast, 94
tomatoes
Baked Eggplant Sandwiches, 161
Balsamic Marinated Tomatoes, 17
Beef Tenderloins, 58–59
Beet Tortilla Mushroom Tacos, 34–35
Caprese Salad Rolls, 13
Creamy Chicken, 89
Creamy Mussels, 40
Eggplant Parmesan, 30
French Tian, 22
Grilled Shrimp, 39
Herbed Flatbread, 110–11
Lamb Chop Birria Tacos, 80–81
Olive Fougasse, 143
Phyllo-Wrapped Seafood Papillote, 43
Rack of Lamb Sandwiches, 153
tomato sauce. *See* Bone Marrow Meatballs; Eggplant Parmesan; French Tian
turkey, 94, 96–97

U-V

vanilla bean
Lime Pavlovas, 214
Mini Pistachio Baklava Cakes, 186
Panna Cotta, 213
Raspberry Babka, 119
vanilla extract
Braided Cinnamon Loaf, 107
Brown Butter Ice Cream, 237
Cookie Choux, 210–11
Lime Cheesecake Gelato, 234
Lime Pavlovas, 214
Mini Pistachio Baklava Cakes, 186
Pineapple Cupcakes, 198
Whipped Ganache Cake, 182
vanilla ice cream, Cookie Choux, 210–11
Vegetables
Baked Beet Salad, 18
Baked Eggplant Rollatini, 25
Balsamic Marinated Tomatoes, 17
Beet Tortilla Mushroom Tacos, 34
Black Red Onion Pies, 26–27
Caprese Salad Rolls, 13
Creamy King Oyster Mushroom Steaks, 21
Eggplant Parmesan, 30
French Tian, 22
Mushroom Wings, 33
Preserved Lemon, 14
Whole-Wheat Shiitake Mushroom Pasta, 29

W

walnut halves, Carrot Loaf Cake, 188–89
wasabi mayonnaise, Tamago Sandwiches, 149
Whipped Ganache Cake, 182–83
Whole-Wheat Shiitake Mushroom Pasta, 29
Worcestershire sauce
Beef Tenderloins, 58–59
Bone Marrow Meatballs, 64–65
Grilled Shrimp, 39
Hamburger Steaks, 73
Lollipop Drumsticks, 90
Reuben Sandwiches, 157

X-Y-Z

zests. *See* lemons; oranges
zucchini, French Tian, 22

Acknowledgments

A huge thank you to everyone who helped make this book possible.

Jessica, your design sense and meticulous work made this book come out beautifully; Christy, thank you for making the manuscript even better with your careful editing; and Brook and the team at DK, thank you for finding me and giving me this opportunity. Without your support and advice, this book would not have seen the light of day.

And to all of you who love Glorious Table, thank you so much. Your support and love have been a constant inspiration to me, and because of you, I find even more joy in cooking and sharing.

About the Author

Gloria Jang is a beloved cooking video creator, known for her inspiring recipes and beautifully crafted food videos. Born in Korea, Gloria began learning to cook at a young age from her mother, starting with traditional Korean dishes and gradually expanding to cuisines from around the world. This growing passion for diverse flavors became the foundation of her global culinary philosophy.

After earning various cooking certifications, Gloria moved to Canada, where she worked as a sushi chef and later ran her own small restaurant. These experiences not only deepened her understanding of food but also shaped her unique style of cooking – one that blends professional technique with personal warmth.

She studied design at university, and her creative background shines through in every piece of content she creates. Her videos go beyond showing the steps of a recipe; they highlight the artistry of food itself, blending visual beauty, thoughtful recipes, and a deep appreciation for flavor to create a feast for both the eyes and the palate.

Gloria's approach to cooking is about more than just making delicious food. Guided by the belief that "food is not only meant to delight the taste buds, but also to heal the heart and be a small remedy for the wounds of the world," she strives to bring warmth and comfort through her creations. Her motto, "Let's make a delicious life," reflects her heartfelt desire to share happiness and healing through the flavors of life.

Motivated by her passion for cooking and her desire to connect with others, Gloria launched her social media channel, Glorious Table (@gloriousTable). What began as a small account on Instagram has grown into a community of more than 2 million followers across Instagram, TikTok, and other platforms, where Gloria shares her love of food, inspiring recipes, and beautifully filmed cooking videos with fans around the globe.

Gloria currently resides in Calgary, Canada, where she continues to explore new flavors and ideas to share with her audience.